INS 23 Course Guide

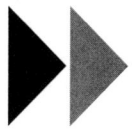

Commercial Insurance
8th Edition

**American Institute for Chartered Property Casualty
Underwriters/Insurance Institute of America**

720 Providence Road • Suite 100 • Malvern, PA 19355-3433

© 2008

American Institute for Chartered Property Casualty Underwriters/Insurance Institute of America

All rights reserved. This book or any part thereof may not be reproduced without the written permission of the copyright holder.

Unless otherwise apparent, examples used in AICPCU/IIA materials related to this course are based on hypothetical situations and are for educational purposes only. The characters, persons, products, services, and organizations described in these examples are fictional. Any similarity or resemblance to any other character, person, product, services, or organization is merely coincidental. AICPCU/IIA is not responsible for such coincidental or accidental resemblances.

This material may contain Internet Web site links external to AICPCU/IIA. AICPCU/IIA neither approves nor endorses any information, products, or services to which any external Web sites refer. Nor does AICPCU/IIA control these Web sites' content or the procedures for Web site content development.

AICPCU/IIA specifically disclaims any implied warranties of merchantability or fitness for a particular purpose. No warranty may be created or extended by sales representatives or written sales materials.

AICPCU/IIA materials related to this course are provided with the understanding that AICPCU/IIA is not engaged in rendering legal, accounting, or other professional service. Nor is AICPCU/IIA explicitly or implicitly stating that any of the processes, procedures, or policies described in the materials are the only appropriate ones to use. The advice and strategies contained herein may not be suitable for every situation.

Information which is copyrighted by and proprietary to Insurance Services Office, Inc. ("ISO Material") is included in this publication. Use of the ISO Material is limited to ISO Participating Insurers and their Authorized Representatives. Use by ISO Participating Insurers is limited to use in those jurisdictions for which the insurer has an appropriate participation with ISO. Use of the ISO Material by Authorized Representatives is limited to use solely on behalf of one or more ISO Participating Insurers.

This publication includes forms which are provided for review purposes only. These forms may not be used, in whole or in part, by any company or individuals not licensed by Insurance Services Office, Inc. (ISO) for the applicable line of insurance and jurisdiction to which this form applies. It is a copyright infringement to include any part(s) of this form within independent company programs without the written permission of ISO.

Eighth Edition • Second Printing • August 2009

ISBN 978-0-89463-376-8

Contents

Study Materials iii
Student Resources. iv
Using This Course Guide iv
INS Advisory Committee. vi
Assignments
   1. Overview of Commercial Insurance 1.1
   2. Commercial Property Insurance, Part I 2.1
   3. Commercial Property Insurance, Part II 3.1
   4. Business Income Insurance 4.1
   5. Commercial Crime and Equipment Breakdown Insurance 5.1
   6. Inland and Ocean Marine Insurance. 6.1
   7. Commercial General Liability Insurance, Part I 7.1
   8. Commercial General Liability Insurance, Part II 8.1
   9. Commercial Auto Insurance 9.1
  10. Businessowners Policies and Farm Insurance 10.1
  11. Workers Compensation and Employers Liability Insurance. 11.1
  12. Miscellaneous Coverages. 12.1
Exam Information 1
Appendix—Sample Policies and Forms 5

Study Materials Available for INS 23

Arthur L. Flitner and Jerome Trupin, *Commercial Insurance,* 2nd ed., 2007, AICPCU/IIA.

INS 23 *Course Guide*, 8th ed., 2008, AICPCU/IIA (includes access code for SMART Online Practice Exams).

INS 23 SMART Study Aids—Review Notes and Flash Cards, 5th ed.

Business Income Insurance: An Introduction (DVD).

Student Resources

Catalog A complete listing of our offerings can be found in *Succeed*, the Institutes' professional development catalog, including information about:

- Current programs and courses
- Current textbooks, course guides, and SMART Study Aids
- Program completion requirements
- Exam registration

To obtain a copy of the catalog, visit our Web site at www.aicpcu.org or contact Customer Service at (800) 644-2101.

How to Prepare for Institute Exams This free handbook is designed to help you by:

- Giving you ideas on how to use textbooks and course guides as effective learning tools
- Providing steps for answering exam questions effectively
- Recommending exam-day strategies

The handbook is printable from the Student Services Center on the Institutes' Web site at www.aicpcu.org, or available by calling Customer Service at (800) 644-2101.

Educational Counseling Services To ensure that you take courses matching both your needs and your skills, you can obtain free counseling from the Institutes by:

- E-mailing your questions to advising@cpcuiia.org
- Calling an Institutes' counselor directly at (610) 644-2100, ext. 7601
- Obtaining and completing a self-inventory form, available on our Web site at www.aicpcu.org or by contacting Customer Service at (800) 644-2101

Exam Registration Information As you proceed with your studies, be sure to arrange for your exam.

- Visit our Web site at www.aicpcu.org/forms to access and print the Registration Booklet, which contains information and forms needed to register for your exam.
- Plan to register with the Institutes well in advance of your exam.

How to Contact the Institutes For more information on any of these publications and services:

- Visit our Web site at www.aicpcu.org
- Call us at (800) 644-2101 or (610) 644-2100 outside the U.S.
- E-mail us at customerservice@cpcuiia.org
- Fax us at (610) 640-9576
- Write to us at AICPCU/IIA, Customer Service, 720 Providence Road, Suite 100, Malvern, PA 19355-3433

Using This Course Guide

This course guide will help you learn the course content and prepare for the exam.

Each assignment in this course guide typically includes the following components:

Educational Objectives These are the most important study tools in the course guide. Because all of the questions on the exam are based on the Educational Objectives, the best way to study for the exam is to focus on these objectives.

Each Educational Objective typically begins with one of the following action words, which indicate the level of understanding required for the exam:

Analyze—Determine the nature and the relationship of the parts.

Apply—Put to use for a practical purpose.

Associate—Bring together into relationship.

Calculate—Determine numeric values by mathematical process.

Classify—Arrange or organize according to class or category.

Compare—Show similarities and differences.

Contrast—Show only differences.

Define—Give a clear, concise meaning.

Describe—Represent or give an account.

Determine—Settle or decide.

Evaluate—Determine the value or merit.

Explain—Relate the importance or application.

Identify or list—Name or make a list.

Illustrate—Give an example.

Justify—Show to be right or reasonable.

Paraphrase—Restate in your own words.

Summarize—Concisely state the main points.

Required Reading The items listed in this section indicate the study materials (the textbook chapter(s), course guide readings, or other assigned materials) that correspond to the assignment.

Outline The outline lists the topics in the assignment. Read the outline before the required reading to become familiar with the assignment content and the relationships of topics.

Key Words and Phrases These words and phrases are fundamental to understanding the assignment and have a common meaning for those working in insurance. After completing the required reading, test your understanding of the assignment's Key Words and Phrases by writing their definitions.

Review Questions The review questions test your understanding of what you have read. Review the Educational Objectives and required reading, then answer the questions to the best of your ability. When you are finished, check the answers at the end of the assignment to evaluate your comprehension.

Application Questions These questions continue to test your knowledge of the required reading by applying what you've studied to "hypothetical" real-life situations. Again, check the suggested answers at the end of the assignment to review your progress.

Sample Exam Your course guide includes either a sample exam (located at the back) or a code for accessing SMART Online Practice Exams (which appears on the inside back cover). Use this supplemental exam material to become familiar with the test format and to practice answering exam questions.

For courses that offer SMART Online Practice Exams, you can both download and print a sample credentialing exam and take full practice exams using the same software you will use when you take your credentialing exam. SMART Online Practice Exams are as close as you can get to experiencing an actual exam before taking one.

More Study Aids

The Institutes also produce supplemental study tools, called SMART Study Aids, for many of our courses. When SMART Study Aids are available for a course, they are listed on both page iii of this course guide and on the first page of each assignment. SMART Study Aids include Review Notes and Flash Cards and are excellent tools to help you learn and retain the information in each assignment.

INS Advisory Committee

The following individuals were instrumental in helping to analyze the audience for the INS program and to design the revisions and updates of the study materials for INS 23.

Patricia M. Arnold, CPCU, ALCM
McCombs School of Business University of Texas at Austin

Gary Grasmann
Insurance Services Office, Inc.

Christine A. Sullivan, CPCU, AIM
Allstate Insurance Company

Jeffrey A. Svestka, CPCU, ARe
Fireman's Fund Insurance Co.

Marcia Tepp, CPCU, ARM, ARP, AIAF, CPIW
Sentry Insurance

Andrew Zagrzejewski, CPCU, CLU, AIC
Farmers Insurance

SEGMENT A

Assignment 1   Overview of Commercial Insurance

Assignment 2   Commercial Property Insurance, Part I

Assignment 3   Commercial Property Insurance, Part II

Assignment 4   Business Income Insurance

Segment A is the first of three segments in the INS 23 course. These segments are designed to help structure your study.

Direct Your Learning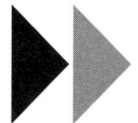

Overview of Commercial Insurance

Educational Objectives

After learning the content of this assignment, you should be able to:

1. Explain how insurance can be viewed as one of several risk management techniques that can be applied through the risk management process.

2. Describe the key characteristics and advantages of the following forms of business organizations:
   - Corporations
   - Partnerships
   - Joint ventures
   - Limited liability companies (LLCs)
   - Unincorporated associations

3. Summarize the purpose of and exposures addressed by each of the various lines of commercial insurance.

4. Describe the components of the Insurance Services Office (ISO) Commercial Package Policy (CPP), including the following:
   - Common Policy Declarations
   - Common Policy Conditions
   - Coverage parts

5. Describe how commercial insurance premiums are determined, including the purpose and application of package modification factors to the ISO CPP program.

6. Define or describe each of the Key Words and Phrases for this assignment.

Study Materials

Required Reading:
- Commercial Insurance
  - Chapter 1

Study Aids:
- SMART Online Practice Exams
- SMART Study Aids
  - Review Notes and Flash Cards—Assignment 1

1.2   Commercial Insurance—INS 23

Outline

▶ **Insurance as a Risk Management Technique**
▶ **Forms of Ownership**
   A. Corporations
   B. Partnerships
   C. Joint Ventures
   D. Limited Liability Companies
   E. Unincorporated Associations
▶ **Lines of Business**
   A. Commercial Property Insurance
   B. Business Income Insurance
   C. Crime Insurance
   D. Equipment Breakdown Insurance
   E. Inland and Ocean Marine Insurance
   F. Commercial General Liability Insurance
   G. Commercial Auto Insurance
   H. Businessowners Insurance
   I. Farm Insurance
   J. Workers Compensation and Employers Liability Insurance
   K. Excess and Umbrella Liability Insurance
   L. Professional Liability Insurance
   M. Management Liability Insurance
   N. Aircraft Insurance
   O. Environmental Insurance
   P. Surety Bonds
▶ **Commercial Insurance Policies**

▶ **ISO Commercial Package Policy Program**
   A. Common Policy Declarations
   B. Common Policy Conditions
      1. Cancellation
      2. Changes
      3. Examination of Books and Records
      4. Inspections and Surveys
      5. Premiums
      6. Transfer of Rights and Duties Under the Policy
   C. Coverage Parts
▶ **Determining Commercial Insurance Premiums**
   A. Rating Fundamentals
   B. Package Modification Factors
▶ **Summary**

   Don't spend time on material you have already mastered. The SMART Review Notes are organized by the Educational Objectives found in each course guide assignment to help you track your study.

For each assignment, you should define or describe each of the Key Words and Phrases and answer each of the Review and Application Questions.

> ## Educational Objective 1
> Explain how insurance can be viewed as one of several risk management techniques that can be applied through the risk management process.

Key Words and Phrases

Commercial insurance (p. 1.3)

Loss exposure (p. 1.3)

Review Questions

1-1 a. Define and give an example of a property loss exposure. (p. 1.4)

b. Define and give an example of a liability loss exposure. (p. 1.4)

c. Define and give an example of a personal loss exposure. (p. 1.4)

1.4 Commercial Insurance—INS 23

1-2. Summarize the risk management process. (p. 1.4)

1-3. List and briefly describe five risk management techniques. (pp. 1.4–1.5)

Application Question

1-4. The Toy Corporation (TC) owns a commercial building located near a large river. TC manufactures children's toys and owns a substantial amount of stock and equipment in its building.

a. Identify at least two property loss exposures TC faces.

b. Identify at least two liability loss exposures TC faces.

c. Identify risk management techniques other than insurance that TC can use to mitigate its risk of fire or explosion and its risk of liability loss when hiring a remodeling contractor.

Educational Objective 2

Describe the key characteristics and advantages of the following forms of business organizations:

- Corporations
- Partnerships
- Joint ventures
- Limited liability companies (LLC)
- Unincorporated associations

Key Words and Phrases

Corporation (p. 1.5)

Partnership (p. 1.6)

Joint venture (p. 1.6)

Limited liability company (LLC) (p. 1.6)

Unincorporated association (p. 1.6)

Review Questions

2-1. Describe, in an insurance context, why the form of ownership is important. (p. 1.5)

2-2. Describe the primary advantage of each of the following forms of ownership.

a. Corporation (p. 1.5)

b. Partnership (p. 1.6)

c. Joint venture (p. 1.6)

d. Limited liability company (LLC) (p. 1.6)

e. Unincorporated association (p. 1.6)

2-3. Explain how corporations and unincorporated associations are similar and how they differ. (pp. 1.6–1.7)

Application Question

2-4. Adele owns Atley Health Products, a California-based company that promotes environment-friendly manufacturing and distribution of natural herb products. Rafael owns a similar company in Chile. Adele and Rafael are considering building a third company in Chile that promotes a similar natural philosophy. However, they plan to sell the company after the building is complete. Explain what type of ownership Adele and Rafael should consider and why, based on the facts presented.

Educational Objective 3
Summarize the purpose of and exposures addressed by each of the various lines of commercial insurance.

Key Word or Phrase
Line of business (p. 1.7)

Review Questions

3-1. Briefly describe, in both the general and narrower sense, what is covered and what is omitted in commercial property insurance. (p. 1.8)

3-2. Distinguish ocean marine insurance from inland marine insurance. (p. 1.9)

3-3. Describe a surety bond and how a contractor might be involved in its use. (p. 1.11)

Application Question

3-4. Family Fare, Inc. (FFI) owns a building in which it operates a restaurant. It also owns furniture, equipment, fixtures, and supplies typical of a restaurant. FFI employs twelve people in the restaurant. It also owns two trucks, which certain employees use to deliver take-out orders. Identify and briefly describe at least five types of insurance (lines of business) FFI needs to cover its loss exposures.

Educational Objective 4

Describe the components of the Insurance Services Office (ISO) Commercial Package Policy (CPP), including the following:

- Common Policy Declarations
- Common Policy Conditions
- Coverage parts

Key Words and Phrases

Monoline policy (p. 1.12)

Package policy (p. 1.12)

Commercial Package Policy (CPP) (p. 1.12)

Common Policy Declarations (p. 1.14)

Common Policy Conditions (p. 1.14)

Coverage part (p. 1.16)

Review Questions

4-1. What are the components of ISO's Commercial Package Policy (CPP)? (p. 1.12)

4-2. What information is shown on a CPP's Common Policy Declarations? (p. 1.14)

4-3. List and briefly describe the six Common Policy Conditions in a CPP. (pp. 1.14–1.16)

4-4. Briefly describe the elements in each coverage part of a CPP. (pp. 1.16–1.17)

4-5. Give six examples of coverage parts that may be used in ISO's Commercial Package Policy. (p. 1.17)

Application Questions

4-6. Danford Grocery is a local vegetable and fruit distributor. Farmers from the surrounding areas bring their produce to Danford, which then purchases the produce and sells it to customers. Identify the necessary components of a CPP for Danford, based on the following loss exposures: the store it owns, the customers on the premises, and Danford's cash transactions.

Educational Objective 5

Describe how commercial insurance premiums are determined, including the purpose and application of package modification factors to the ISO CPP program.

Key Words and Phrases

Rate (p. 1.17)

Commercial Lines Manual (CLM) (p. 1.18)

Package modification factors (p. 1.18)

Review Questions

5-1. Describe two ways that a commercial insurance premium can be calculated. (pp. 1.17–1.18)

5-2. How do insurers convert loss costs in a *Commercial Lines Manual* (CLM) to rates that can be used to rate a policy? (p. 1.18)

5-3. Explain how a package discount is determined. (p. 1.19)

5-4. What do package modification factors reflect? (p. 1.19)

5-5. Briefly describe what a package modification factor of 0.85 means. (p. 1.19)

Application Question

5-6. Underwriter Julie is preparing a CPP for a real estate firm. Julie determines that, if rated as a monoline policy, the firm's premium for the general liability coverage part would equal $25,450. A package modification factor of 0.80 applies to the premium. What is the discounted premium the firm will pay if Julie issues a package policy instead of a monoline policy for the general liability coverage part?

Answers to Assignment 1 Questions

NOTE: These answers are provided to give students a basic understanding of acceptable types of responses. They often are not the only valid answers and are not intended to provide an exhaustive response to the questions.

Educational Objective 1

1-1   a. A property loss exposure is defined as the possibility that a person or an organization will sustain a financial loss as the result of the damaging, destruction, taking, or loss of use of property in which that person or organization has a financial interest. An example of a property loss exposure is the possibility that a tornado will damage a building.

   b. A liability loss exposure is defined as the possibility that a person or an organization will sustain a financial loss as the result of a claim by someone seeking monetary damages or some other legal remedy. An example of a liability loss exposure is the possibility that a customer who is hospitalized for food poisoning immediately after eating in a restaurant will sue the restaurant owner for damages.

   c. A personal loss exposure is defined as the possibility of financial loss to a person caused by injury, sickness, or death. Anyone who could be injured on the job or in an auto accident has a personal loss exposure.

1-2. The risk management process can be summarized in the following six steps:

   (1) Identifying loss exposures

   (2) Analyzing loss exposures

   (3) Examining the feasibility of risk management techniques

   (4) Selecting the appropriate risk management techniques

   (5) Implementing the selected risk management techniques

   (6) Monitoring results and revising the risk management program

1-3. Risk management techniques include the following:

   - Insurance—enables a person or an organization to transfer the financial consequences of a loss to an insurer

   - Avoidance—occurs when an organization avoids an identified loss exposure by choosing not to own a particular item of property or not to engage in a particular activity

   - Loss control—includes any measure to prevent losses from occurring (such as storing gasoline in sealed, approved containers) or to reduce the size of losses that do occur (such as installing an automatic sprinkler system in a building)

   - Retention—occurs when an organization pays all or part of its own losses (also known as self-insurance)

   - Noninsurance transfer—occurs when an organization (such as a building owner) obtains the promise of a second, noninsurance organization (such as a remodeling contractor) to pay for certain losses for which the first organization would otherwise be responsible

1-4. Possible loss exposures faced by TC might include the following:
 a. Property loss exposures—TC faces the possibility of fire or flood (and other perils) damaging its building. TC also has the possibility of the same perils damaging its stock and equipment.
 b. Liability loss exposures—TC could sustain a financial loss from a claim if a toy it manufactures is defective and injures a child. Also, TC might face the possibility of a suit if a customer is injured on TC's premises.
 c. To mitigate its risk of fire or explosion, TC can use the loss control risk management technique. To mitigate its risk of liability loss when hiring a remodeling contractor, TC can use the noninsurance transfer risk management technique.

Educational Objective 2

2-1. The form of ownership is important in an insurance context because it affects the insurability of the business and it determines, to some extent, exactly how the named insured should be identified on the policy.

2-2. The primary advantage of each form of ownership is as follows:
 a. Corporation—It limits the owners' liability for the corporations' contracts and torts.
 b. Partnership—Income flows to each partner and is taxable at that individual's rate, rather than at a rate that would apply to a corporation.
 c. Joint venture—It can be formed quickly, and participants can pool resources in order to pre-empt competitors while sharing the risks of an undertaking.
 d. Limited liability company (LLC)—It provides its owners the limited liability of a corporation and the tax advantages of a partnership.
 e. Unincorporated association—It can be easily formed and is not subject to many of the taxes commonly levied on corporations.

2-3. Corporations and unincorporated associations are similar in that they can be both for-profit and not-for-profit. However, because an unincorporated association is not a legal entity like a corporation, its members can be held individually liable for the association's activities.

2-4. Adele and Rafael should consider forming a joint venture when building their overseas company. A joint venture will fulfill their desire to dissolve the relationship after the building is sold to another investor. Joint ventures are also often used as an expedited means to enter new markets, especially foreign markets.

Educational Objective 3

3-1. Commercial property insurance covers commercial buildings and their contents against loss caused by fire, windstorm, and many other causes of loss, or perils. Commercial property insurance (in its narrower meaning) provides little, if any, coverage for property while it is in transit or otherwise away from the insured location. Commercial property insurance omits most crime-related perils as well as mechanical or electrical breakdown or steam boiler explosion.

3-2. Ocean marine insurance differs from inland marine insurance in that ocean marine insurance conforms to the international meaning of marine insurance, whereas inland marine insurance includes a wide variety of risks that in the United States were first insured by marine underwriters. These risks include property in domestic transit, mobile equipment, buildings in the course of construction, property essential to transportation or communication (such as bridges, tunnels, and radio and television towers), and many other classes of property that typically involve an element of transportation.

3-3. A surety bond is defined as an agreement by one party (the surety) to answer for the failure of another (the principal) to perform as the principal has promised. Contract surety bonds are widely used to guarantee that a contractor (the principal) will complete a building project according to specifications and within a stated time frame, that the contractor will pay certain bills for labor and materials, and that the contractor's work will be free from defects for a specified period.

3-4. FFI needs the following types of insurance, among others:
- Commercial property insurance—insurance to cover its building and contents against perils such as fire, windstorm, and so forth
- Business income insurance—coverage to protect FFI in case it suffers a financial loss from lost income and/or increased expenses due to physical damage (such as fire) to its building or contents
- Commercial general liability insurance—insurance to cover the loss exposure of a suit or claim for damages arising from the restaurant operation, such as a customer becoming ill after eating FFI's food
- Commercial automobile insurance—insurance to cover liability and physical damage losses arising from the ownership and use of the two trucks
- Workers compensation and employers liability insurance—insurance to cover FFI's legal obligation to pay benefits for employees' job-related injuries or illnesses

Educational Objective 4

4-1. The components of ISO's Commercial Package Policy include the following:
- Common Policy Declarations
- Common Policy Conditions
- Two or more coverage parts

4-2. The following information is shown on a CPP's Common Policy Declarations:
- Policy number
- Names of the insurer and the producer
- Name, address, and business description of the named insured
- Effective date and expiration date of the policy
- Premium for each coverage part included in the policy
- Total premium

The Common Policy Declarations also includes a general statement, known as the "in consideration" clause, in which the insurer agrees with the named insured to provide the insurance as stated in the policy in return for the payment of premium and subject to all the terms of the policy.

4-3. The six Common Policy Conditions in a CPP are as follows:
(1) Cancellation—The insured may cancel the policy at any time by mailing or delivering written notice of cancellation to the insurer. If two or more insureds are listed in the declarations,

only the one listed first ("the first named insured") can request cancellation. The insurer can cancel the policy by mailing or delivering written notice of cancellation to the first named insured. In almost every state, the Cancellation condition is superseded by state law, and a state-specific cancellation endorsement is added to the policy.

(2) Changes—The CPP policy can be changed only by a written endorsement issued by the insurer. Such changes may be made, with the insurer's consent, upon the request of the first named insured. Only the first named insured has the authority to request policy changes, and the insurer is authorized to make changes upon the request of the first named insured without specific permission of any other insured.

(3) Examination of Your Books and Records—The insurer reserves the right to examine and audit the insured's books and records related to the policy at any time during the policy period and for up to three years after the termination of the policy.

(4) Inspections and Surveys—The insurer has the right, but not the obligation, to inspect the insured's premises and operations at any reasonable time during the policy period. Such inspections are important in determining the insurability of the insured's property and operations, in setting proper insurance rates, and in making loss control recommendations.

(5) Premiums—The first named insured is responsible for paying the premium under the policy. The insurer must also pay any return premium under the policy to the first named insured.

(6) Transfer of Rights and Duties Under the Policy—The insured cannot transfer any rights or duties under the policy to any other person or organization without the written consent of the insurer. The transfer of rights and duties condition also provides specifically for the automatic transfer of coverage upon the death of an individual named insured. Upon death, the insured's rights and duties under the policy are automatically transferred to the insured's legal representative, or, if the insured's legal representative has not yet been appointed, to any person having proper temporary custody of the insured property.

4-4. Each coverage part of a CPP contains the following elements:
- A declarations page that pertains only to that coverage part
- One or more coverage forms, which contain insuring agreements, exclusions, and other policy provisions
- Applicable endorsements, which modify the terms of the coverage form(s) to fit the needs of the particular insured

4-5. The following are examples of coverage parts that can be included in an ISO Commercial Package Policy:
- Commercial property
- Commercial general liability
- Commercial crime
- Equipment breakdown
- Commercial inland marine
- Commercial auto

4-6. The necessary components of a commercial package policy for Danford are as follows:
- Common policy declarations
- Common policy conditions
- Commercial property coverage part
  - Dec page
  - Coverage forms
  - Causes of loss forms
  - Conditions
- Commercial general liability coverage part
  - Dec page
  - Coverage form
- Commercial crime coverage part
  - Dec page
  - Coverage forms

Educational Objective 5

5-1. One way to calculate a commercial insurance premium is by dividing the rate by the unit amount, and then multiplying that value by the amount of insurance.

Another way to reach the same result is to establish the number of exposure units by dividing the amount of insurance by the unit amount, and then multiplying the number of units by the rate.

5-2. Insurers convert CLM loss costs to rates that can be used to rate a policy by calculating a loss cost multiplier to cover other expenses that it will incur (such as underwriting, marketing, and taxes). In addition, a charge is usually added to allow for possible errors in the insurer's predictions. An allowance for insurer profit may also be added.

5-3. The package discount is determined by applying the appropriate package modification factors to the premiums for the eligible coverage parts included in the policy.

5-4. Package modification factors reflect the type of business (apartment, office, mercantile, and so forth), the particular coverage part being rated, and other eligibility requirements.

5-5. A package modification factor of 0.85 means that the premium for that coverage part will be 85 percent of the premium that would apply if the coverage part were issued in a monoline policy.

5-6. If Julie issues a package policy instead of a monoline policy for the general liability coverage part of the real estate firm's CPP, the discounted premium will equal $25,450 × 0.80, or $20,360.

Direct Your Learning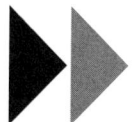

Commercial Property Insurance, Part I

Educational Objectives

After learning the content of this assignment, you should be able to:

1. Describe the following documents that are included in a commercial property coverage part:
   - Commercial property declarations
   - Commercial property coverage forms
   - Causes of loss forms
   - Commercial Property Conditions
   - Endorsements
2. Identify covered property and property not covered under the Building and Personal Property Coverage Form (BPP).
3. Describe each of the additional coverages and coverage extensions included in the BPP.
4. Describe the application of limits of insurance and deductibles in commercial property insurance.
5. Describe each of the conditions appearing in the loss conditions or additional conditions section of the BPP.
6. Explain how each of the following optional coverages printed in the BPP modifies the basic coverage of the BPP:
   - Agreed value
   - Inflation guard
   - Replacement cost
   - Extension of replacement cost to personal property of others
7. Describe the purpose and the operation of each of the following modifications of the BPP:
   - Functional Building Valuation endorsement
   - Functional Personal Property Valuation endorsement
   - Value Reporting Form
   - Peak Season Limit of Insurance endorsement
8. Describe the operation of blanket insurance and its advantages over specific insurance.
9. Explain whether, and for what amount, the BPP and any applicable optional coverages would cover a described loss.
10. Define or describe each of the Key Words and Phrases for this assignment.

Study Materials

Required Reading:
- Commercial Insurance
  - Chapter 2

Study Aids:
- SMART Online Practice Exams
- SMART Study Aids
  - Review Notes and Flash Cards—Assignment 2

2.1

Outline

▶ **Overview of the Commercial Property Coverage Part**
  A. Commercial Property Declarations
  B. Commercial Property Coverage Form
  C. Causes of Loss Form
  D. Commercial Property Conditions
  E. Endorsements

▶ **Building and Personal Property Coverage Form (BPP)**
  A. Covered Property
    1. Building
    2. Business Personal Property of the Insured
    3. Personal Property of Others
  B. Property Not Covered
  C. Additional Coverages and Coverage Extensions
    1. Additional Coverages
    2. Coverage Extensions
  D. Limits of Insurance
  E. Deductible
  F. Loss Conditions
    1. Abandonment
    2. Appraisal
    3. Duties in the Event of Loss or Damage
    4. Loss Payment
    5. Recovered Property
    6. Vacancy
    7. Valuation
  G. Additional Conditions
    1. Coinsurance
    2. Mortgageholder
  H. Optional Coverages
    1. Agreed Value
    2. Inflation Guard
    3. Replacement Cost
    4. Extension of Replacement Cost to Personal Property of Others
  I. Functional Building and Personal Property Valuation Endorsements

▶ **Insuring Fluctuating Values**
  A. Value Reporting Form
    1. Penalties for Improper Reporting
    2. Determining Premium
  B. Peak Season Limit of Insurance Endorsement

▶ **Blanket Insurance**
  A. Coinsurance Requirement for Blanket Insurance
  B. Advantages of Blanket Insurance
  C. Combining the Agreed Value Option With Blanket Insurance

▶ **Summary**

Reduce the number of Key Words and Phrases that you must review. SMART Flash Cards contain the Key Words and Phrases and their definitions, allowing you to set aside those cards that you have mastered.

For each assignment, you should define or describe each of the Key Words and Phrases and answer each of the Review and Application Questions.

> ## Educational Objective 1
> Describe the following documents that are included in a commercial property coverage part:
> - Commercial property declarations
> - Commercial property coverage forms
> - Causes of loss forms
> - Commercial Property Conditions
> - Endorsements

Key Words and Phrases

Commercial property coverage part (p. 2.4)

Commercial property declarations page (p. 2.4)

Commercial property coverage form (p. 2.5)

Building and Personal Property Coverage Form (BPP) (p. 2.5)

Causes of loss form (p. 2.5)

Commercial Property Conditions (p. 2.7)

Review Questions

1-1. Briefly describe the five documents that constitute a commercial property coverage part. (p. 2.4)

1-2. What specific information is contained in the commercial property declarations page? (pp. 2.4–2.5)

1-3. What elements are part of every commercial property coverage form? (p. 2.5)

Application Question

1-4. Walter operates a used-tire recycling business in East St. Louis. He visits Georgine, his insurance agent, to obtain commercial property insurance. Georgine is uneasy about crime and loss experience in Walter's neighborhood. In response to Walter's application for commercial property insurance, how might Georgine tailor the coverage part to address her underwriting concerns?

Educational Objective 2

Identify covered property and property not covered under the Building and Personal Property Coverage Form (BPP).

Key Word or Phrase

Improvements and betterments (p. 2.9)

Review Questions

2-1. Give two examples of different types of property included within each of the following categories of covered property under the Building and Personal Property Coverage Form (BPP):

  a. Building (p. 2.8)

  b. Business personal property of the insured (p. 2.9)

  c. Personal property of others (pp. 2.9–2.10)

2-2. Give three reasons why certain kinds of property are specifically not covered under the BPP. (pp. 2.10–2.11)

Application Question

2-3. Jamal and Keisha own a used celebrity guitar business and conduct most of their sales via their Web site. Their warehouse and office operations are housed in a large building, which is insured under a BPP. The office contains their Web servers, currently valued at $300,000. Two years ago, they purchased a separate EDP equipment policy to cover their computer hardware. They have kept the policy in force, but they have not increased the original $200,000 amount of insurance. A computer room fire destroys all of their Web servers. How much will each policy provide in covering the loss?

Educational Objective 3
Describe each of the additional coverages and coverage extensions included in the BPP.

Review Questions

3-1. Explain how the insured can benefit from the following additional coverages that are automatically included in the BPP:

a. Debris removal (pp. 2.11–2.12)

b. Preservation of property (p. 2.13)

c. Fire department service charge (p. 2.13)

d. Pollutant cleanup and removal (p. 2.13)

e. Increased cost of construction (p. 2.13)

f. Electronic data (p. 2.14)

2.8 Commercial Insurance—INS 23

3-2. From the viewpoint of the insured, explain the specific benefits and limitations of each of the following coverage extensions in the BPP:

a. Newly acquired or constructed property (p. 2.14)

b. Personal effects and property of others (p. 2.15)

c. Valuable papers and records—cost of research (p. 2.15)

d. Property off-premises (p. 2.16)

e. Outdoor property (p. 2.16)

f. Non-owned detached trailers (p. 2.16)

Application Question

3-3. Sadeer runs a successful surgery center in San Diego, California. He insures his building under a BPP. As the business grows, he finds an opportunity to acquire another building in nearby La Jolla for another surgery center. The insurable value of his new location is $600,000. How does the BPP respond to his new need for building coverage? What actions, if any, should Sadeer take to be insured at both locations?

Educational Objective 4
Describe the application of limits of insurance and deductibles in commercial property insurance.

Review Questions

4-1. How is it possible for an insurer to pay more than the limit of insurance to an insured in any one policy year? (p. 2.17)

4-2. How can an insured collect the full BPP policy limit for a building loss, even if there is a deductible? (p. 2.18)

4-3. Why do higher deductibles appeal to insureds and to underwriters? (p. 2.18)

Application Question

4-4. Carl owns a souvenir store in Roswell, New Mexico. He insures his store under a BPP with a $400,000 building limit and a $1,000 deductible. Calculate how the policy would pay for losses valued at each of the following amounts:

a. $800

b. $25,000

c. $415,000

Commercial Property Insurance, Part 1

Educational Objective 5
Describe each of the conditions appearing in the loss conditions or additional conditions section of the BPP.

Key Words and Phrases

Abandonment condition (p. 2.19)

Appraisal condition (p. 2.19)

Proof of loss (p. 2.21)

Actual cash value (ACV) (p. 2.22)

Coinsurance condition (p. 2.24)

Review Questions

5-1. With regard to the BPP:

    a. Describe the procedure presented in the Appraisal condition. (p. 2.19)

b. What are the insured's duties in the event of a loss? (pp. 2.20–2.21)

c. Under what circumstances might the insurer deny payment of a claim? (p. 2.21)

d. Describe the insurer's options in settling a claim. (p. 2.21)

e. Explain how the vacancy conditions affect the insurer's obligation to pay a loss. (p. 2.22)

5-2. Explain how loss to each of the following is valued under the BPP:

   a. Stock (p. 2.23)

   b. Glass (p. 2.23)

   c. Improvements and betterments replaced by the insured (p. 2.23)

   d. Improvements and betterments not replaced (p. 2.23)

   e. Valuable papers and records (p. 2.23)

f. Property other than that specifically listed (p. 2.23)

5-3. Describe the rights granted to a mortgageholder that is named on the declarations page of a commercial property policy. (p. 2.24)

Application Questions

5-4. Tarnton Greeting Card Company is insured under a Building and Personal Property Coverage Form (BPP). A fire at Tarnton's warehouse on October 15 destroyed most of its stock of holiday greeting cards.

    a. Tarnton notified its insurer of the loss as required under the loss conditions section of the coverage form. Identify two other duties in the event of a loss that are imposed on Tarnton by the BPP.

    b. Most of Tarnton's inventory had already been sold but had not been delivered to customers. The remaining inventory had not been sold. Explain how the value of its inventory would be established under the valuation provision of the BPP.

5-5. An office building with an actual cash value of $300,000 is covered under a BPP, subject to an 80 percent coinsurance provision.

   a. What is the minimum amount of insurance that must be purchased on this building on an ACV basis to avoid a coinsurance penalty?

   b. Assume that the owner purchased $180,000 coverage (ACV) on the building. What amount would the owner be paid in the event of a $100,000 covered loss (ACV) to the building? Disregard any deductible that might apply.

5-6. The contents of Tony's Toy Store are insured on an ACV basis under a BPP with an 80 percent coinsurance requirement and a limit of insurance of $150,000. A $1,000 deductible applies to all covered losses. A fire caused $60,000 damage (ACV) to the contents of the store. At the time of the fire, the contents had an ACV of $300,000. How much will Tony's insurer pay for this loss? Show your calculations.

Educational Objective 6

Explain how each of the following optional coverages printed in the BPP modifies the basic coverage of the BPP:

- Agreed value
- Inflation guard
- Replacement cost
- Extension of replacement cost to personal property of others

Key Words and Phrases

Agreed Value optional coverage (p. 2.26)

Inflation Guard optional coverage (p. 2.26)

Replacement Cost optional coverage (p. 2.27)

Review Questions

6-1. List the four optional coverages available in the BPP. (p. 2.25)

6-2. Describe the purpose and operation of the Agreed Value optional coverage in the BPP. (p. 2.26)

6-3. When the insured chooses the Replacement Cost option under the BPP, how is the Coinsurance condition affected? (p. 2.26)

Application Question

6-4. Sadie owns a call center business in Rochester, New York, and insures her building and personal property under a BPP. Because communications technology changes so rapidly, she leases all of her phone equipment. According to the lease agreement, she is responsible for the replacement cost of the leased phone equipment in the event it is damaged. What should Sadie do to ensure that she has insurance coverage sufficient to meet the obligations of her lease agreement?

> **Educational Objective 7**
>
> Describe the purpose and the operation of each of the following modifications of the BPP:
>
> - Functional Building Valuation endorsement
> - Functional Personal Property Valuation endorsement
> - Value Reporting Form
> - Peak Season Limit of Insurance endorsement

Key Words and Phrases

Functional replacement cost (p. 2.28)

Value Reporting Form (p. 2.29)

Peak Season Limit of Insurance endorsement (p. 2.30)

Review Questions

7-1. Explain how and why the functional valuation endorsements may be used to change the loss settlement provision in a commercial property policy. (p. 2.28)

7-2. Explain how the interior walls of an older building could be used to illustrate functional replacement cost. (p. 2.28)

7-3. Explain how loss recovery is limited if property is not replaced using functional replacement cost. (p. 2.28)

7-4. How does the Value Reporting Form address the needs of a business with fluctuating inventory values? (p. 2.29)

7-5. How does the Peak Season Limit of Insurance endorsement address the needs of a business with fluctuating inventory values? (p. 2.30)

7-6. Explain why a peak season endorsement, rather than a value reporting form, is better suited to small businesses that have regular fluctuations in inventory. (p. 2.30)

Application Question

7-7. Tomoko recently opened a card and gift shop and purchased coverage under a Value Reporting Form. Explain why a business like Tomoko's might need to purchase coverage under a Value Reporting Form.

Educational Objective 8

Describe the operation of blanket insurance and its advantages over specific insurance.

Key Words and Phrases

Specific insurance (pp. 2.30–2.31)

Blanket insurance (p. 2.31)

Review Questions

8-1. Explain how an insured with blanket insurance would meet coinsurance requirements. (p. 2.31)

8-2. What is a major advantage of blanket insurance? (p. 2.32)

8-3. Jack owns and operates restaurants in several different locations. However, he is not sure of the insurable value at each location. Describe Jack's duties in this situation if he had the following kinds of insurance:

a. Specific insurance (p. 2.30)

b. Blanket insurance (p. 2.31)

Application Question

8-4. A costume rental and sales company that has stores in ten large cities including New Orleans and Hollywood ships costumes from all of its stores to New Orleans before Mardi Gras and to Hollywood when it receives contracts to supply film productions. Describe the benefits that blanket insurance for the store's personal property would provide in ensuring adequate coverage for its costumes.

Educational Objective 9

Explain whether, and for what amount, the BPP and any applicable optional coverages would cover a described loss.

Application Question

9-1. A two-story antique store owned by Chris was damaged by fire. The building is a restored Victorian mansion insured on an ACV basis under a BPP. The features of the building include original hardwood floors, hand-carved woodwork, and a slate roof. The limit of insurance is $280,000. The policy has an 80 percent coinsurance requirement, and a $1,000 deductible that applies to all covered losses. The fire caused $72,000 in damages (ACV) to Chris's building. At the time of the fire, the building had an ACV of $400,000, a market value of $500,000, and a functional replacement cost of $250,000.

  a. What dollar amount will Chris be paid for this loss? Show your calculations.

  b. Explain how your answer would change if there was a Functional Building Valuation Endorsement attached to the policy and whether you would recommend this to Chris.

Answers to Assignment 2 Questions

NOTE: These answers are provided to give students a basic understanding of acceptable types of responses. They often are not the only valid answers and are not intended to provide an exhaustive response to the questions.

Educational Objective 1

1-1. A commercial property coverage part consists of the following five documents:
   (1) Commercial property declarations, which provides basic information about the policyholder and the insurance provided
   (2) One or more commercial property coverage forms that contain an insuring agreement and related provisions
   (3) One or more causes of loss forms (basic, broad, and special) that allow the insured to select or the underwriter to offer a range of covered perils
   (4) Commercial property conditions, a component which contains conditions (as its name suggests) applicable to all commercial property coverage forms
   (5) Any applicable endorsements, available to tailor commercial property coverage to meet specialized needs of the insured or underwriting concerns of the insurer

1-2. The commercial property declarations page contains the following specific information:
   - A description of the property insured
   - The kinds and amounts of coverage provided and the covered causes of loss (basic, broad, or special)
   - A list of mortgagees, if any
   - The deductible amount
   - A list of the property coverage forms and endorsements attached to the policy
   - The applicable coinsurance percentage(s)
   - Any optional coverages

1-3. Every commercial property coverage form contains the following elements:
   - Insuring agreement
   - Delineation of the property covered and not covered
   - Additional coverages and coverage extensions
   - Provisions and definitions that apply only to that coverage form

1-4. In the commercial property coverage part, Georgine might include more than one causes of loss form, so that one causes of loss form (such as the special form) may apply to buildings, while another (such as the broad form) may apply to personal property, thereby restricting perils covered. Georgine may also attach endorsements that eliminate any exposures that she is unwilling to insure.

Educational Objective 2

2-1. Examples of categories of covered property under the Building and Personal Property Coverage form (BPP) include the following:
   a. Building:
   - Completed additions
   - Fixtures
   - Permanently installed machinery
   - Personal property used to service building

   b. Business personal property of the insured:
   - Office furniture
   - Merchandise held for sale

   c. Personal property of others:
   - Lawn mowers in repair shops
   - Customers' clothing in dry cleaner facilities

2-2. Some kinds of property are specifically not covered under the BPP for the following three reasons:
   (1) May be illegal to insure
   (2) May not be subject to loss by the perils insured against
   (3) Can be insured better using other forms

2-3. Because the EDP policy specifically describes the computer hardware, its coverage is primary and will cover the loss for its $200,000 limit. Jamal and Keisha's BPP policy will then cover the remaining $100,000 of the loss as business personal property.

Educational Objective 3

3-1. The insured can benefit from the following additional coverages included in the BPP:
   a. Debris removal—Removal of debris resulting from a covered cause of loss during the policy period
   b. Preservation of property—"Any direct physical loss or damage" to the covered property while being moved
   c. Fire department service charge—The fire department charges for services to control or extinguish a fire if assumed by contract prior to loss or required by local ordinance (up to $1,000)
   d. Pollutant cleanup and removal—Expenses to extract pollutants from land or water at the premises if the release, discharge, dispersal, seepage, migration, or escape of the pollutants is the result of a covered cause of loss occurring during the policy period (up to $10,000 per location)
   e. Increased cost of construction—The additional cost to rebuild in compliance with building laws, not to exceed the lesser of 5 percent of the limit of insurance or $10,000
   f. Electronic data—$2,500 of coverage per policy year for electronic data damage

3-2. The coverage extensions in the BPP provide the following benefits and limitations to the insured:
   a. Newly acquired or constructed property:
      - Benefits—Automatically covers a new building constructed at the premises in the declarations and can provide automatic coverage at other locations
      - Limitations—Limits coverage to $250,000; limits coverage at other locations to newly acquired buildings used as a warehouse or for same purpose as building in the declarations; limits business personal property to $100,000; excludes property at a fair or an exhibition
   b. Personal effects and property of others:
      - Benefits—Covers the property of others in the care, custody, or control of the insured (higher limits available); includes loss of personal effects owned by an individual insured, its partner, officer, or employee while on the premises
      - Limitations—Limits coverage on all property to $2,500 at each described location; excludes theft
   c. Valuable papers and records—Cost of research:
      - Benefits—Covers the cost of research and reconstruction of information in destroyed records
      - Limitations—Limits coverage to $2,500 at each described location unless a higher limit in the declarations
   d. Property off-premises:
      - Benefits—Covers property while temporarily at a location not owned, leased, or operated by the insured
      - Limitations—Limits coverage to $10,000; excludes coverage for stock or property in or on a vehicle, unless the property is in the care of the insured's sales personnel, or at a fair or an exhibition
   e. Outdoor property
      - Benefits—Covers loss to outdoor fences, radio and television antennas including satellite dishes, signs not attached to buildings, and trees, shrubs, and plants for loss by fire, lightning, explosion, riot or civil commotion, and aircraft
      - Limitations—Limits coverage to $1,000 and not more than $250 for any one tree, shrub, or plant; excludes loss by windstorm, vehicles, and vandalism
   f. Non-owned detached trailers:
      - Benefits—Extends the insured's business personal property coverage to include loss to a trailer that the insured has leased from others to expand office space or provide additional storage or work space, if the insured has a contractual responsibility to pay for loss to the trailer.
      - Limitations—Applies only while the trailer is not attached to a motor vehicle. The limit is $5,000 unless a higher limit is shown in the policy.

3-3. Because the new building's purpose will be similar to that of Sadeer's existing building, the Newly Acquired or Constructed Property coverage extension of the BPP provides Sadeer with automatic coverage for the newly acquired building for up to 30 days or the policy expiration date. However, the maximum amount of coverage is $250,000 for the new building. Because the new building is valued at $600,000, Sadeer should take immediate steps to purchase building insurance for that amount.

Educational Objective 4

4-1. It is possible for an insurer to pay more than the limit of insurance to an insured in any one policy year in either of the following ways:
- Payments are made under coverage extension and additional coverages, in addition to the policy limit.
- Insured sustains multiple losses (other than under the Pollutant Cleanup and Electronic Data coverage extensions) during the policy year.

4-2. An insured can collect the full BPP policy limit for a building loss even if there is a deductible because the limit applies to loss in excess of the deductible. That is, the deductible is subtracted from the loss, not the limit of insurance. For example, if the building is insured for $800,000 with a $5,000 deductible and a building loss of $815,000 ensues, the loss payment is calculated as $815,000 − $5,000 = $810,000. The $810,000 exceeds the policy limit, so the loss payment is $800,000.

4-3. Higher deductibles appeal to insureds because the insured pays a reduced premium for taking a higher deductible. Higher deductibles appeal to underwriters because the underwriter likes to save the insurer the expense of handling small claims. The underwriter may require a higher deductible for an insured with frequent small losses.

4-4. Carl's BPP with a $400,000 building limit and a $1,000 deductible would pay the following for losses:
   a. $800 loss—BPP pays nothing.
   b. $25,000 loss—BPP pays $24,000.
   c. $415,000—BPP pays $400,000.

Educational Objective 5

5-1. a. The steps for the procedure in the appraisal clause of the BPP include the following:
   - The insured or the insurer disagree on the value of the property or the amount of loss.
   - Either party makes a written demand for an appraisal.
   - Each party appoints an appraiser, and the two appraisers appoint an umpire.
   - Each appraiser prepares a statement of property value and amount of loss.
   - The appraisers submit the items of conflict to the umpire.
   - A decision agreed to by any two of the three is binding on all parties.

   b. The insured's duties in the event of loss include the following:
   - Notify the police if the loss might have resulted from a violation of law.
   - Promptly notify the insurer of the loss (how, when, and where the loss occurred).
   - Protect the property from further loss and keep a record of expenses incurred.
   - Prepare an inventory of the damaged and undamaged property.
   - Permit the insurer to inspect the property and records and take samples for testing and analysis.
   - Submit to examination under oath.
   - Cooperate with the insurer in the adjustment of the loss.
   - Send a signed, sworn proof of loss to the insurer within sixty days after the insurer requests one.

c. The insurer can deny payment of a claim for lack of coverage under the policy or failure of the insured to comply with the policy conditions.
d. The insurer's options in settling a claim include the following:
- Pay the amount of loss or damage.
- Pay the cost of repairing or replacing the damaged property.
- Take over all or any part of the property and pay its agreed or appraised value.
- Repair, rebuild, or replace the damaged property with other property of like kind and quality.
e. If the building has been vacant for more than sixty consecutive days before the loss occurred, the insurer will not pay for loss from certain perils (vandalism, most sprinkler leakage, breakage of building glass, water damage, theft, or attempted theft). Payment for loss by other perils is reduced by 15 percent.

5-2. Insured losses are valued by the BPP as follows:
a. Stock—at ACV, except that stock sold and not delivered is valued at selling price less discounts and unincurred costs
b. Glass—valued at replacement cost for safety glazing if required by law
c. Improvements and betterments replaced by insured—valued at actual cash value
d. Improvements and betterments not replaced—valued at percentage of cost based on remaining life of lease
e. Valuable papers and records—valued at cost of blank material plus cost of transcription or copying (coverage extension of $2,500 research cost)
f. Property other than that specifically listed—valued at actual cash value

5-3. A mortgageholder named on the declarations page of a commercial property policy would have the following rights:
- Payment for any claim for loss on the covered mortgaged property
- Notification of cancellation or nonrenewal

5-4. a. Two other duties in the event of a loss imposed on Tarnton by the BPP are that Tarnton is required to separate damaged and undamaged property and that Tarnton must permit the insurer to inspect its property and records.
b. Under the valuation provision of the BPP, Tarnton would establish the value of its inventory by valuing stock that had not been sold at actual cash value. The stock that had been sold but not delivered would be valued at selling price, less any expenses and discounts that would have applied if delivery had been completed.

5-5. a. The minimum amount of insurance that must be purchased on an ACV basis to avoid a coinsurance penalty is calculated as follows:
0.80 × $300,000 = $240,000.
b. The amount the owner would be paid in the event of a $100,000 covered loss (ACV) is as follows:
$$\$180,000/\$240,000 \times \$100,000 = \$75,000.$$

5-6. Tony's BPP policy will pay the following to the contents of Tony's Toy Store insured on an actual cash value basis in the event of a fire loss:

[$150,000/0.80($300,000) × $60,000] − 1,000 = (5/8 × $60,000) − $1,000 = $37,500 − $1,000

Loss payment = $36,500.

Educational Objective 6

6-1. The four optional coverages available in the BPP are as follows:

(1) Agreed value

(2) Inflation guard

(3) Replacement cost

(4) Extension of replacement cost to personal property of others

6-2. The purpose of the Agreed Value optional coverage in the BPP is to remove the uncertainty as to whether the amount of insurance carried complies with the Coinsurance condition. The option suspends the Coinsurance condition if the insured carries the amount of insurance that the insurer and insured agree to be the property's full value.

6-3. When the insured chooses the Replacement Cost option under the BPP, the Coinsurance condition continues to apply, but the amount of insurance required by the Coinsurance condition is calculated by multiplying replacement cost by the coinsurance percentage if the claim is made on a replacement cost basis.

6-4. Sadie should select the Replacement Cost optional coverage, and she should further elect to have the personal property of others valued at replacement cost. In that way, the amount of the loss to the leased phone equipment is calculated according to the terms of the lease (but the amount of loss cannot exceed the replacement cost of the property or the applicable limit of insurance).

Educational Objective 7

7-1. The functional valuation endorsements provide loss settlement based on the cost of replacing the damaged property with similar property that can perform the same function. Insurers use these endorsements for insureds unwilling to purchase amounts of insurance in excess of the market value of their buildings. Also, insurers avoid moral and morale hazards that might result from writing amounts of insurance that exceed the market value of the property.

7-2. The interior walls of an older building could be used to illustrate functional replacement cost as follows: If the interior walls were constructed of three-coat plaster on wire lath, the walls could be replaced using sheetrock. The sheetrock walls would be functionally equivalent to the previous walls but would cost far less than an exact replacement.

7-3. If property is not replaced using functional replacement cost, recovery is limited to the smallest of the following:

- The limit of insurance
- The market value of the building or personal property
- The functional replacement cost

7-4. With the Value Reporting Form, the policy premium is based on the insured's reports of actual property values during the policy period. Thus, the insured pays for the amount of insurance it actually needs instead of having to pay for an amount of insurance that is more than needed during most of the year. The limit for the Value Reporting Form can be set high enough to cover the highest anticipated value during the policy period, but the insured will only have to pay for the amount of insurance needed to cover actual values.

7-5. The Peak Season Limit of Insurance endorsement provides differing amounts of insurance for specified time periods during the policy term.

7-6. Although a value reporting form might be more effective at matching coverage to exposure, a peak season endorsement might be better for small businesses that have regular fluctuations in inventory. This is true because many small businesses do not have accounting systems of sufficient sophistication to generate the required reports accurately and on time. Furthermore, many insurers would decline to issue a value reporting form for a small insured because the premium might not be large enough to warrant the added expense of processing the reports and calculating the final premium.

7-7. A card and gift shop is usually a seasonal business, and Tomoko's shop will likely have widely fluctuating values for its stock. Using the Value Reporting Form, Tomoko will be required to report the value of the insured business personal property to the insurer periodically during the policy period. As long as Tomoko reports values accurately and on time, the insurer will pay the full amount of any loss that occurs, even if the values on hand at the time of the loss are greater than those last reported.

Educational Objective 8

8-1. An insured with blanket insurance would meet coinsurance requirements by purchasing more insurance than otherwise would be required. This is true because the minimum coinsurance clause is 90 percent, but the rates are the same as for 80 percent coinsurance. The insured with blanket insurance must insure to 90 percent of value to avoid a coinsurance penalty but does not receive the 5 percent discount that applies to specific insurance with a 90 percent coinsurance clause.

8-2. An advantage of blanket insurance is that the full blanket limit can be applied to any one loss. The minimum amount of blanket insurance to comply with coinsurance would fully protect property at each location.

8-3. a. If Jack had specific insurance, he would either have to purchase a higher amount of insurance to provide a cushion against error in estimating insurable values or risk an uninsured loss.

b. If Jack had blanket insurance, assuming the restaurant locations are not likely to be damaged by the same occurrence (such as a hurricane that devastates a wide area), the minimum amount of insurance needed to comply with coinsurance would be sufficient to protect Jack's properties fully.

8-4. Blanket insurance covering personal property at all of the stores would provide a single limit of coverage for all of the costumes regardless of their location. Blanket coverage would provide coverage for the entire inventory regardless of its location. If scheduled insurance was written for the costumes, the values reflected at the various locations would have to either change with the inventory fluctuations or be written for the maximum possible inventory to provide adequate coverage.

Educational Objective 9

9-1. The dollar amount Chris will be paid for this loss is calculated as follows:

a. 0.80 × $400,000 = $320,000
   ($280,000/$320,000 × $72,000) − $1,000 = $62,000.

b. For functional replacement, the loss would be limited to the smallest of the following: (1) the limit of insurance, (2) the market value of the building, or (3) the functional replacement cost. The lowest of these limits is $250,000. The deductible would apply, but coinsurance does not apply. Therefore, the amount payable would be $72,000 − $1,000 (deductible) = $71,000. Such an endorsement is probably a good idea for Chris, who might otherwise be unable to purchase coverage equal to or approaching the $400,000 ACV or $500,000 market value because such coverage is too costly or because insurers are unwilling to write an amount so far in excess of the functional replacement cost. The Functional Building Valuation endorsement will cover, at least, the cost to replace the building so that he can continue his business.

Direct Your Learning

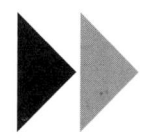

ASSIGNMENT 3

Commercial Property Insurance, Part II

Educational Objectives

After learning the content of this assignment, you should be able to:

1. Identify the perils covered and the perils excluded or limited by the following:
   - Causes of Loss—Basic Form
   - Causes of Loss—Broad Form
   - Causes of Loss—Special Form

2. Explain how and why each of the following coverage forms differs from the Building and Personal Property Coverage Form (BPP):
   - Builders Risk Coverage Form
   - Condominium Association Coverage Form
   - Condominium Commercial Unit-Owners Coverage Form

3. Explain how each of the following endorsements modifies the BPP:
   - Ordinance or Law Coverage
   - Spoilage Coverage
   - Manufacturers' Consequential Loss Assumption
   - Brands and Labels
   - Flood Coverage
   - Earthquake and Volcanic Eruption Coverage

4. Describe the following conditions expressed in the Commercial Property Conditions Form:
   - Concealment, Misrepresentation, or Fraud
   - Control of Property
   - Insurance Under Two or More Coverages
   - Legal Action Against Us
   - Liberalization
   - No Benefit to Bailee
   - Other Insurance
   - Policy Period, Coverage Territory
   - Transfer of Rights of Recovery Against Others to Us

5. Describe the aspects of coverage and other factors that affect commercial property insurance premiums.

6. Define or describe each of the Key Words and Phrases for this assignment.

Study Materials

Required Reading:
- Commercial Insurance
  - Chapter 3
- "Terrorism Coverage and Exclusions," Course Guide Reading 3-1

Study Aids:
- SMART Online Practice Exams
- SMART Study Aids
  - Review Notes and Flash Cards—Assignment 3

3.1

Outline

- **Causes of Loss Forms**
- **Causes of Loss—Basic Form**
    - A. Covered Causes of Loss
        1. Fire
        2. Lightning
        3. Explosion
        4. Windstorm or Hail
        5. Smoke
        6. Aircraft or Vehicles
        7. Riot or Civil Commotion
        8. Vandalism
        9. Sprinkler Leakage
        10. Sinkhole Collapse
        11. Volcanic Action
    - B. Exclusions
        1. Anti-Concurrent Causation Wording
        2. Ordinance or Law
        3. Earth Movement
        4. Governmental Action
        5. Nuclear Hazard
        6. Utility Services
        7. War and Military Action
        8. Water
        9. "Fungus," Wet Rot, Dry Rot, and Bacteria
        10. Other Exclusions
    - C. Additional Coverage—Limited Coverage for "Fungus," Wet Rot, Dry Rot, and Bacteria
- **Causes of Loss—Broad Form**
    - A. Covered Causes of Loss
        1. Falling Objects
        2. Weight of Snow, Ice, or Sleet
        3. Water Damage
    - B. Additional Coverage—Collapse
- **Causes of Loss—Special Form**
    - A. Exclusions and Limitations
        1. Exclusions and Limitations Unique to the Special Form
        2. Theft-Related Exclusions and Limitations
    - B. Additional Coverage—Collapse
    - C. Coverage Extensions
        1. Property in Transit
        2. Water Damage, Other Liquids, Powder or Molten Material Damage
        3. Glass
- **Other Commercial Property Coverage Forms**
    - A. Builders Risk Coverage Form
        1. Eligible Property and Insureds
        2. Covered Property
        3. Coverage Extensions
        4. Causes of Loss
        5. Need for Adequate Insurance
        6. When Coverage Ceases
        7. Other Provisions
    - B. Condominium Coverage Forms
        1. Condominium Association Coverage Form
        2. Condominium Commercial Unit-Owners Coverage Form
    - C. Insurance for Highly Protected Risks
- **Endorsements**
    - A. Ordinance or Law Coverage
    - B. Spoilage Coverage
    - C. Manufacturers' Consequential Loss Assumption
    - D. Brands and Labels
    - E. Flood Coverage
    - F. Earthquake and Volcanic Eruption Coverage

▶ **Commercial Property Conditions**
   A. Concealment, Misrepresentation, or Fraud
   B. Control of Property
   C. Insurance Under Two or More Coverages
   D. Legal Action Against Us
   E. Liberalization
   F. No Benefit to Bailee
   G. Other Insurance
   H. Policy Period, Coverage Territory
   I. Transfer of Rights of Recovery Against Others to Us

▶ **Rating Commercial Property Coverage**
   A. Aspects of Coverage
      1. Limit of Insurance
      2. Covered Causes of Loss
      3. Coinsurance Percentage
      4. Deductible Amount
      5. Optional Coverages
   B. Other Factors
      1. Construction
      2. Occupancy
      3. Protection
      4. Exposure
      5. Location
   C. Class Rates and Specific Rates

▶ **Summary**

▶ **Terrorism Coverage and Exclusions**
   (Course Guide Reading 3-1)

s.m.a.r.t. tips — Actively capture information by using the open space in the SMART Review Notes to write out key concepts. Putting information into your own words is an effective way to push that information into your memory.

Reading 3-1

Terrorism Coverage and Exclusions

The terrorist attacks of September 11, 2001, changed the insurance landscape in the United States. Along with the rest of the country, insurers saw the enormous loss exposure that terrorist acts pose. The American Academy of Actuaries estimates that a major terrorist attack on New York City using chemical, nuclear, or biological weapons could cause more than $700 billion in insured losses.[1] The events of September 11, 2001, highlighted catastrophic exposures that were previously overlooked. For example, underwriters traditionally regarded office workers as a low-risk classification for insurance such as workers compensation. However, the terrorist attacks caused huge losses for the insurers of the office tenants in the World Trade Center.

The Terrorism Risk Insurance Act (TRIA)

Many insurers felt that the terrorism threat was too large and unpredictable for the industry to properly price the coverage or insure the risk without financial reinforcement from the federal government. In response, Congress passed the Terrorism Risk Insurance Act (TRIA) in 2002. It expired December 31, 2005, and was replaced with the Terrorism Risk Insurance Extension Act (TRIEA), which was scheduled to expire on December 31, 2007. The main features of TRIEA are as follows:

- TRIEA applies to most property-casualty lines of business except commercial auto, professional liability (other than directors and officers insurance), surety, and a few others.
- TRIEA requires all insurers to offer certified terrorism coverage for all lines of insurance addressed by the act. "Certified terrorism" is defined as a violent act certified by the Secretary of the Treasury to have been committed by a foreign person or interest to coerce or influence U.S. policy and to have resulted in at least $5 million in insured damage.
- The provision of TRIEA that provides for federal reimbursement is triggered only when industry-wide insured damages exceed $50 million in 2006 or $100 million in 2007.
- Reimbursement to insurers for payment of certified terrorism losses is subject to a deductible equal to 17.5 percent (2006) or 20 percent (2007) of the insurer's direct earned premiums in the prior year.
- The federal government's share of losses over the deductible is 90 percent in 2006 and 85 percent in 2007.[2]

TRIEA applies only to foreign terrorist acts. Domestic terrorism, such as the 1995 Oklahoma City bombing, is not covered.

Terrorism Endorsements

In addition to TRIEA-mandated coverage, insurers use several endorsements to handle terrorism exposures. The endorsements filed by Insurance Services Office (ISO) include the Exclusion of Terrorism endorsement and the Exclusion of Terrorism Involving Nuclear, Biological or Chemical Terrorism endorsement.

The Exclusion of Terrorism endorsement excludes damage resulting from terrorist acts carried out by means of nuclear, biological, or chemical materials, provided that the insured damage in the U.S., Puerto Rico, and Canada totals more than $25 million. (The $25 million trigger is for all insured damage, not just damage to the insured's property.)

The Exclusion of Terrorism Involving Nuclear, Biological or Chemical Terrorism endorsement is similar to the Exclusion of Terrorism endorsement, but does not contain a dollar amount-of-loss trigger.

Both endorsements contain wording that provides coverage for direct fire losses when required by laws of the state where the property is located.

In addition to these endorsements, ISO has filed numerous state-specific endorsements to comply with state terrorism laws. Some states have not approved terrorism exclusions.

ISO has developed contingent endorsements to be attached to policies expiring after December 31, 2007, if TRIEA is not renewed. The Conditional Exclusion of Terrorism (Relating to Disposition of Federal Terrorism Risk Insurance Act) endorsement eliminates certified terrorism coverage from the policy. ISO and others developing insurance forms will need to provide other coverage options and exclusions if TRIEA is not renewed.

Many elected officials hope that the insurance industry will be able to provide terrorism coverage without federal reinforcement. Some insurers currently offer stand-alone terrorism coverage, but many observers doubt that the industry can independently provide the required amounts of coverage, fearing that the potential dollar losses exceed the collective surplus (funds available to pay new claims) of the industry.

READING NOTES

1. "Major Attack on NYC Seen Costing Insurers $778B," *Business Insurance Online*, March 20, 2006, www.businessinsurance.com/cgi-bin/news.pl?newsId=7469 (accessed March 20, 2006).

2. Robert Blumber and Ben Tucker, "Marketwatch: Terrorism Insurance 2005—Highlights of the TRIA Extension," Marsh, Inc., 2005, solutions.marsh.com/terrorism/documents/MarshTRIAExtensionupdate200512.pdf (accessed November 1, 2006).

For each assignment, you should define or describe each of the Key Words and Phrases and answer each of the Review and Application Questions.

Educational Objective 1

Identify the perils covered and the perils excluded or limited by the following:

- Causes of Loss—Basic Form
- Causes of Loss—Broad Form
- Causes of Loss—Special Form

Key Words and Phrases

Causes of Loss—Basic Form (p. 3.4)

Concurrent causation doctrine (p. 3.8)

Causes of Loss—Broad Form (p. 3.11)

Causes of Loss—Special Form (p. 3.13)

Review Questions

1-1. List the covered causes of loss in the Causes of Loss—Basic Form. (p. 3.4)

1-2. Identify the causes of loss that are excluded under the Causes of Loss—Basic Form. (pp. 3.7–3.11)

1-3. Identify the causes of loss that are covered under the broad form that are not covered under the basic form. (p. 3.11)

1-4. What are the advantages to the insured of purchasing the Causes of Loss—Special Form? (p. 3.14)

1-5. Why does the special form contain several exclusions that are not found in the basic or broad form? (pp. 3.14–3.15)

1-6. Describe the Additional Coverage—Collapse that is included in both the broad form and the special form. (p. 3.12)

1-7. Give an example of a loss that would be covered under each of the following additional coverage extensions of the special form:

   a. Property in transit (p. 3.17–3.18)

   b. Water damage, other liquids, powder or molten material damage (p. 3.18)

Application Questions

1-8. The Murphy Corporation has a commercial property policy with a Causes of Loss—Basic Form covering its building. Explain whether each of the following losses would be covered under Murphy's policy. If not, identify a causes-of-loss form, if any, that would cover the loss.

   a. A windstorm damaged Murphy's roof.

   b. During a major storm, the river that runs near Murphy's property overflowed its banks. The rising water seeped into Murphy's building, damaging the hardwood floors.

c. Vandals broke several windows in Murphy's building.

d. An employee driving one of Murphy's trucks accidentally backed into Murphy's building and damaged an exterior wall.

e. Heavy earthquake shocks caused structural damage to Murphy's building.

1-9. Coverage for Jones's building and business personal property is currently subject to a Causes of Loss—Broad Form. When Jones renews his property insurance, he will purchase coverage subject to a Causes of Loss—Special Form, rather than a broad form. Briefly explain how each of the following will be affected by this change in the causes of loss form:

a. The coverage for Jones's building and business personal property

b. The premium for Jones's property coverage

> ## Educational Objective 2
> Explain how and why each of the following coverage forms differs from the Building and Personal Property Coverage Form (BPP):
> - Builders Risk Coverage Form
> - Condominium Association Coverage Form
> - Condominium Commercial Unit-Owners Coverage Form

Key Words and Phrases

Builders Risk Coverage Form (p. 3.18)

Condominium Association Coverage Form (p. 3.22)

Condominium Commercial Unit-Owners Coverage Form (p. 3.23)

Loss assessment coverage (p. 3.24)

Miscellaneous real property coverage (p. 3.24)

Insurance for highly protected risks (HPR) (p. 3.24)

Review Questions

2-1. Explain how the coverage of a Builders Risk Coverage Form (plus Causes of Loss—Special Form) would differ from a BPP (plus special form) with regard to each of the following:

   a. Covered property (pp. 3.18–3.19)

   b. Covered causes of loss (p. 3.20)

2-2. Summarize the following provisions in the Builders Risk Coverage Form:

   a. Need for adequate insurance (p. 3.20–3.21)

   b. When coverage ceases (p. 3.21)

2-3. Describe the circumstances under which each of the following covers appliances, fixtures, improvements, and alterations contained within individual units of a condominium building:

a. Condominium Association Coverage Form (p. 3.22)

b. Condominium Commercial Unit-Owners Coverage Form (pp. 3.23–3.24)

2-4. What characteristic do properties qualifying for HPR insurance generally have? (p. 3.24)

Application Questions

2-5. Lawton Builders, Inc. (LBI) is constructing a commercial building that it estimates will have a value of $250,000 upon completion. Construction has already begun, and the current value of the completed part of the building is $25,000. LBI is interested in purchasing a Builders Risk Coverage Form on this building.

a. What amount of insurance would LBI be required to carry on its builders risk policy? Explain.

b. How would the causes of loss to be covered under LBI's policy be determined?

c. How can LBI obtain coverage for theft of its building materials on the building site?

d. If LBI is unable to find a buyer for its building upon completion, how long will the builders risk coverage continue?

2-6. The Bellevue Condominium Association owns a twenty-story condominium building containing 200 office condominiums owned by individual owners.

　　a. What ISO property coverage form could Bellevue use to cover its building?

　　b. What ISO property coverage form could each individual owner of the office condominiums use?

c. What can an individual unit owner do to protect against assessments made by Bellevue because of damage to the building caused by a covered loss?

Educational Objective 3

Explain how each of the following endorsements modifies the BPP:

- Ordinance or Law Coverage
- Spoilage Coverage
- Manufacturers' Consequential Loss Assumption
- Brands and Labels
- Flood Coverage
- Earthquake and Volcanic Eruption Coverage

Key Words and Phrases

Ordinance or Law Coverage endorsement (p. 3.25)

Spoilage Coverage endorsement (p. 3.26)

Manufacturers' Consequential Loss Assumption endorsement (p. 3.26)

Brands and Labels endorsement (p. 3.26)

Review Questions

3-1. Briefly describe the three coverages provided by the Ordinance or Law Coverage endorsement. (p. 3.25)

3-2. Under the Spoilage Coverage endorsement, what must cause the spoilage of perishable stock in order for the spoilage to be covered? (p. 3.26)

3-3. What are two actions that the Brands and Labels endorsement permits the insured to take when the insurer takes covered property as salvage? (p. 3.26)

3-4. In general, where must a building be located in order for a private insurer to be willing to insure the property against flood by endorsement to the insured's commercial property policy? (p. 3.27)

3-5. What is the principal way in which the two ISO earthquake endorsements differ? (pp. 3.27–3.28)

Application Question

3-6. Robust, a toy manufacturer, has constructed its new factory in coastal southern California. It specializes in toy trucks, bulldozers, and cranes that are high-quality replicas of full-sized equipment. The company is contracted by many of the manufacturers of the full-sized equipment to build these replicas and mass-produce them. Robust's new factory is insured by a commercial property policy with a special causes of loss form. What additional endorsements would you add to its policy, and why would you add them?

> ## Educational Objective 4
> Describe the following conditions expressed in the Commercial Property Conditions Form:
> - Concealment, Misrepresentation, or Fraud
> - Control of Property
> - Insurance Under Two or More Coverages
> - Legal Action Against Us
> - Liberalization
> - No Benefit to Bailee
> - Other Insurance
> - Policy Period, Coverage Territory
> - Transfer of Rights of Recovery Against Others to Us

Key Word or Phrase
Subrogation (p. 3.31)

Review Questions

4-1. Explain the following conditions in the Commercial Property Conditions:

  a. Concealment, misrepresentation, or fraud (pp. 3.28–3.29)

  b. Control of property (p. 3.29)

c. Insurance under two or more coverages (p. 3.29)

d. Liberalization (p. 3.30)

e. Other insurance (pp. 3.30–3.31)

f. Transfer of rights of recovery against others (p. 3.31)

4-2. Describe the two requirements an insured must meet before legal action can be brought against an insurer to enforce a commercial property policy. (p. 3.30)

4-3. Explain how the "no benefit to bailee" clause protects bailors' property. (p. 3.30)

Application Question

4-4. Zelles Hospital uses Ambrose Laundry as its laundry service for linens and uniforms. Ambrose experienced a fire in which $20,000 worth of Zelles's laundry was destroyed. Ambrose has stated that it is not liable for the damage and that Zelles should collect the value of the laundry from its own commercial property insurance. Explain whether you agree with Ambrose's statement.

Educational Objective 5
Describe the aspects of coverage and other factors that affect commercial property insurance premiums.

Key Words and Phrases
Specific rating (p. 3.35)

Class rating (pp. 3.35–3.36)

Review Questions

5-1. Identify the aspects of coverage that affect the premium for commercial property coverage. (p. 3.32)

5-2. What other factors affect commercial property premiums? (p. 3.34)

5-3. How is specific rating different from class rating? (pp. 3.35–3.36)

Application Question

5-4. Etchley Corporation owns a red brick building that it occupies as a retail clothing store. Etchley has purchased a commercial property policy from Radley Insurance Company with a Causes of Loss—Broad Form on this building. The policy has a limit of $500,000 on the building on a replacement cost basis with a 90 percent coinsurance clause and a $1,000 deductible. Because Etchley's building is located fifteen miles from the nearest fire department and twenty miles from a police station, it has installed a sprinkler system and a burglar alarm.

   a. In rating Etchley's commercial property policy, what factors will Radley consider?

b. How will the factors you identified in part (a) affect the premium for this policy?

Educational Objective 6
Describe terrorism coverages and exclusions by endorsement and the major features of the Terrorism Risk Insurance Act, including applicable lines of business, certified terrorism, and the obligations of the federal government.

Review Questions

6-1. Which major property-casualty lines of business are not covered by TRIEA? (Course Guide Reading 3-1, p. 3.4)

6-2. What select set of terrorist acts are addressed by TRIEA, and who determines which acts qualify under TRIEA as certified terrorism? (Course Guide Reading 3-1, p. 3.4)

6-3. During 2007, how is the federal government's share of certified terrorism losses determined? (Course Guide Reading 3-1, p. 3.4)

Application Question

6-4. Green Tomato Insurance Group (GTIG) is a property-casualty insurer writing business in 12 midwestern U.S. states. GTIG had $600 million in direct earned premiums in 2006. GTIG incurred $75 million of certified terrorism losses during 2007. What is the federal government's share of those losses?

Answers to Assignment 3 Questions

NOTE: These answers are provided to give students a basic understanding of acceptable types of responses. They often are not the only valid answers and are not intended to provide an exhaustive response to the questions.

Educational Objective 1

1-1. The covered causes of loss in the Causes of Loss—Basic Form are as follows:
- Fire
- Lightning
- Explosion
- Windstorm or hail
- Smoke
- Aircraft or vehicles
- Riot or civil commotion
- Vandalism
- Sprinkler leakage
- Sinkhole collapse
- Volcanic action
- Fungus, wet rot, dry rot, and bacteria (provided as an additional limited coverage)

1-2. The following covered causes of loss are excluded under the Causes of Loss—Basic Form:
- Ordinance or law
- Earth movement
- Governmental action
- Nuclear hazard
- Utility services
- War and military action
- Water
- Fungus, wet rot, dry rot, and bacteria
- Artificially generated electric currents
- Rupture or bursting of water pipes
- Leakage of water or steam
- Explosion of steam boilers, steam pipes, steam turbines, or steam engines
- Mechanical breakdown
- Loss resulting from the neglect of the insured to use all reasonable means to save and preserve property at and after the time of loss

1-3. The causes of loss covered under the broad form that are not covered under the basic form include the following:
- Falling objects
- Weight of snow, ice, or sleet
- Water damage

1-4. An insured purchasing the Causes of Loss—Special Form has coverage for the following:
- Causes of loss omitted or excluded under the broad form (such as theft)
- Unanticipated losses (any loss other than those specifically excluded)
- All accidental losses unless the insurer can prove an excluded peril caused the loss (shift in burden of proof)

1-5. The special form contains several exclusions that are not found in the basic or broad form because of its open-ended (all risks except those excluded) approach to coverage, in comparison with the basic and broad forms, which simply list the covered causes of loss. The additional exclusions in the special form eliminate coverage for many difficult-to-insure perils that are not covered under the basic and broad forms because they are not listed as covered perils in those forms.

1-6. The Additional Coverage—Collapse, included in both the broad form and the special form, provides coverage for loss resulting from collapse of a building or any part of a building if the collapse is caused by one or more of the following:
- The covered causes of loss under the broad form
- Hidden decay
- Hidden insect or vermin damage
- Weight of people or personal property
- Weight of rain that collects on a roof
- Use of defective materials or construction methods if the collapse occurs during the course of construction
- Collapse of personal property inside a building

1-7. Covered losses under the following additional coverage extensions of the special form include the following:
   a. Property in transit—The insured's notebook computer is destroyed when the car driven by the insured collides with a truck. The insured's additional coverage would pay for the cost of repairing or replacing the notebook computer.
   b. Water damage, other liquids, powder or molten material damage —Water escapes from a water pipe that ruptures inside a wall of the insured's building and damages the floor and the ceiling below. The additional coverage would pay the cost of tearing out the wall (and restoring it) in order to repair the broken pipe.

1-8. A commercial property policy with a Causes of Loss—Basic Form provides the following coverage:
   a. Windstorm damage would be covered because windstorm is a covered peril under the basic form.
   b. Damage from rising water would not be covered because of flood exclusion. Flood is not a covered peril under any of the causes-of-loss forms. (Murphy needs to purchase coverage through the National Flood Insurance Program or by endorsement to its commercial property policy.)

c. The broken windows would be covered because vandalism is a covered cause of loss. (Although the vandalism peril once excluded glass breakage, that exclusion was eliminated in the 2000 revision.)

d. The damage to the exterior wall would not be covered because the basic form excludes vehicle damage caused by vehicles owned by the insured or operated in the insured's business. Murphy would need a special form to cover this loss.

e. The structural damage would not be covered because of the earthquake exclusion. Murphy needs one of the earthquake endorsements.

1-9. Coverage changes resulting from a change from a BPP Causes of Loss—Broad Form to a Causes of Loss—Special Form would include the following:

a. With the special form, Jones's building and business personal property form will have coverage for accidental and unforeseen risks of direct physical loss subject to exclusions and limitations expressed in the form. With the broad form, Jones's building and business personal property form had coverage for the listed perils.

b. The premium for property coverage would generally increase because the special form covers more causes of loss.

Educational Objective 2

2-1. Coverage provided by a Builders Risk Coverage Form (plus Causes of Loss—Special Form) differs from a BPP (plus special form) in the following ways:

a. Covered property—The builders risk form, unlike the BPP, covers foundations and temporary structures assembled on the work site (such as scaffolding).

b. Covered causes of loss—When the special form is attached to a builders risk form, it excludes collapse that occurs during construction.

2-2. Provisions in the Builders Risk Coverage Form include the following:

a. The Need for Adequate Insurance Provision is similar to a 100 percent coinsurance clause requiring the insured to carry insurance at least equal to the actual cash value of the completed building.

b. The When Coverage Ceases provision states that coverage under the builders risk form terminates at the earliest of the following:

- The expiration date shown in the declarations
- The date of cancellation
- The date when the property is accepted by the purchaser
- When the insured's interest in the property ceases
- When the insured abandons construction not intending to complete it
- Either 90 days after the construction is completed or 60 days after the building is occupied in whole or in part or is put to its intended use, unless the insurer indicates otherwise in writing

2-3. a. The Condominium Association Coverage Form covers appliances, fixtures, improvements, and alterations contained within individual units if the condominium association agreement requires the association to insure them.

b. The Condominium Commercial Unit-Owners Coverage Form covers only "your business personal property" and personal property of others. These coverages are basically the same as in the BPP. Fixtures, improvements, and alterations that are part of the building and owned by the unit owner are included in the definition of "your business personal property" in the unit-owners form.

2-4. Properties qualifying for HPR insurance generally have a proactive management determined to control the risk of property loss.

2-5.
a. LBI needs a limit of $250,000 in order to satisfy the "need for adequate insurance" condition in the builders risk form, which requires the insured to carry insurance in an amount that is at least equal to the actual cash value of the building on completion.
b. The builders risk form must be combined with a basic, broad, or special causes-of-loss form. It is the causes-of-loss form that LBI must choose that will determine what causes of loss are covered.
c. Because none of the causes-of-loss forms cover uninstalled building materials, LBI would need a special endorsement (Builders Risk—Theft of Building Materials, Fixtures, Machinery, Equipment) to cover this exposure.
d. The builders risk coverage ceases 90 days after construction is completed (unless the insurer agrees to extend the coverage for a longer period).

2-6. The Bellevue Condominium Association, which owns a twenty-story condominium building containing 200 office condominiums owned by individual owners, could use the following coverage forms:
a. Bellevue could use the Condominium Association Coverage Form to cover the condominium building.
b. An individual owner could use the Condominium Commercial Unit-Owners Form to cover an individual office condominium.
c. An individual owner could purchase the optional loss assessment coverage to cover his or her unit-owner's share of any assessment made by the association against all unit owners because of physical loss or damage to condominium property caused by a covered cause of loss.

Educational Objective 3

3-1. The Ordinance or Law Coverage Endorsement provides the following three coverages:
(1) Coverage A covers the value of the undamaged portion of the building that must be demolished because of a building law.
(2) Coverage B covers the cost to demolish the undamaged portion of a building and remove its debris.
(3) Coverage C covers the increased cost to repair or rebuild the property.

3-2. The Spoilage Coverage Endorsement covers spoilage resulting from a power outage or an on-premises breakdown or contamination of the insured's refrigerating, cooling, or humidity control equipment.

3-3. The Brands and Labels Endorsement permits the insured to stamp the word "salvage" on the merchandise and to remove brands or labels, provided neither of these measures will physically damage the merchandise.

3-4. Private insurers will typically provide flood coverage by endorsement to their commercial property policies if the building is located outside high-hazard flood zones.

3-5. The main difference between the two earthquake endorsements is that one is written for the full policy limit (and subject to its coinsurance requirement), whereas the other endorsement can be written subject to a sublimit that is not subject to a coinsurance requirement.

3-6. The following additional endorsements should be added to the toy manufacturer's policy:
- An Earthquake and Volcanic Eruption Endorsement would be required due to the location of the factory.
- Brands and Labels Endorsement would be beneficial if stock was damaged. The toys might be repainted or relabeled and sold as salvage without damaging Robust's reputation for quality products.

Educational Objective 4

4-1. Commercial Property Conditions include the following:
   a. Concealment, misrepresentation, or fraud—The commercial property coverage part is void if the insured conceals or misrepresents any material fact or commits any fraudulent act related to the coverage.
   b. Control of property—Coverage will not be affected by acts or omissions of persons other than the insured if the others are not acting under the direction or control of the insured. Also, a violation of a policy condition at one location will not affect coverage at any other location.
   c. Insurance under two or more coverage parts—The total payment under all applicable coverage parts is limited to the actual amount of the loss.
   d. Liberalization—If the insurance company adopts a revision that would broaden the coverage under the commercial property coverage part and does not charge an additional premium, the broader coverage is extended automatically to outstanding policies.
   e. Other insurance—If an insured has more than one policy covering a given loss, the total recovery from all applicable insurance is limited to an amount not to exceed the actual loss sustained. If the other insurance is provided by another policy subject to the same plan, terms, and conditions, then each policy pays that proportion of the loss that its policy limit bears to the total policy limits of all applicable policies. If the other insurance is not subject to the same conditions as the ISO commercial property coverage part, then the policy subject to the commercial property coverage part provisions is excess over the other insurance.
   f. Transfer of rights of recovery against others—The insurance company can recover the amount paid for a covered loss from any party causing the loss or otherwise legally liable for the loss. If the insured takes any action eliminating the insurer's right of recovery, the insurer may not be required to pay the loss.

4-2. The two requirements an insured must meet before legal action can be brought against an insurer to enforce a commercial property policy are as follows:
   (1) The insured must have complied with all conditions of the policy, including those in the coverage part and the common policy conditions, as well as the applicable loss conditions.
   (2) The action must be brought within two years after the date on which the direct physical loss occurred.

4-3. Bailees sometimes try to limit their liability by contractual provisions stating that they are not liable for damage to property in their possession if the damage is recoverable under insurance carried by the bailor. The "no benefit to bailee" clause defeats such provisions in the bailment contract and reinforces the insurance company's right of subrogation against the bailee.

4-4. One of the conditions of the policy is that it will not benefit a bailee. Ambrose is a bailee and responsible for the damage to the laundry. Although Zelles's commercial property insurance will cover the damage to the laundry, it is Ambrose's responsibility to pay the damages.

Educational Objective 5

5-1. The aspects of coverage that affect the premium for commercial property coverage are the limit of insurance, covered causes of loss, and optional coverages selected. Coinsurance and deductibles can be used to decrease this premium.

5-2. The following factors also affect commercial property premiums:
- Construction—Type of building (frame, joisted masonry, noncombustible, masonry noncombustible, modified fire resistive, and fire resistive)
- Occupancy—Type of activity conducted inside the building
- Protection—Private or public protection (sprinkler systems, local fire departments)
- Exposure—Risk created by neighboring buildings
- Location—Geographic area

5-3. Specific rating develops rates that reflect the exposure to loss of a particular business. Class rating develops rates that reflect the average probability of loss for businesses within a large group of similar risks by generalizing about the probabilities of loss within these groups.

5-4. a. Etchley's insurer will consider the following factors:
- Construction (brick)
- Occupancy (retail clothing store)
- Causes-of-loss form (broad)
- Building limit ($500,000)
- Coinsurance (90%)
- Deductible ($1,000)
- Location (territory)
- Fire protection (15 miles from fire station, sprinkler system)

b. These factors will affect the premium as follows:
- The brick (masonry) construction will carry a lower rate than a frame building but a higher one than a fire-resistive building.
- Occupancies are rated according to how risky they are. The occupancy (retail clothing store) would probably not be considered particularly hazardous and would carry an average rate.
- The Causes of Loss—Broad Form would have a higher premium than a basic form but a lower premium than a Special Form.

- The building limit is used to determine the exposure unit to be multiplied by the rate to determine the premium. (Property rates are usually per $100 of insurance, so in this case: 5,000 × rate = premium.)
- Tower's premium would be reduced because its coinsurance percentage is higher than 80 percent and its deductible is higher than the base deductible.
- A "territorial multiplier" would be applied based on the exposure involved at the location (Anytown).
- Although a high rate would apply because the building is many miles from the nearest fire station, a credit would probably be given for the sprinkler system.

NOTE: The burglar alarm and the distance from the police station would probably not be considered in this case. Property rates are generally based on fire protection; also, since the broad form does not include theft coverage, crime protection is not a valid factor.

The replacement cost option does not affect the rate (but it does affect the amount of insurance Tower needs to satisfy the coinsurance requirement).

Terrorism coverage, if applicable, might also have a bearing on the premium.

Educational Objective 6

6-1. TRIEA applies to most property and casualty lines of business except commercial auto, professional liability (other than D&O), surety, and a few others.

6-2. TRIEA applies only to foreign terrorist acts. Domestic terrorism, such as the Oklahoma City bombing in 1995, is not covered. Certified terrorism is a violent act certified by the Secretary of the Treasury to have been committed by a foreign person or interest to coerce or influence U.S. policy and to have resulted in at least $5 million in insured damage.

6-3. During 2007, reimbursement for certified terrorism losses by the federal government to insurers is subject to a deductible equal to 20 percent of the insurer's direct earned premiums in the prior year. The federal government's share of losses over the deductible is 90 percent in 2006 and 85 percent in 2007.

6-4. During 2007, reimbursement for certified terrorism losses by the federal government to GTIG is subject to a deductible equal to 20 percent of GTIG's 2006 direct earned premiums, which is calculated as 0.2 × $600 million = $120 million. Because GTIG's terrorism losses ($75 million) are below the calculated deductible for 2007, the federal government will not share the losses.

Direct Your Learning

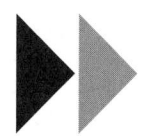

ASSIGNMENT 4

Business Income Insurance

Educational Objectives

After learning the content of this assignment, you should be able to:

1. Describe the following aspects of the business income loss exposure:
   - Measurement of business income losses
   - Effect of business interruption on expenses
   - Property and perils involved in business income losses
2. Given a simple case, calculate the amount of a business income loss.
3. Describe the coverage provided by the insuring agreements, additional coverages, and the coverage extension in the following business income coverage (BIC) forms:
   - Business Income (and Extra Expense) Coverage Form
   - Business Income (Without Extra Expense) Coverage Form
4. Describe the exclusions in the causes of loss forms that apply specifically to business income coverage.
5. Describe the loss conditions and coinsurance provision of the BIC.
6. Explain how each of the following optional coverages affects business income coverage:
   - Maximum period of indemnity
   - Monthly limit of indemnity
   - Business income agreed value
   - Extended period of indemnity
7. Describe the Extra Expense Coverage Form and the types of businesses for which it is appropriate.
8. Explain how each of the following endorsements affects business income coverage:
   - Business Income From Dependent Properties
   - Ordinary Payroll Limitation or Exclusion
   - Power, Heat and Refrigeration Deduction
   - Ordinance or Law—Increased Period of Restoration
9. Explain how business income coverage is rated.
10. Explain whether, and for what amount, the BIC and any applicable optional coverages and endorsements would cover a described loss.
11. Define or describe each of the Key Words and Phrases for this assignment.

Study Materials

Required Reading:
- Commercial Insurance
  - Chapter 4

Study Aids:
- SMART Online Practice Exams
- SMART Study Aids
  - Review Notes and Flash Cards—Assignment 4

Outline

- **Business Income Loss Exposure**
  - A. Measurement of Business Income Losses
  - B. Effect of Business Interruption on Expenses
    1. Continuing Expenses
    2. Extra Expenses
  - C. Property and Perils Involved in Business Income Losses
- **Business Income Coverage Forms**
  - A. Business Income Insuring Agreement
  - B. Extra Expense Insuring Agreement
  - C. Additional Coverages and Coverage Extension
    1. Expenses to Reduce Loss
    2. Civil Authority
    3. Alterations and New Buildings
    4. Extended Business Income
    5. Interruption of Computer Operations
    6. Newly Acquired Locations
  - D. Exclusions
    1. Off-Premises Services Interruption
    2. Finished Stock
    3. Antennas
    4. Delay and Suspension, Lapse, or Cancellation of Agreements
    5. Extra Expense Due to Suspension, Lapse, or Cancellation of Agreements
    6. Other Consequential Losses
  - E. Limits of Insurance
  - F. Loss Conditions
    1. Appraisal
    2. Duties in the Event of Loss
    3. Loss Determination
    4. Loss Payment
  - G. Coinsurance
  - H. Optional Coverages
    1. Maximum Period of Indemnity
    2. Monthly Limit of Indemnity
    3. Business Income Agreed Value
    4. Extended Period of Indemnity
- **Other Forms and Endorsements**
  - A. Extra Expense Coverage Form
  - B. Business Income From Dependent Properties
  - C. Ordinary Payroll Limitation or Exclusion
  - D. Power, Heat and Refrigeration Deduction
  - E. Ordinance or Law—Increased Period of Restoration
  - F. Other Endorsements
- **Rating Business Income Coverage**
- **Summary**

Use the SMART Online Practice Exams to test your understanding of the course material. You can review questions over a single assignment or multiple assignments, or you can take an exam over the entire course. The questions are scored, and you are shown your results. (You score essay exams yourself.)

For each assignment, you should define or describe each of the Key Words and Phrases and answer each of the Review and Application Questions.

> ## Educational Objective 1
> Describe the following aspects of the business income loss exposure:
> - Measurement of business income losses
> - Effect of business interruption on expenses
> - Property and perils involved in business income losses

Key Words and Phrases

Business income insurance (p. 4.4)

Net income (p. 4.4)

Profit (p. 4.4)

Net loss (p. 4.4)

Continuing expenses (p. 4.5)

Noncontinuing expenses (p. 4.5)

Extra expenses (p. 4.5)

Review Questions

1-1. How can business income losses be measured? (pp. 4.4–4.5)

1-2. Give three examples of normal operating expenses that could continue during a short business interruption. (p. 4.5)

1-3. Give three examples of extra expenses that might be incurred to continue operations after a physical loss. (pp. 4.5–4.6)

1-4. In order for business income insurance to apply, what must occur, according to the usual business income insuring agreement? (p. 4.7)

Application Question

1-5. Surewell Aircraft manufactures small single-engine aircraft. It annually assembles 100 aircraft at its plant in Arizona from composite-material bodies manufactured in Mexico and engines manufactured in England specifically for Surewell's aircraft. Analyze Surewell's business income loss exposures.

Educational Objective 2
Given a simple case, calculate the amount of a business income loss.

Review Questions

2-1. What financial figures (expected and actual amounts) are involved in the calculation of business income losses? (pp. 4.4–4.5)

2-2. Identify the types of expenses that must be considered when measuring a business income loss. (pp. 4.4–4.5)

Application Question

2-3. Sal's Candy Shop suffered a fire and was shut down for six months while a new shop was built. During those six months, Sal's revenues were nil, compared with the $60,000 of revenue that would have been earned for that period if the loss had not occurred. Sal's operating expenses for the six-month shutdown were only $5,000, compared with the $30,000 in expenses that would have been incurred under normal conditions. Calculate the amount of Sal's business income loss for the six-month shutdown.

Educational Objective 3

Describe the coverage provided by the insuring agreements, additional coverages, and the coverage extension in the following business income coverage (BIC) forms:

- Business Income (and Extra Expense) Coverage Form
- Business Income (Without Extra Expense) Coverage Form

Key Words and Phrases

Business Income (and Extra Expense) Coverage Form (p. 4.7)

Business Income (Without Extra Expense) Coverage Form (p. 4. 7)

Business income (p. 4.8)

Period of restoration (p. 4.8)

Expenses to Reduce Loss (p. 4.10)

Civil Authority additional coverage (pp. 4.10–4.11)

Extended Business Income (EBI) additional coverage (p. 4.11)

Review Questions

3-1. Describe the application of the following terms found in the business income insuring agreement, as indicated in the following context:

　　a. What must the "suspension" result from? (p. 4.8)

　　b. What are the "operations" in relation to business activities of the insured and rental value coverage? (p. 4.8)

c. When does the "period of restoration" begin and end? (p. 4.9)

3-2. Explain how extra expenses to repair or replace property are treated differently than other extra expenses in the Extra Expense insuring agreement. (p. 4.9)

3-3. Explain the purpose of the following additional coverages in the business income coverage form (BIC):

a. Alterations and New Buildings (p. 4.11)

b. Interruption of Computer Operations (p. 4.12)

Application Question

3-4. Shortly before opening their new yoga studio business, Anton and Lynne decided to sell yoga merchandise in a small room of the studio. Stocking the merchandise consumed more of their operating budget than they had anticipated. They decided to buy the less expensive Business Income (Without Extra Expense) coverage to offset the cost of the merchandise.

A month after they purchased the insurance, several of the studio's windows were broken as a result of a windstorm, which ruined most of the merchandise. In an attempt to fill customer orders, Anton and Lynne paid $2,000 in overnight shipping costs to replace the damaged goods. Had they not paid for expedited shipping, they would have lost $3,000 in merchandise sales. Explain whether their Business Income (Without Extra Expense) coverage will pay for the overnight shipping cost.

Educational Objective 4
Describe the exclusions in the causes of loss forms that apply specifically to business income coverage.

Review Questions

4-1. Where must a power failure occur in order for the off-premises services interruption exclusion to apply? (p. 4.13)

4-2. With regard to business income coverage, the causes of loss forms exclude any loss resulting from damage to a manufacturer's finished stock. How, then, can a manufacturer insure its loss of profit on finished stock? (p. 4.14)

4-3. In what circumstances, if any, would business income insurance (under ISO forms) cover an increase in business income loss resulting from a delay in rebuilding because of the interference of strikers? (pp. 4.14–4.15)

Application Question

4-4. Sherina owns a small retail bakery. The bakery is insured under a commercial package policy that includes the Business Income (and Extra Expense) Coverage Form and the Causes of Loss—Special Form. Explain whether coverage applies in each of the following situations:

a. An ice storm caused a utility service failure, resulting in frozen water pipes that subsequently leaked at the leased premises. As a result of the ensuing water damage, the bakery had to close its doors for three days.

b. In a subsequent loss, Sherina's bakery was unusable for two weeks because of a small oven fire. However, she neglected to advertise that the bakery had reopened after two weeks. As a result, Sherina experienced lower than normal sales for two weeks after her bakery reopened.

Educational Objective 5
Describe the loss conditions and coinsurance provision of the BIC.

Key Word or Phrase
Probable maximum loss (PML) (p. 4.18)

Review Questions

5-1. Summarize the loss determination condition in the BIC. (p. 4.16)

5-2. What are the different coinsurance percentages that can be used with the BIC? (p. 4.17)

5-3. How is the denominator of the business income coinsurance formula calculated? (p. 4.17)

5-4. Describe the circumstances in which each of the following coinsurance percentages might be appropriate. (p. 4.19)

   a. 50 percent

   b. 125 percent

5-5. In addition to the maximum length of time it would take to restore the property, what factors should an insured consider in estimating the PML for business income loss? (p. 4.19)

Application Question

5-6. Susan's Sporting Goods is insured for $60,000 under a business income coverage form that contains a 50 percent coinsurance clause. Following a fire, Susan was forced to close her store for one month before she could reopen for business. If the fire had not occurred, Susan's net income and operating expenses at the store for the twelve months following the policy inception date would have been $180,000. For the month that the store was closed, Susan's business income loss (net income lost plus continuing operating expenses) was $12,000. What dollar amount will Susan recover from her insurer for this business income loss? (Hint: Don't overlook the coinsurance clause.) Show your calculations.

Educational Objective 6

Explain how each of the following optional coverages affects business income coverage:

- Maximum period of indemnity
- Monthly limit of indemnity
- Business income agreed value
- Extended period of indemnity

Key Words and Phrases

Maximum Period of Indemnity coverage option (p. 4.20)

Monthly Limit of Indemnity coverage option (p. 4.20)

Business Income Agreed Value coverage option (p. 4.21)

Extended Period of Indemnity coverage option (p. 4.22)

Review Questions

6-1. Identify the two optional business income coverages that eliminate the coinsurance provision. (p. 4.19)

6-2. When is the only time insureds should add the Maximum Period of Indemnity coverage option to their business income insurance? (p. 4.20)

6-3. Describe the two steps necessary to activate the Business Income Agreed Value coverage option. (p. 4.21)

6-4. Why is the Extended Period of Indemnity coverage option so attractive to insureds such as the owners of restaurants and clothing stores? (p. 4.22)

Application Questions

6-5. Brad is an insured who purchased BIC with a $60,000 policy limit. If Brad chose a Monthly Limit of Indemnity option with a fraction of 1/6, what is the maximum amount he would recover for any business income loss during any period of thirty consecutive days of interrupted operations? Show your calculations.

6-6. Wilson's Widget Company has a BIC with an agreed value of $400,000. Describe how covered losses will be calculated in the following scenarios:

   a. Wilson carried $400,000 of insurance.

   b. Wilson carried $200,000 of insurance.

Educational Objective 7
Describe the Extra Expense Coverage Form and the types of businesses for which it is appropriate.

Key Word or Phrase
Extra Expense Coverage Form (p. 4.22)

Review Questions

7-1. Identify the types of businesses that might choose the Extra Expense Coverage Form instead of the Business Income (and Extra Expense) Coverage Form, and explain why. (pp. 4.22–4.23)

7-2. The Extra Expense Coverage Form and the Business Income (and Extra Expense) Coverage Form both cover extra expenses due to a business interruption. How do they differ in covering extra expenses? (pp. 4.22–4.23)

7-3. Explain why the extra expense coverage provided by the Business Income (and Extra Expense) Coverage Form is a better alternative for most businesses than the Extra Expense Coverage Form. (pp. 4.22–4.23)

Application Question

7-4. A newspaper publisher is insured for $150,000 under an Extra Expense Coverage Form with 40–80–100 limits of liability. After the publisher suffered a loss that was covered under its Extra Expense Coverage Form, it took 21 days for operations to return to normal. The publisher incurred extra expenses of $75,000 during those 21 days. What dollar amount, if any, will the publisher recover from its insurer for this extra expense loss? Show your calculations.

Educational Objective 8

Explain how each of the following endorsements affects business income coverage:

- Business Income From Dependent Properties
- Ordinary Payroll Limitation or Exclusion
- Power, Heat and Refrigeration Deduction
- Ordinance or Law—Increased Period of Restoration

Key Words and Phrases

Dependent property exposure (p. 4.23)

Ordinary Payroll Limitation or Exclusion endorsement (p. 4.24)

Power, Heat and Refrigeration Deduction endorsement (p. 4.24)

Ordinance or Law—Increased Period of Restoration endorsement (p. 4.25)

Review Questions

8-1. Explain why a business organization might select each of the following:

　　a. Business Income From Dependent Properties endorsement (p. 4.23)

b. Ordinary Payroll Limitation or Exclusion endorsement (p. 4.24)

c. Ordinance or Law—Increased Period of Indemnity endorsement (pp. 4.24–4.25)

8-2. Describe the two types of Business Income From Dependent Properties endorsements. (pp. 4.23–4.24)

8-3. Explain why care must be exercised in selecting the Power, Heat, and Refrigeration Deduction endorsement. (p. 4.24)

Application Question

8-4. Val operates a card and gift shop in a local shopping mall. Many people who shop at the one large department store in the mall also buy cards and gifts from Val's shop. Identify and describe the type of insurance Val might consider purchasing to protect her business against the possibility of fire causing the department store to shut down for an extended period.

Educational Objective 9
Explain how business income coverage is rated.

Review Questions

9-1. In what way is rating business income coverage closely related to rating property coverage? (p. 4.25)

9-2. Identify the three aspects of coverage that modify the base rate for business income coverage. (pp. 4.24–4.26)

9-3. Explain how business income coverage is rated. (pp. 4.25–4.26)

Application Question

9-4. Millie's Card Shop and Springtown Florist are two businesses located in the same strip mall. Each shop has the same level of sales and number of employees. Explain why the rates for the business income coverage for these two shops would be different.

Educational Objective 10

Explain whether, and for what amount, the BIC and any applicable optional coverages and endorsements would cover a described loss.

Review Questions

10-1. Explain whether an unendorsed BIC offers immediate coverage after a physical loss occurs. (p. 4.25)

10-2. Explain why an insured's unendorsed BIC would not cover fire at the operations of a supplier on whom the insured is dependent, and identify two endorsements that would provide coverage. (pp. 4.23–4.24)

10-3. Explain whether an unendorsed BIC covers an increase in the period of restoration resulting from compliance with building ordinances or laws. (pp. 4.24–4.25)

Application Question

10-4. For each of the following losses, indicate what dollar amount, if any, each insurer will pay:

a. Jada owns a coffee shop in California and is insured with a BIC (and Extra Expense) Coverage Form. A recent tornado ripped the siding from two-thirds of the building and broke four picture windows in front of her shop. Jada paid two contractors a total of $25,000 in overtime to work around the clock to repair her siding and broken windows so that the business could reopen promptly.

b. Nafeem is an insured with a BIC (Without Extra Expense) Coverage Form. In an attempt to reduce business income loss, Nafeem incurred $2,000 in expenses while attempting to extinguish the fire at his restaurant before the fire engines arrived.

c. Tony is the owner of a beachfront resort that reopened after extensive repairs were made following a severe hurricane. However, a month after the hotel was repaired, the beaches were still in disarray, and as a result, Tony suffered $200,000 in lost income because of fewer tourists to the island.

Answers to Assignment 4 Questions

NOTE: These answers are provided to give students a basic understanding of acceptable types of responses. They often are not the only valid answers and are not intended to provide an exhaustive response to the questions.

Educational Objective 1

1-1. A business income loss can be measured as the reduction in the firm's net income (the difference between what the firm would have earned had no loss occurred and what the firm actually did earn during the period of interruption).

1-2. Three examples of normal operating expenses that could continue during a short interruption are payroll of key employees, debt repayments, and taxes.

1-3. Three examples of extra expenses are the cost to rent temporary office space, overtime wages to employees, and overnight air shipment of needed repair parts.

1-4. In order for business income insurance to apply, there must be an interruption of operations caused by property damage from a covered peril to property at locations or situations described in the policy, resulting in a loss of business income and/or extra expense.

1-5. Surewell's business income loss exposures include the following:
- Loss of income from the manufacture and sales of the aircraft.
- Extra expenses to rent equipment and a facility while its plant is being restored.
- Two key suppliers provide aircraft bodies and engines. Damage to either of these plants could shut down Surewell's production and sales.

Educational Objective 2

2-1. The financial figures involved in the calculation of business income loss are expected and actual amounts of revenue, expenses, and net profit or net loss.

2-2. All changes in expenses must be considered when measuring a business income loss. For example, during a business interruption, some of the firm's expenses (called continuing expenses) will continue, and other expenses (called noncontinuing expenses) will not continue. A business can also incur extra expenses during a business interruption.

2-3. Sal's actual revenues and expenses during the shutdown are compared below with the revenues and expenses that would have been expected had no loss occurred.

	Expected	Actual
Revenue	$60,000	$0
Expenses	30,000	5,000
Profit (net loss)	$30,000	($5,000)

The net loss that actually occurred is expressed as "($5,000)" on a financial statement. In mathematical terms, this number is expressed as "minus $5,000" or "–$5,000."

Sal's business income loss for the six-month shutdown is $35,000, which is the amount by which Sal's expected net income for this period was reduced because of the shutdown. This amount can be calculated by subtracting the actual net loss from the expected profit:

$$\$30{,}000 - (\$5{,}000) = \$35{,}000.$$

In other words, $30,000 minus a negative $5,000 equals $35,000.

Educational Objective 3

3-1. The significance of "suspension," "operations," and "period of restoration" in the business income insuring agreement is as follows:

   a. The "suspension" must result from direct physical loss or damage to real or personal property caused by a covered cause of loss and occurring at the "premises" described in the declarations.

   b. The "operations" of the insured are (1) the business activities of the insured that occur at the premises described in the declarations or (2) in the case of rental value coverage, the "tenantability" (suitability for occupancy) of the described premises.

   c. The "period of restoration" begins seventy-two hours after the physical loss occurs and ends when the property is (or should have been) restored to use with reasonable speed.

3-2. Extra expenses to repair or replace property are treated differently than other extra expenses in the Extra Expense insuring agreement. Extra expenses to repair or replace property are covered only to the extent that they actually reduce the business income loss. Other extra expenses, such as the costs to move to a temporary location, increased rent at the temporary location, rental of substitute equipment (furniture, fixtures, or machinery), and the cost of substitute services such as data processing are covered in full, subject to the policy limit and are not limited to the amount by which they reduce the extra expense loss. Coverage applies even if the business income loss is not reduced at all.

3-3. a. The purpose of the Alterations and New Buildings additional coverage is to provide coverage for loss of income resulting from a delay in beginning operations if the delay results from damage at the described premises by a covered cause of loss to any of the following:

   - New buildings or structures, either completed or under construction
   - Alterations or additions to existing buildings
   - Machinery, equipment, supplies, or building materials located on or within 100 feet of the described premises (provided they are used in the construction, alterations, or additions or are incidental to the occupancy of new buildings)

   b. The purpose of the Interruption of Computer Operations additional coverage is to provide $2,500 of coverage for all loss of business income or extra expense when business operations are suspended due to an interruption of computer operations resulting from the destruction or corruption of electronic data caused by a covered cause of loss.

3-4. Under Business Income (Without Extra Expense) coverage, Anton and Lynne's insurer will pay the $2,000 overnight shipping cost because doing so will reduce the $3,000 business income loss that would have been incurred had they not paid for the expedited shipping. Conversely, if the cost to ship the merchandise did not reduce the business income loss, the Business Income (Without Extra Expense) coverage would not cover the expedited shipping.

Educational Objective 4

4-1. The off-premises services interruption exclusion applies only if the power failure or loss of utility service occurs outside of a covered building (for example, a fire at a public utility's generating station).

4-2. A manufacturer can insure its loss of profit on finished stock by having the Manufacturer's Selling Price (Finished Stock Only) endorsement added to its building and personal property coverage.

4-3. The delay exclusion applies only if the strikers interfering with the work are on the insured premises. Thus, the exclusion would not apply to delay resulting from strikes occurring elsewhere, such as at the premises of a key supplier.

4-4. a. If a covered cause of loss occurs at the described premises because of a power or utility service failure (such as freezing of and subsequent leaking from water pipes), causing a suspension of operations and a resulting reduction in business income, business income coverage applies—but only for loss of business income resulting from the damage caused by the covered peril.

   b. The Extended Business Income (EBI) additional coverage in Sherina's policy would cover the reduction in business income occurring during the two weeks after her property was restored to use.

Educational Objective 5

5-1. The loss determination condition states that the business income loss is determined on the basis of the following:

- The net income of the business before the loss occurred
- The probable net income of the business if no loss had occurred
- The operating expenses that must continue during the period of restoration to permit the insured to resume operations with the quality of service that existed prior to loss
- Other relevant sources of information

5-2. The coinsurance percentages that can be used with the BIC are 50, 60, 70, 80, 90, 100, 125, or no coinsurance.

5-3. The denominator of the BIC coinsurance formula is determined by multiplying the coinsurance percentage by the sum of the insured's net income (whether profit or loss) plus all operating expenses (less certain exceptions) that would have been incurred in the absence of a loss for the twelve-month period beginning at the inception or last anniversary date of the policy. This sum of net income and operating expenses for one year is called the coinsurance basis.

5-4. a. A 50 percent coinsurance might be appropriate if the insured's probable maximum business income loss was less than 50 percent of the insured's coinsurance basis (net income and operating expenses for one year). The insured would be able to satisfy the coinsurance provision with an amount of insurance that was only half of the probable maximum loss (PML).

   b. A 125 percent coinsurance might be appropriate if the insured's PML for business income loss was 125 percent or more of the insured's coinsurance basis.

5-5. Other factors that should be considered in setting PML for a business income loss are (1) the effect of peak seasons, (2) seasonal variations in construction, (3) changes in income and expenses during the period of restoration, (4) noncontinuing expenses, and (5) extended business income and extra expenses.

5-6. Susan's Sporting Goods will recover the following from her insurer for a business income loss resulting from a fire:

$$\text{Loss payment} = \left(\frac{\text{Amount of insurance carried}}{\text{Amount of insurance required}}\right) \times \text{Loss amount.}$$

0.50 × $180,000 = $90,000 (insurance required)
$60,000 = amount of insurance carried
$12,000 = business income loss
$60,000/$90,000 × $12,000 = $8,000.

Educational Objective 6

6-1. The optional coverages that eliminate the coinsurance requirement are the Maximum Period of Indemnity and the Monthly Limit of Indemnity coverages.

6-2. The only time insureds should add the Maximum Period of Indemnity coverage option to their business income insurance is when they feel certain that any suspension of operations will last no more than four months.

6-3. In order to activate the Business Income Agreed Value coverage option, two steps are necessary. First, the insured must furnish to the insurer a completed business income report/worksheet showing the following:

- The insured's actual data for the most recent twelve months' accounting period before the date of the worksheet
- Estimated data for the twelve months immediately following the inception of the coverage

Second, the agreed value must be entered in the declarations. The agreed value must be at least equal to the product obtained by multiplying the coinsurance percentage shown in the declarations by the estimated net income and operating expenses shown on the worksheet for the twelve months following the inception of the optional coverage.

6-4. The Extended Period of Indemnity coverage option extends the extended business income (EBI) additional coverage to include business income losses that continue for more than thirty days after the property is restored. This option is attractive to insureds such as the owners of restaurants and clothing stores because they depend on repeat business and would have a hard time returning to normal income levels within thirty days after reopening following a severe loss.

6-5. With a Monthly Limit of Indemnity option with a fraction of 1/6 and a policy limit of $60,000, the maximum amount that Brad would recover for any business income loss during any period of thirty consecutive days of interrupted operations would be $10,000, calculated as 1/6 × $60,000.

6-6. a. Because Wilson carries insurance at least equal to the agreed value of $400,000, the losses will be paid in full up to the amount of insurance.

b. Because Wilson carries $200,000 of insurance, which is less than the agreed value of $400,000, only half of its covered losses will be paid (calculated as $200,000/$400,000 = ½).

Educational Objective 7

7-1. The types of businesses that might choose the Extra Expense Coverage Form instead of the Business Income (and Extra Expense) Coverage Form are service businesses and organizations such as banks, hospitals, newspapers, and insurance agencies that have a minimal business income exposure and therefore wish to buy only extra expense insurance.

7-2. The Extra Expense Coverage Form has percentage limitations that restrict the amount recoverable for losses with periods of restoration sixty days or less. Otherwise, the Extra Expense Coverage Form is essentially the same as the extra expense coverage under the Business Income (and Extra Expense) Coverage Form.

7-3. The extra expense coverage provided by the Business Income (and Extra Expense) Coverage Form is a better alternative for most businesses because it does not contain percentage limitations.

7-4. An amount equal to 40 percent of the $150,000 policy limit would be available for the first 30 days following the loss. This would be 0.40 × $150,000, which equals $60,000. Although the loss was $75,000, only $60,000 would be paid. (This loss demonstrates that a better choice for this insured might have been the Business Income (and Extra Expense) Coverage Form, which provides extra expense coverage without the monthly percentage limitations.)

Educational Objective 8

8-1. a. Business Income From Dependent Properties endorsement: An insured may be so dependent on a single supplier or a single customer that damage to the property of the supplier or customer could interrupt the insured's operations. This endorsement covers the insured's loss of business income resulting from direct damage to property at the premises of a business on which the insured is dependent.

   b. Ordinary Payroll Limitation or Exclusion endorsement: An insured may be willing to lay off unskilled workers during a business interruption and recall them when operations resume. In that case, the insured may wish to limit or exclude coverage for payroll expense so that this expense will also be excluded from the coinsurance calculation, allowing the insured to carry a lower limit of insurance and still comply with the coinsurance requirement. This endorsement accomplishes these changes.

   c. Ordinance or Law—Increased Period of Indemnity endorsement: The BIC does not cover any increase in the period of restoration resulting from compliance with building ordinances or laws. This endorsement provides coverage for the additional time required to comply with such ordinances or laws when repairing or rebuilding covered property.

8-2. The two types of Business Income From Dependent Properties endorsements are as follows:

   (1) Business Income From Dependent Properties Endorsement—Broad Form. The broad form endorsement extends the business income coverage (BIC) to include loss from damage to property at other locations, subject to the BIC's regular limit of insurance.

   (2) Business Income From Dependent Properties Endorsement—Limited Form. The limited form endorsement is used to provide different limits for dependent property exposures.

8-3. Care must be exercised in selecting the Power, Heat, and Refrigeration Deduction endorsement for the following reasons:
- Some firms are subject to minimum "energy" charges even if they are shut down.
- Premium savings might not be available unless the excluded energy expenses are a substantial portion of the insured's operating expenses, because the rate for business income coverage is increased when this endorsement is added.

8-4. Val needs to have the Business Income From Dependent Properties endorsement attached to her business income policy. This endorsement would protect her against loss of income resulting from direct damage to the department store.

Educational Objective 9

9-1. Rating business income coverage is closely related to rating property coverage because the same perils that damage covered property also cause the business income loss.

9-2. The three aspects of coverage that modify the base rate for business income coverage are as follows:
(1) The type of business being insured
(2) The coinsurance percentage at which the business income coverage is being written
(3) The coverage options the insured has chosen

9-3. Rating business income coverage begins with the base rate for building coverage written at 80 percent coinsurance. This base rate is multiplied by rating factors that reflect the type of coverage provided. The final premium for business income coverage can be calculated after the business income rate, including all modifications for optional coverages, has been determined.

9-4. Business income rates are based on (1) the type of business being insured, (2) the coinsurance percentage written, and (3) the coverage options chosen. Items 2 and 3 might be different for the two shops, or the two shops could have differing business interruption loss exposures. Springtown Florist might have a longer expected delay in reopening following a loss if the coolers are damaged. It would be unable to accept shipments of flowers until such repairs are made. Millie's Card Shop would have little delay in reopening and resuming business.

Educational Objective 10

10-1. Because an unendorsed BIC's period of restoration begins seventy-two hours after the physical loss occurs, an unendorsed BIC does not offer immediate coverage after a physical loss occurs. The seventy-two hour deductible can be reduced to twenty-four hours or eliminated entirely by endorsement for an additional premium.

10-2. An insured's unendorsed BIC would not cover fire at the operations of a supplier on whom the insured is dependent because the loss of business income must result from direct damage to the insured's property. The Business Income From Dependent Properties—Broad Form and the Business Income From Dependent Properties—Limited Form are two endorsements available to provide coverage for covered loss exposures.

10-3. The unendorsed BIC would cover loss of business income for only sixty days and would not cover any increase in the period of restoration resulting from compliance with building ordinances or laws. The Ordinance or Law—Increased Period of Restoration endorsement covers business income loss during the additional time required to comply with building ordinances or laws.

10-4. a. The additional cost Jada paid as overtime would be payable as an extra expense, but only to the extent that it actually reduced the business income loss. Thus, if reopening earlier reduced the business income loss by $30,000, Jada's insurer would pay the $25,000 overtime charges she incurred (subject to the limit of insurance).

b. Under the BIC (Without Extra Expense) Coverage Form, Nafeem's insurer would not pay the $2,000 Nafeem incurred while attempting to extinguish the fire at his restaurant. Under this coverage, the insurer agrees to pay any necessary expenses incurred by the named insured (except the cost of extinguishing a fire) to reduce the business income loss.

c. Tony will not recoup the $200,000 in lost income due to the hurricane. Extended Business Income (EBI) additional coverage is coverage for business income losses that continue after the period of restoration ends; the coverage begins when the damaged property has been restored and ends when the insured's business returns to normal, subject to a maximum of thirty days. However, EBI additional coverage does not apply to business income lost as a result of unfavorable business conditions caused by the effect of the covered cause of loss in the insured's area.

SEGMENT B

Assignment 5   Commercial Crime and Equipment Breakdown Insurance

Assignment 6   Inland and Ocean Marine Insurance

Assignment 7   Commercial General Liability Insurance, Part I

Assignment 8   Commercial General Liability Insurance, Part II

Segment B is the second of three segments in the INS 23 course. These segments are designed to help structure your study.

Direct Your Learning

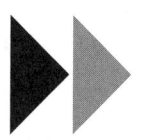

Assignment 5

Commercial Crime and Equipment Breakdown Insurance

Educational Objectives

After learning the content of this assignment, you should be able to:

1. Describe the following eight insuring agreements contained in the Insurance Services Office, Inc., (ISO) Commercial Crime Coverage Form and policy:
   - Employee Theft
   - Forgery or Alteration
   - Inside the Premises—Theft of Money and Securities
   - Inside the Premises—Robbery or Safe Burglary of Other Property
   - Outside the Premises
   - Computer Fraud
   - Funds Transfer Fraud
   - Money Orders and Counterfeit Paper Currency

2. Identify the causes of loss, types of property, and locations that can be covered by the Commercial Crime Coverage Form and related endorsements.

3. Describe the following crime exclusions:
   - General exclusions
   - Exclusions applicable only to employee theft
   - Exclusions applicable to inside the premises and outside the premises
   - Exclusions applicable only to computer fraud
   - Exclusions applicable only to funds transfer fraud

Study Materials

Required Reading:
- Commercial Insurance
  - Chapter 5
  - Chapter 6

Study Aids:
- SMART Online Practice Exams
- SMART Study Aids
  - Review Notes and Flash Cards—Assignment 5

5.1

4. Describe the following conditions applicable to the crime form:
   - Interests insured
   - Where coverage applies
   - When coverage applies
   - Claims provisions

5. Explain how each of the endorsements available in the ISO crime program modifies the coverage forms.

6. Summarize the differences between the ISO government crime forms and the ISO commercial crime forms.

7. Describe the Surety and Fidelity Association of America financial institution bonds used by financial institutions to insure crime loss exposures.

8. Explain why equipment breakdown insurance is often needed in addition to building and personal property insurance.

9. Summarize the ten insuring agreements and the coverages that an equipment breakdown policy can provide.

10. Describe the three types of exclusions typically found in equipment breakdown policies.

11. Summarize the limits and sublimits typically included in equipment breakdown policies.

12. Describe the following policy conditions that are unique to equipment breakdown policies:
    - Suspension
    - Valuation
    - Deductibles
    - Joint or disputed loss agreement
    - Jurisdictional inspections

13. Given a case, determine whether a described loss would be covered, and any loss amount payable, under the Equipment Breakdown Protection Coverage Form.

14. Define or describe each of the Key Words and Phrases for this assignment.

Outline

- **ISO Commercial Crime Program**
  - A. Basic Crime Insuring Agreements
    1. Employee Theft
    2. Forgery or Alteration
    3. Inside the Premises—Theft of Money and Securities
    4. Inside the Premises—Robbery or Safe Burglary of Other Property
    5. Outside the Premises
    6. Computer Fraud
    7. Funds Transfer Fraud
    8. Money Orders and Counterfeit Paper Currency
  - B. Exclusions
    1. General Exclusions
    2. Exclusions Applicable Only to Employee Theft
    3. Exclusions Applicable Only to Inside the Premises and Outside the Premises
    4. Exclusions Applicable Only to Computer Fraud
    5. Exclusions Applicable Only to Funds Transfer Fraud
  - C. Crime Policy Conditions
    1. Interests Insured
    2. Where Coverage Applies
    3. When Coverage Applies
    4. Claims Provisions
  - D. Endorsements
  - E. Government Crime Forms
- **Financial Institution Bonds**
- **Summary (Chapter 5)**
- **Overview of Equipment Breakdown Insurance**
- **Insuring Agreements**
  - A. Property Damage
  - B. Expediting Expenses
  - C. Business Income and Extra Expense (or Extra Expense Only)
  - D. Spoilage Damage
  - E. Utility Interruption
  - F. Newly Acquired Premises
  - G. Ordinance or Law
  - H. Errors and Omissions
  - I. Brands and Labels
  - J. Contingent Business Income and Extra Expense (or Extra Expense Only)
- **Exclusions**
  - A. Exclusions That Duplicate Commercial Property Exclusions
  - B. Exclusions of Perils Covered Under Other Policies
  - C. Exclusions Unique to Equipment Breakdown Policies
- **Limits of Insurance**
  - A. Ammonia Contamination
  - B. Hazardous Substance
  - C. Consequential Loss
  - D. Water Damage
  - E. Data and Media
- **Conditions**
  - A. Suspension
  - B. Valuation
  - C. Deductibles
  - D. Joint or Disputed Loss Agreement
  - E. Jurisdictional Inspections
- **Summary (Chapter 6)**

s.m.a.r.t. tips — The SMART Online Practice Exams product contains a final practice exam. You should take this exam only when you have completed your study of the entire course. Take this exam under simulated exam conditions. It will be your best indicator of how well prepared you are.

5.4 Commercial Insurance—INS 23

For each assignment, you should define or describe each of the Key Words and Phrases and answer each of the Review and Application Questions.

Educational Objective 1

Describe the following eight insuring agreements contained in the Insurance Services Office (ISO) Commercial Crime Coverage Form and policy:

- Employee Theft
- Forgery or Alteration
- Inside the Premises—Theft of Money and Securities
- Inside the Premises—Robbery or Safe Burglary of Other Property
- Outside the Premises
- Computer Fraud
- Funds Transfer Fraud
- Money Orders and Counterfeit Paper Currency

Key Words and Phrases

Commercial crime insurance (p. 5.4)

Discovery form (p. 5.4)

Loss sustained form (p. 5.4)

Theft (p. 5.6)

Forgery (p. 5.10)

Alteration (p. 5.10)

Robbery (p. 5.13)

Custodian (p. 5.13)

Safe burglary (p. 5.14)

Messenger (p. 5.15)

Computer fraud coverage (p. 5.16)

Review Questions

1-1. Under what circumstances, if any, is each of the following included in the definition of "employee" in the Commercial Crime Coverage Form?

    a. Temporary personnel (p. 5.7)

    b. Leased employees (p. 5.7)

c. Corporate directors (p. 5.7)

d. Corporate officers (p. 5.7)

1-2. How does the limit of insurance apply to employee theft coverage when an employee has embezzled money on several different occasions? (pp. 5.8–5.9)

1-3. Explain the automatic termination condition applicable to employee theft coverage. (p. 5.9)

Application Question

1-4. Fernwood Insurance Agency (FIA) is insured under a Commercial Crime Coverage Form that includes the employee theft insuring agreement with a limit of $100,000. Indicate whether FIA's employee theft insurance would cover each of the following losses. If FIA's employee theft insurance would not cover a loss, explain why.

   a. One of FIA's employees, a bookkeeper, wrote several unauthorized paychecks to herself and tricked FIA's treasurer into signing the checks.

   b. FIA's president discovered that Hal, one of FIA's most successful producers (an employee of the agency), had dishonestly pocketed several thousand dollars worth of travel advances over a period of several months. When Hal's misdeeds were discovered, he paid back the money and apologized, and FIA's president decided to give Hal another chance. A few months later, Hal stole, and left town with, nearly $50,000 in policy premiums that had been collected by the agency. When FIA made an employee theft claim, the claim adjuster's investigation revealed Hal's prior misconduct.

Educational Objective 2

Identify the causes of loss, types of property, and locations that can be covered by the Commercial Crime Coverage Form and related endorsements.

Review Questions

2-1. Give an example of alteration that would be covered by the forgery or alteration insuring agreement. (pp. 5.10–5.11)

2-2. What perils, in addition to theft, are covered by the Inside the Premises—Theft of Money and Securities insuring agreement? (pp. 5.11–5.12)

2-3. What types of property are covered by the two coverage extensions to the Inside the Premises—Theft of Money and Securities insuring agreement? (pp. 5.11–5.12)

Application Questions

2-4. Parne Manufacturing Company is insured under a commercial package policy that includes the BPP and the Causes of Loss—Special Form. Should either of the following crime coverages be added to Parne's policy? (Assume that Parne is exposed to loss that would be covered by each of the following coverages.) Explain each of your answers.

   a. Inside the Premises—Robbery or Safe Burglary of Other Property

   b. Outside the Premises

2-5. County College is insured under a Commercial Crime Coverage Form that includes the insuring agreement for Inside the Premises—Theft of Money and Securities. Indicate whether that insuring agreement would cover each of the following losses that resulted from a single occurrence at the college's office. If the insuring agreement would not cover a loss, explain why.

   a. The thieves broke into the building, damaging a door.

   b. The thieves broke into a safe, damaging it severely.

c. The thieves stole money from the safe.

d. The thieves stole negotiable securities from the safe.

e. The thieves stole student records from an unlocked file cabinet.

Educational Objective 3

Describe the following crime exclusions:

- General exclusions
- Exclusions applicable only to employee theft
- Exclusions applicable to inside the premises and outside the premises
- Exclusions applicable only to computer fraud
- Exclusions applicable only to funds transfer fraud

Review Questions

3-1. Identify the exclusions of the Commercial Crime Coverage Form applicable to all of the insuring agreements. (p. 5.19)

3-2. Identify the exclusions of the Commercial Crime Coverage Form applicable only to the Employee Theft insuring agreement. (pp. 5.20–5.21)

3-3. Identify the exclusions of the Commercial Crime Coverage Form applicable only to the inside the premises and outside the premises agreements. (pp. 5.21–5.23)

3-4. Identify the exclusions of the Commercial Crime Coverage Form applicable only to the Computer Fraud insuring agreement. (p. 5.23)

3-5. Identify the exclusions of the Commercial Crime Coverage Form applicable only to Fund Transfer Fraud. (p. 5.23)

Application Question

6-6. A bookstore is insured under a Commercial Crime Coverage Form that includes the insuring agreement for Inside the Premises—Theft of Money and Securities. During a burglary, thieves vandalized the bookstore office by smashing several desks and computer monitors. Indicate whether that insuring agreement would cover the damage to the desks and the monitors.

Educational Objective 4

Describe the following conditions applicable to the crime form:

- Interests insured
- Where coverage applies
- When coverage applies
- Claims provisions

Review Questions

4-1. When must a loss event occur in order to be covered under each of the following?

   a. Loss sustained crime form (p. 5.25)

   b. Discovery crime form (p. 5.25)

4-2. When must a loss event *be discovered* in order to be covered under each of the following?

   a. Loss sustained crime form (pp. 5.25–5.26)

   b. Discovery crime form (pp. 5.25–5.26)

4-3. Under what circumstances will a loss sustained form cover a loss occurring before that policy's inception date? (pp. 5.25–5.26)

Application Question

4-4. For nine consecutive years with the same insurer, Emily has insured her souvenir shop under the loss sustained version of the ISO Commercial Crime Coverage Form, which includes the Employee Theft insuring agreement. Her policy limit during the entire span has been $100,000. During the ninth year of coverage, she learns that her staff accountant, Jerome, has been embezzling $35,000 in July (her peak season) for each of the last six years. In total, Jerome has stolen $210,000 from Emily's business. How much can Emily recover from her insurer for the losses?

Educational Objective 5

Explain how each of the endorsements available in the ISO crime program modify the coverage forms.

Review Questions

5-1. How does the Employee Theft—Name or Position Schedule Endorsement modify the regular employee theft insuring agreement? (p. 5.29)

5-2. Describe the loss exposure covered by the Clients' Property endorsement. (p. 5.29)

5-3. Describe the loss exposure covered by the Extortion—Commercial Entities endorsement. (p. 5.29)

Application Questions

5-4. For each of the following situations, identify (1) the specific peril involved and (2) whether an insuring agreement or a coverage endorsement of the ISO commercial crime program would cover the loss.

   a. A messenger taking money to the bank was stopped by a person holding a gun and told to hand over the money. Fearing for her life, the messenger surrendered the money.

   b. A thief hid in a store until after closing time and removed merchandise from the store shelves. The thief broke a window and escaped with the merchandise.

   c. An employee increased the amount that had been written on a check by his employer and kept the difference between the two amounts.

d. A "smash and grab" thief broke a show window of the insured store and stole several items of valuable merchandise. The incident was witnessed by two of the store's sales clerks.

e. All of the cash, checks, and charge card receipts in a store were lost in a fire that occurred when the store was open for business.

5-5. Video/Audio Store sells televisions and audio equipment. Many of the store's customers pay for their purchases with cash or checks.

a. Identify four causes of crime loss that might affect Video/Audio Store.

b. Identify the crime *insuring agreements* or coverage *endorsements* that would be appropriate to cover the causes of loss identified in your answer to part (a).

Educational Objective 6

Summarize the differences between the ISO government crime forms and the ISO commercial crime forms.

Review Questions

6-1. Why has ISO developed separate government crime forms? (p. 5.30)

6-2. Compare the two employee theft insuring agreements that are contained in each of the government crime forms. (p. 5.30)

6-3. How does the policy territory for employee theft coverage in ISO government crime forms differ from ISO commercial crime forms? (p. 5.30)

Application Question

6-4. A governing council insures for employee theft loss under an unendorsed ISO government crime form with a $300,000 limit. During the policy period, it is discovered instantly when the treasurer steals $400,000 and leaves the country. Explain how much, if any, of the loss will be covered.

Educational Objective 7
Describe the Surety and Fidelity Association of America financial institution bonds used by financial institutions to insure crime loss exposures.

Key Word or Phrase
Financial institution bond (pp. 5.30–5.31)

Review Questions

7-1. Explain why a policy that covers the crime loss exposures of financial institutions is called a bond. (p. 5.31)

7-2. Identify the types of organizations that are insured under financial institution bonds. (p. 5.31)

7-3. List the six insuring agreements of the financial institution bond known as Standard Form No. 24 (also referred to as the "bankers blanket bond"). (p. 5.31)

Application Question

7-4. Megan runs a finance company. She visits Scott, her insurance agent, in a nearby town in order to obtain insurance for her crime exposures. Scott explains the various insuring agreements, endorsements, conditions, and exclusions under the ISO commercial crime forms so that Megan may select the coverage that best matches her insurance needs. What else should Scott do, or do differently, to be certain that Megan purchases appropriate insurance?

Educational Objective 8

Explain why equipment breakdown insurance is often needed in addition to building and personal property insurance.

Key Word or Phrase

Equipment breakdown insurance (p. 6.3)

Review Questions

8-1. If a business is insured under a BPP, why might there also be a need for equipment breakdown insurance? (p. 6.3)

8-2. Few insurers have the expertise to underwrite and provide risk control services for equipment breakdown insurance; how do they provide this coverage for their customers? (p. 6.4)

8-3. The effects of equipment breakdown are potentially catastrophic. How does this affect the insurer and the insured? (p. 6.4)

Application Question

8-4. Bruce owns an apartment building. He removed the old-fashioned gas-fired steam boiler that provided heat to the units and replaced it with a geothermal, earth-friendly heating system. Bruce is insured under a BPP. Because there is no steam boiler on the premises, does he need an equipment breakdown policy in addition to his BPP coverage?

Educational Objective 9

Summarize the ten insuring agreements and the coverages that an equipment breakdown policy can provide.

Key Words and Phrases

Expediting expenses coverage (p. 6.8)

Contingent business income and extra expense coverage (p. 6.12)

Review Questions

9-1. What is the covered cause of loss in an equipment breakdown policy? (p. 6.5)

9-2. What property is covered by the property damage insuring agreement of an equipment breakdown policy? (pp. 6.6–6.7)

9-3. Identify ten insuring agreements of the ISO Equipment Breakdown Form. (p. 6.6)

Application Question

9-4. Freddie owns a steakhouse. He has equipment breakdown coverage, and his policy includes the Spoilage Damage insuring agreement. Freddie closes his restaurant on Tuesdays. Late Monday night, an employee leaves the meat freezer door open. This is not discovered until Wednesday afternoon. Several thousands of dollars' worth of gourmet meats and sauce are ruined. Will the Spoilage Damage insuring agreement pay for loss caused by this spoilage of perishable goods?

Educational Objective 10
Describe the three types of exclusions typically found in equipment breakdown policies.

Review Questions

10-1. Give an example of exclusions that duplicate commercial property exclusions. (p. 6.12)

10-2. Give an example of exclusions of perils covered under other policies. (p. 6.13)

10-3. Give an example of an exclusion that is unique to equipment breakdown policies. (p. 6.13)

Application Question

10-4. Patti's employee leasing firm operates out of an office building that she owns. She is insured for equipment breakdown under an ISO Equipment Breakdown Form. An inspector from her insurer contacts her to schedule a safety inspection. Patti agrees, but notes that her staff maintenance man conducted a full pressure test on the steam boiler in the basement the previous week. Before the insurer can conduct the safety inspection, the boiler explodes and damages the foundation. Which exclusion, if any, could prevent Patti from recovering loss amounts from her insurer?

Educational Objective 11

Summarize the limits and sublimits typically included in equipment breakdown policies.

Review Questions

11-1. Describe the operation of limits and sublimits in equipment breakdown policies. (p. 6.13)

11-2. Identify the five types of loss that are subject to a special sublimit under the Equipment Breakdown Protection Coverage Form. (pp. 6.13–6.14)

11-3. How is "hazardous substance" defined in the provision specifying the Hazardous Substance sublimit? (p. 6.14)

Application Question

11-4. Moshe is a manager for a large manufacturing company. He has secured equipment breakdown coverage from an insurer that uses the ISO form. His policy limit is $250,000. A valve internal to his steam boiler fails during the policy period, causing water to leak from the boiler and ruin some finished products that were stored near the boiler. The value of the destroyed products is $43,000. How will the equipment breakdown coverage respond to this loss?

Educational Objective 12

Describe the following policy conditions that are unique to equipment breakdown policies:

- Suspension
- Valuation
- Deductibles
- Joint or disputed loss agreement
- Jurisdictional inspections

Key Words and Phrases

Suspension condition (p. 6.15)

Joint or Disputed Loss Agreement (p. 6.17)

Review Questions

12-1. What is the reason for the strict terms of the Suspension condition? (p. 6.15)

12-2. Describe how the Valuation condition establishes the loss valuation of covered property. (pp. 6.15–6.16)

12-3. What are four types of deductibles that can be used in an Equipment Breakdown Protection Coverage Form? (p. 6.17)

Application Question

12-4. Jason is an insurance broker and a CPCU who strives to put his customers' needs above his own. He places commercial insurance with several different insurers in order to find the best coverages and best prices for his clients. Often, he finds the best value in BPP coverage with Fernley Mutual Insurance Company, and the best value in equipment breakdown coverage with Granton Insurance Company. Jason makes an effort to do the best for his customers on the underwriting end, and he also wants to make sure that their claims are handled promptly. What condition should Jason be certain is included in both the BPP from Fernley and the equipment breakdown policy from Granton?

Educational Objective 13

Given a case, determine whether a described loss would be covered, and any loss amount payable, under the Equipment Breakdown Protection Coverage Form.

Application Question

13-1. A pressurized vessel at Radley Manufacturing Company's (RMC) factory exploded, causing the losses described as follows. Indicate which of the following losses can ordinarily be insured under an equipment breakdown insurance policy:

- Destruction of the pressure vessel
- Damage to a customer's goods for which RMC was legally liable
- Damage to RMC's building and contents
- The increased cost to repair RMC's building because of a building ordinance
- Damage to a neighboring building owned by K&L Warehousers
- Injury to one of RMC's employees
- Injury to a business guest in RMC's building
- Loss of business income resulting from the suspension of operations because of the explosion

Answers to Assignment 5 Questions

NOTE: These answers are provided to give students a basic understanding of acceptable types of responses. They often are not the only valid answers and are not intended to provide an exhaustive response to the questions.

Educational Objective 1

1-1. The Commercial Crime Coverage Form defines "employee" in the following circumstances:

   a. Temporary personnel (or "temps") are employees provided they meet the three basic criteria given in the definition.

   b. The ISO definition of employee includes leased employees. Some non-ISO crime policies do not cover leased employees unless they are added by endorsement.

   c. Corporate directors are considered employees while performing duties usual to an employee.

   d. Corporate officers are employees as long as they meet the basic criteria of the definition.

1-2. The limit of insurance as it applies to employee theft coverage is the most that the insured can collect for all embezzlement committed by that employee, even if the employee has committed dishonest acts on several different occasions.

1-3. The Termination as to Any Employee condition contains two distinct parts. The first part provides automatic termination of employee theft coverage with respect to any employee who has committed a dishonest act as soon as the act is known to the insured or any partner, officer, director, or LLC member or manager not in collusion with the employee. Coverage on the employee is terminated regardless of whether the act was committed against the insured or others (before or after the employee was hired by the insured) and whether the employer learns of it before or after policy inception. The second part of the condition gives the insurer the right to cancel coverage with respect to any employee by providing thirty days' advance notice to the insured.

1-4. Fernwood Insurance Agency (FIA)'s coverage under a Commercial Crime Coverage Form that includes the employee theft insuring agreement provides the following coverage:

   a. Unauthorized paychecks signed by treasurer would qualify as "money." Therefore, theft by an employee of those checks would be covered.

   b. Hal's theft of premiums is not covered. Because FIA's president was aware of Hal's previous dishonesty, coverage on Hal was automatically canceled in accordance with the Termination as to Any Employee condition.

Educational Objective 2

2-1. An example of alteration that would be covered by the forgery or alteration insuring agreement is as follows: The insured pays an independent contractor with a check for $10,000, and the contractor changes the amount of the check to $100,000.

2-2. The Inside the Premises—Theft of Money and Securities insuring agreement also covers "disappearance and destruction," which encompass loss by virtually any perils that are not otherwise excluded.

2-3. The extensions to the Inside the Premises—Theft of Money and Securities insuring agreement provide coverage extensions of the money and securities coverage, which apply to loss or damage to (1) the premises, if the insured is the owner or is liable for the damage, and (2) containers holding covered property caused by safe burglary or attempted safe burglary.

2-4. a. Inside the Premises—Robbery or Safe Burglary of Other Property coverage should not be added to Parne's commercial package policy because Parne already has coverage for this exposure under its BPP with Causes of Loss—Special Form.

b. Adding Outside the Premises coverage could be beneficial to Parne because the BPP, even with the special form, provides little coverage for property off the insured premises.

2-5. A Commercial Crime Coverage Form that includes the insuring agreement for "Inside the Premises—Theft of Money and Securities" would provide the following loss coverage for County College:

a. Door damaged during theft would be covered under the extension for damage to the premises.

b. Safe damaged during theft would be covered under the extension for damage to safes and other containers.

c. Money stolen from safe would be covered.

d. Negotiable securities stolen from safe would be covered.

e. Stolen student records from unlocked cabinet would not be covered. Student records are not "money" or "securities."

Educational Objective 3

3-1. The ten general exclusions applicable to any of the crime insuring agreements are as follows:

(1) Nuclear

(2) Pollution

(3) War and Military Action

(4) Acts Committed by You, Your Partners or Your Members

(5) Acts of Employees Learned of by You Prior to the Policy Period

(6) Acts of Employees, Managers, Directors, Trustees or Representatives

(7) Confidential Information

(8) Government Action

(9) Indirect Loss

(10) Legal Fees, Costs and Expenses

3-2. The Commercial Crime Coverage Form exclusions that apply to the Employee Theft insuring agreement only are: Inventory Shortages, Trading, and Warehouse Receipts.

3-3. The Commercial Crime Coverage Form exclusions that apply only to inside the premises and outside the premises are as follows:

- Accounting or Arithmetical Errors or Omissions; Exchanges or Purchases
- Fire
- Money Operated Devices
- Motor Vehicles or Equipment and Accessories

- Transfer or Surrender of Property
- Vandalism
- Voluntary Parting With Title to or Possession of Property

3-4. The Commercial Crime Coverage Form exclusions that apply only to the Computer Fraud insuring agreement are as follows:
- Credit Card Transactions
- Fund Transfer Fraud
- Inventory Shortages

3-5. The Commercial Crime Coverage Form exclusion that applies only to Fund Transfer Fraud is loss due to the use of a computer to transfer money, securities, or other property.

3-6. A Commercial Crime Coverage Form that includes the insuring agreement for Inside the Premises—Theft of Money and Securities would not cover the loss, because vandalism is excluded under that insuring agreement.

Educational Objective 4

4-1. A loss event must occur under the following circumstances in order to be covered under the specified form:
   a. Loss sustained form—A loss event must occur at some time during the policy period. (Subject to specific rules, a loss sustained form will also cover some losses that occurred under prior policies.)
   b. Discovery form—A loss event must occur at any time before the policy expires, even if that is before the policy inception date. (If a discovery form is subject to a retroactive date, the loss event must occur on or after the retroactive date.)

4-2. A loss event must be discovered under the following circumstances in order to be covered under the specified form:
   a. Loss sustained form—A loss event must be discovered during the policy period or within one year after the policy period.
   b. Discovery form—A loss event must be discovered during the policy period or within sixty days after the policy period. (A one-year discovery period applies to losses affecting employee benefit plans.)

4-3. A loss sustained form will cover a loss occurring before its inception date if the loss meets all four of the following criteria:
   (1) The loss is *discovered* during the policy period shown in the Declarations.
   (2) The loss *occurred* while prior insurance, issued by the same insurer or an affiliated insurer, was in effect.
   (3) The current insurance became effective when the prior insurance was canceled.
   (4) The loss would have been covered by the present insurance if the insurance had been in force at the time of loss.

4-4. Even though Emily is insured under the loss sustained version, these losses can be covered (up to the policy limit) by the policy currently in effect. Under the Loss Sustained During Prior Insurance Issued by Us or Any Affiliate condition, the insurer agrees to pay a loss (that would be covered by the present insurance) that is discovered during the policy period and occurred while prior insurance issued by the same insurer was in effect. The current policy applies but the most the insurer will pay is the amount recoverable under the prior insurance, if it had remained in effect. Therefore, Emily may collect the $100,000 policy limit.

Educational Objective 5

5-1. The Employee Theft—Name or Position Schedule Endorsement covers employee theft only if it is committed by an employee whose name or position has been listed in the policy. This coverage is more restrictive than the regular employee theft insuring agreement.

5-2. The Clients' Property endorsement covers theft, committed by the insured's employees, of clients' property within clients' premises.

5-3. The Extortion—Commercial Entities endorsement covers loss due to surrender of money, securities, or other property as a result of (1) a threat of bodily harm to an employee, director, trustee, partner, member, manager, or proprietor; or (2) a threat to do damage to the insured's premises.

5-4. The stated peril might be covered by the following insuring agreement or coverage endorsement of the ISO commercial crime program:
- a. The policy defines theft as unlawful taking; robbery qualifies as theft. This peril can be covered by the Outside the Premises insuring agreement.
- b. The policy defines theft as unlawful taking; burglary qualifies as theft. This peril can be covered by the Inside the Premises—Theft of Other Property endorsement or by the Inside the Premises—Robbery or Burglary of Other Property endorsement.
- c. The peril is theft and can be covered by the Employee Theft insuring agreement.
- d. The peril is robbery (theft) and can be covered by the Inside the Premises—Robbery or Safe Burglary of Other Property insuring agreement; or by the Inside the Premises—Theft of Other Property endorsement.
- e. The peril is fire or simply "destruction" and can be covered by the Inside the Premises—Theft of Money and Securities insuring agreement.

5-5. a. Four causes of crime loss that might affect Video/Audio Store include: Employee theft; theft by outsiders of money, securities, and other property; computer fraud; and funds transfer fraud. (Other correct answers are possible.)
   b. These causes of loss can be insured with the following insuring agreements or coverage endorsements:
   - Employee Theft
   - Inside the Premises—Theft of Money and Securities
   - Inside the Premises—Theft of Other Property (by Endorsement)
   - Outside the Premises
   - Computer Fraud
   - Funds Transfer Fraud

Educational Objective 6

6-1. ISO has developed separate government crime forms because government units have different exposures and coverage requirements imposed by law.

6-2. The government crime forms have two employee theft agreements. One provides "per loss coverage" (the limit applies separately to each loss), and the other provides "per employee coverage" (the limit applies separately to each employee).

6-3. In the government crime forms, the policy territory for employee theft coverage does not include Canada except for coverage under the ninety-day worldwide travel extension for employee theft.

6-4. The government crime forms contain two additional exclusions not included in the commercial crime forms. These exclusions eliminate coverage for loss caused by any employee required by law to be individually bonded or any treasurer or tax collector. Therefore, there is no coverage for this loss.

Educational Objective 7

7-1. Policies that cover the crime loss exposures of financial institutions were developed by the Surety and Fidelity Association of America (SFAA) and are called "bonds" because one of the key coverages that they provide is employee dishonesty insurance, which was traditionally called a "fidelity bond."

7-2. The types of organization insured under financial institution bonds include banks, savings and loan associations, credit unions, stock brokerages, finance companies, and insurers.

7-3. Form No. 24 includes the following six insuring agreements (Agreements D and E are optional.):
   A. Fidelity
   B. On Premises
   C. In Transit
   D. Forgery or Alteration
   E. Securities
   F. Counterfeit Money

7-4. Scott has made a fundamental error. Entities eligible for financial institution bonds, such as finance companies, are not eligible for the ISO commercial crime forms. Scott should instead be discussing financial institution forms, developed by the SFAA, ISO, or independent insurers.

Educational Objective 8

8-1. A business insured under a BPP may also need equipment breakdown insurance because the types of equipment covered by equipment breakdown insurance are covered under the Building and Personal Property Coverage Form (BPP), but only with regard to the perils insured against by the causes of loss forms used with the BPP. The commercial property causes of loss forms exclude electrical breakdown, mechanical breakdown, and steam boiler explosion, all of which can damage such equipment and the other property around it. Equipment breakdown insurance can fill this coverage gap, covering physical damage to both the covered equipment and other property of the insured that results from the accidental breakdown of covered equipment. Equipment breakdown insurance can also cover business income, extra expense, and other losses resulting from such physical damage.

8-2. Many insurers provide equipment breakdown insurance in their package policies through reinsurance arrangements with insurers that specialize in equipment breakdown coverage.

8-3. Because of the potentially catastrophic effects of equipment breakdown, loss prevention is a key goal for both the equipment breakdown insurer and the insured. Therefore, the inspection and risk control services provided by equipment breakdown insurers are an important part of their services. An insurer's inspection expenses for equipment breakdown coverage often equal or exceed its loss payments.

8-4. Bruce may need equipment breakdown coverage because there are many types of equipment other than boilers whose mechanical breakdown can cause great damage not covered by the BPP. Examples of other mechanical breakdown include short-circuits in electrical systems, breakdown of commercial laundry equipment that Bruce may have installed for residents, compressors and tubes for the air conditioner, or voltage fluctuations in the phone system.

Educational Objective 9

9-1. The covered cause of loss in an equipment breakdown policy is "breakdown" of "covered equipment."

9-2. Covered property included in the property damage insuring agreement of an equipment breakdown policy consists of property owned by the named insured (building or personal property) and property that is in the named insured's care, custody, or control and for which the named insured is legally liable.

9-3. The ten insuring agreements of the ISO Equipment Breakdown Form are as follows:
(1) Property Damage
(2) Newly Acquired Premises
(3) Expediting Expenses
(4) Ordinance or Law
(5) Business Income and Extra Expense
(6) Errors and Omissions
(7) Spoilage Damage
(8) Brands and Labels
(9) Utility Interruption
(10) Contingent Business Income and Extra Expense

9-4. Because the spoilage did not result from a breakdown of covered equipment, the spoiled goods are not covered. In order for coverage to apply, the spoilage must be due to the lack or excess of power, light, heat, steam, or refrigeration.

Educational Objective 10

10-1. Examples of exclusions that duplicate commercial property exclusions are: ordinance or law, nuclear hazard, war or military action, water, and neglect to preserve property from further damage.

10-2. Examples of exclusions of perils covered under other policies are: fire, windstorm or hail, explosion (other than explosion of a steam boiler, piping, turbine or engine; electric steam generator; or gas turbine), war, and earth movement, regardless of whether the insured has other insurance covering these perils.

10-3. An example of an exclusion unique to equipment breakdown policies is the testing exclusion. Equipment breakdown policies exclude certain types of testing because it can pose significantly increased risk of loss.

10-4. None of the exclusions will affect coverage. Had the explosion occurred *during* testing, it would have been excluded.

Educational Objective 11

11-1. Equipment breakdown insurance is written subject to one overall limit, which is the most that the insurer will pay for all loss or damage resulting from any one breakdown. If a separate limit (known as a sublimit) is shown for an individual insuring agreement, that limit is the most that the insurer will pay under that insuring agreement for any one breakdown covered by the individual insuring agreement. This value is included in the overall limit. When the word "included" is shown for an individual insuring agreement, that insuring agreement is subject to the overall limit for each breakdown.

11-2. The five types of loss that may be subject to a sublimit under the Equipment Breakdown Protection Coverage Form are as follows:
   (1) Ammonia contamination
   (2) Hazardous substance cleanup
   (3) Consequential loss
   (4) Water damage
   (5) Data and media

11-3. "Hazardous substance" is defined to mean any substance, other than ammonia, declared to be hazardous to health by a government agency.

11-4. The equipment breakdown form excludes most types of water damage, such as flooding, backup of sewers, and discharge from a sprinkler system or domestic water system. The water damage sublimit ($25,000 unless otherwise noted in the declarations) applies to water damage losses that are not otherwise excluded. An example of water damage that would be covered is damage to the insured's merchandise resulting from leakage of water from a steam boiler as the result of a breakdown. The water damage sublimit restricts to $25,000 the amount that Moshe could collect for this loss. (Depending on the nature of the damage to the ruined equipment, the Consequential Loss sublimit might also restrict the loss payment to $25,000. Consequential loss, limited to $25,000, is the reduction in value of undamaged parts of the finished products that became unmarketable as a result of physical loss or damage to another part of the products, such as the circuit boards.)

Educational Objective 12

12-1. The terms of the Suspension condition are strict because of the enormous loss potential of some equipment breakdown exposures. The Suspension condition allows a boiler inspector or another representative of the insurer to act immediately when imminent danger of an accident exists. Most insureds want a loss-free operation and willingly cooperate when a dangerous situation is discovered. Therefore, the Suspension condition is seldom invoked. However, it serves as a last resort that the insurer can use when the insured cannot or will not cooperate in remedying a dangerous situation.

12-2. Subject to several exceptions, the Valuation condition establishes that covered property under the Equipment Breakdown Protection Coverage Form is valued on a replacement cost basis. The insurer agrees to pay the smallest of the following amounts for a covered loss:

- The cost to repair the damaged property with property of the same kind, capacity, size, or quality
- The cost to replace the damaged property on the same site or another site
- The amount the insured actually spends that is necessary to repair or replace the damaged property

12-3. Four types of deductibles that can be used in an Equipment Breakdown Protection Form are as follows:

(1) Dollar deductible

(2) Time deductible

(3) Multiple of daily value deductible

(4) Percentage of loss deductible

12-4. Jason should be sure that each policy includes the Joint or Disputed Loss Agreement, which is a condition that addresses claim situations in which the insured's equipment breakdown insurer and the insured's commercial property insurer disagree on which insurer covers a loss. In such a scenario, each insurer pays half the loss to quickly indemnify the insured and then resolve their differences.

Educational Objective 13

13-1. All of the described losses at RMC, caused by a pressurized vessel explosion, can usually be insured under an equipment breakdown policy except for damage to a neighboring building owned by K&L Warehouses, injury to one of RMC's employees, and injury to a business guest in RMC's building.

Direct Your Learning

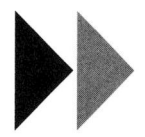

Assignment 6

Inland and Ocean Marine Insurance

Educational Objectives

After learning the content of this assignment, you should be able to:

1. Explain how and why inland marine insurance developed, including the role of the Nationwide Marine Definition.

2. Describe the following aspects of inland marine loss exposures:
   - Items subject to loss
   - Causes of loss
   - Economic or financial effect of loss

3. Distinguish between the filed and nonfiled classes of inland marine insurance.

4. Describe the purpose and distinguishing provisions of each type of nonfiled inland marine policies described in this assignment.

5. Describe the property covered by each of the filed inland marine forms discussed in this assignment.

6. Explain why judgment rating is often needed for pricing inland and ocean marine insurance.

7. Describe the loss exposures faced by owners of cargo and vessels in overseas trade.

8. Describe the following types of ocean marine insurance, including the policy provisions commonly found in each:
   - Cargo insurance
   - Hull insurance
   - Protection and indemnity insurance

9. Recommend an ocean or inland marine policy form to cover a described exposure.

10. Define or describe each of the Key Words and Phrases for this assignment.

Study Materials

Required Reading:
- Commercial Insurance
  - Chapter 7

Study Aids:
- SMART Online Practice Exams
- SMART Study Aids
  - Review Notes and Flash Cards—Assignment 6

Outline

- **Development of Inland Marine Insurance**
- **Inland Marine Exposures**
    A. Items Subject to Loss
        1. Goods in Domestic Transit
        2. Property in the Possession of Bailees
        3. Movable Equipment and Unusual Property
        4. Property of Certain Dealers
        5. Instrumentalities of Transportation and Communication
    B. Covered Causes of Loss
    C. Economic or Financial Effect of Loss
- **Inland Marine Insurance**
    A. Nonfiled Inland Marine Coverages
        1. Contractors Equipment
        2. Builders Risk
        3. Transit
        4. Motor Truck Cargo Liability
        5. Difference in Conditions
        6. Electronic Data Processing Equipment
        7. Bailees
        8. Instrumentalities of Transportation and Communication
    B. Filed Inland Marine Coverages
        1. Commercial Articles
        2. Camera and Musical Instrument Dealers
        3. Equipment Dealers
        4. Physicians and Surgeons Equipment
        5. Signs
        6. Theatrical Property
        7. Film
        8. Floor Plan
        9. Jewelers Block
        10. Mail
        11. Accounts Receivable
        12. Valuable Papers and Records
    C. Rating Inland Marine Coverage
- **Ocean Marine Exposures**
- **Ocean Marine Insurance**
    A. Cargo Insurance
        1. Valuation of Property
        2. Warehouse to Warehouse Clause
        3. Covered Causes of Loss
        4. Sue and Labor Expenses
        5. General Average and Salvage Charges
    B. Hull Insurance
        1. Covered Causes of Loss
        2. Types of Policies
        3. Valuation of Property
        4. Types of Loss Covered
        5. Collision Liability Clause
    C. Protection and Indemnity
    D. Rating Ocean Marine Insurance
- **Summary**

s.m.a.r.t. tips — When you take the randomized full practice exams in the SMART Online Practice Exams product, you are using the same software you will use when you take the actual exam. Take advantage of your time and learn the features of the software now.

For each assignment, you should define or describe each of the Key Words and Phrases and answer each of the Review and Application Questions.

Educational Objective 1

Explain how and why inland marine insurance developed, including the role of the Nationwide Marine Definition.

Key Words and Phrases

Ocean marine insurance (p. 7.3)

Inland marine insurance (p. 7.3)

Marine insurance (p. 7.3)

Nationwide Marine Definition (p. 7.4)

Review Questions

1-1. In the early 1900s, United States insurers were restricted to writing only one of which broad categories of insurance? (p. 7.3)

1-2. How did the early restrictions lead to the concept and terminology of "inland marine?" (pp. 7.3–7.4)

1-3. What is the purpose of the Nationwide Marine Definition? (p. 7.4)

Application Question

1-4. Sisterdale Insurance Company has developed a new policy to provide property insurance for electronic data processing equipment. It would like to offer this policy in the 14 states where it currently conducts business. For competitive reasons, Sisterdale would like to get this product to market quickly. How can the Nationwide Marine Definition be helpful to Sisterdale in this regard?

Educational Objective 2

Describe the following aspects of inland marine loss exposures:

- Items subject to loss
- Causes of loss
- Economic or financial effect of loss

Key Words and Phrases

Common carriers (p. 7.5)

Contract carriers (p. 7.5)

Private carriers (p. 7.5)

Bill of lading (p. 7.5)

Bailment (p. 7.6)

Bailor (p. 7.6)

Bailee (p. 7.6)

Review Questions

2-1. What categories of property are covered under commercial inland marine insurance? (p. 7.5)

2-2. In what circumstances is a common carrier liable to a shipper for damage to the shipper's cargo that occurs while the cargo is being transported by the carrier? (p. 7.5)

2-3. What determines the liability of a contract carrier? (p. 7.5)

2-4. Why are terms of sale important in evaluating the transit loss exposure of a shipper or receiver of sold goods? (p. 7.6)

2-5. Why do many bailees want insurance that covers damage to customers' property regardless of whether the bailees are legally liable for the damage? (pp. 7.6–7.7)

2-6. What valuation methods are used in inland marine policies? (p. 7.8)

Application Question

2-7. Mickey owns a specialized self-storage facility. Customers pay a monthly fee to lease a small climate-controlled space in which to store fine wines. Each customer has a contract with Mickey that declares the value of the wine. Due to faulty switches, the climate control system fails in many storage units. This is not discovered for several months. As a result of the humidity and heat, much of the wine is ruined. Explain Mickey's obligation to his customers and how the loss amounts are likely to be valued.

Educational Objective 3
Distinguish between the filed and nonfiled classes of inland marine insurance.

Key Words and Phrases
Filed classes (p. 7.9)

Nonfiled classes (p. 7.10)

Review Questions

3-1. What characteristics are common to the filed classes of inland marine business? (p. 7.9)

3-2. What characteristics are common to the nonfiled classes of inland marine business? (p. 7.10)

3-3. Why are the nonfiled classes of inland marine insurance more flexible than the filed classes? (p. 7.11)

Application Question

3-4. Callaway Insurance Company writes property coverages in six states in the U.S. northwest. It wishes to expand its inland marine business into neighboring states. If its goal is to begin issuing policies as soon as possible, should it seek to expand its business in filed classes or nonfiled classes?

Inland and Ocean Marine Insurance 6.9

> ## Educational Objective 4
> Describe the purpose and distinguishing provisions of each type of nonfiled inland marine policies described in this assignment.

Key Words and Phrases

Contractors equipment floater (p. 7.10)

Builders risk policy (p. 7.11)

Soft costs coverage (p. 7.11)

Installation floater (p. 7.12)

Trip transit policy (p. 7.12)

Annual transit policy (p. 7.12)

Motor truck cargo liability policy (p. 7.13)

Difference in conditions (DIC) policy (p. 7.13)

Electronic data processing (EDP) equipment floater (p. 7.14)

Warehouse operators legal liability policy (p. 7.15)

Bailees' customers policy (p. 7.15)

Review Questions

4-1. What is the purpose of the rental reimbursement coverage that is often added by endorsement to contractors equipment floaters? (p. 7.11)

4-2. What property does an inland marine builders risk policy typically cover other than the building under construction? (pp. 7.11–7.12)

4-3. Describe the coverage territory that often applies to an annual transit policy. (p. 7.12)

4-4. What are the principal reasons for buying a difference in conditions (DIC) policy? (pp. 7.13–7.14)

Application Question

4-5. Identify the type of nonfiled inland marine insurance policy that would provide coverage for each of the following loss exposures:

   a. A manufacturing company regularly uses its own trucks to deliver finished products to customers.

   b. A construction company owns several pieces of mobile equipment that remain at a construction site until the construction project is completed.

   c. A computer services company owns several computers that it uses to develop software packages for local businesses.

d. Smith Warehouse needs legal liability coverage for the property of others being stored with Smith.

e. Ian owns a dry cleaning business and wants to cover customers' goods without regard to his legal liability.

Educational Objective 5
Describe the property covered by each of the filed inland marine forms discussed in this assignment.

Key Words and Phrases
Commercial Articles Coverage Form (p. 7.16)

Camera and Musical Instruments Dealers Coverage Form (p. 7.16)

Equipment Dealers Coverage Form (p. 7.16)

Physicians and Surgeons Equipment Coverage Form (p. 7.16)

Signs Coverage Form (p. 7.16)

Theatrical Property Coverage Form (p. 7.17)

Film Coverage Form (p. 7.17)

Floor Plan Coverage Form (p. 7.17)

Jewelers Block Coverage Form (p. 7.17)

Mail Coverage Form (p. 7.17)

Accounts Receivable Coverage Form (p. 7.18)

Valuable Papers and Records Coverage Form (p. 7.18)

Review Questions

5-1. What types of property, other than the insured's medical instruments and equipment, can be insured under the Physicians and Surgeons Equipment Coverage Form? (p. 7.16)

5-2. Why do businesses need the coverage provided under the Signs Coverage Form? (p. 7.16)

5-3. What coverage is provided by the Film Coverage Form? (p. 7.17)

Application Question

5-4. Identify a filed inland marine coverage form that would be appropriate for insuring each of the following types of property:

   a. A medical doctor who treats homebound patients needs a policy to cover the contents of her medical bag.

   b. A store owner wants to insure his business records because he is concerned that damage to these records will make him unable to collect outstanding debts.

   c. A professional photographer needs coverage for his cameras and other equipment.

Educational Objective 6

Explain why judgment rating is often needed for pricing inland and ocean marine insurance.

Key Word or Phrase

Judgment rating (p. 7.19)

Review Questions

6-1. Which inland marine rates are included in the CLM? (pp. 7.18–7.19)

6-2. Explain why judgment rating is often used in pricing nonfiled inland marine policies. (p. 7.19)

6-3. Beyond the underwriter's judgment, what else influences rates for the nonfiled classes of inland marine insurance? (p. 7.19)

Application Question

6-4. Russell is a junior underwriter at an independent insurance agency. He receives an application from a prospective insured seeking motor truck cargo liability insurance. He consults the CLM, but discovers that this is an unfiled class of inland marine business. As a junior underwriter, he is hesitant to apply judgment rating. How might Russell best price this risk?

Educational Objective 7
Describe the loss exposures faced by owners of cargo and vessels in overseas trade.

Key Word or Phrase
Freight (p. 7.19)

Review Questions

7-1. What types of loss exposures does overseas trade by oceangoing vessels create for cargo owners? (p. 7.19)

7-2. What types of loss exposures does overseas trade by oceangoing vessels create for shipowners? (p. 7.19)

Application Question

7-3. Nathan runs a shipping business on the U.S. eastern seaboard. His primary business is transporting liquid fertilizer to and from ports in Florida, Georgia, and New Jersey. On one voyage, the ship's captain neglects the controls, and the ship collides with another vessel loaded with shipments of electronics, damaging both the vessel and its contents. Crew on both ships are injured, and fertilizer is spilled into coastal waterways. What ocean marine exposures are involved for Nathan's shipping business?

Educational Objective 8

Describe the following types of ocean marine insurance, including the policy provisions commonly found in each:

- Cargo insurance
- Hull insurance
- Protection and indemnity insurance

Key Words and Phrases

Voyage policy (p. 7.20)

Open cargo policy (p. 7.20)

Warehouse to warehouse clause (p. 7.21)

Sue and labor clause (p. 7.22)

General average (p. 7.22)

Particular average (p. 7.22)

Hull insurance (p. 7.22)

Perils of the seas (p. 7.22)

Collision liability clause (p. 7.24)

Protection and indemnity (P&I) insurance (p. 7.24)

Review Questions

8-1. How does a voyage cargo policy differ from an open cargo policy? (p. 7.20)

8-2. Explain how each of the following affects the coverage provided in a cargo policy:

   a. Warehouse to warehouse clause (p. 7.21)

   b. Sue and labor clause (p. 7.22)

8-3. Distinguish between general average and particular average. (p. 7.22)

8-4. What causes of loss are typically covered in a hull insurance policy? (p. 7.22)

8-5. Explain how property is normally valued under a hull policy. (pp. 7.23–7.24)

8-6. How does the collision liability clause affect the coverage provided by a hull policy? (p. 7.24)

8-7. What types of loss are covered by protection and indemnity (P&I) insurance? (pp. 7.24–7.25)

Application Questions

8-8. The *Steamer* is an oceangoing freighter insured under a hull policy, which contains a collision liability clause and a P&I policy. As the *Steamer* was leaving harbor, a steering error by the captain caused the vessel to collide with another vessel, the *Piston*. The collision caused damage to both vessels, as well as to their cargoes. Three crew members on the *Steamer* were injured. Which of the two policies covering the *Steamer* will pay for the following losses that resulted from the collision?

a. Damage to the *Steamer*

b. Damage to the *Piston*

c. Damage to cargo owned by others aboard the *Steamer*

d. Damage to cargo aboard the *Piston*

e. Bodily injury to the three crew members on the *Steamer*

8-9. The *Malvern*, an oceangoing vessel, is insured under a hull policy that contains a collision liability clause. The *Malvern* is also covered by P&I insurance. Identify two sources of liability claims that may be covered by the P&I insurance on the *Malvern*.

Educational Objective 9

Recommend an ocean or inland marine policy form to cover a described exposure.

Application Questions

9-1. Ruben owns a store in which he sells agricultural equipment. The equipment manufacturer holds the title to the tractors and other devices on display in Ruben's store. Both Ruben and the manufacturer want to be protected against accidental loss or damage to the agricultural equipment. What ocean or inland marine policy form might best cover this exposure?

9-2. Sandra is the general manager of a college radio station. Due to the popularity of its programs, the station wants to broadcast to a wider location than is possible with the broadcasting tower services it now leases from another party. Sandra arranges for the station to build its own radio broadcast tower and seeks to protect that investment with insurance. What ocean or inland marine policy form might best cover this exposure?

9-3. Donna operates a riverboat cruise ship that caters to cigar smokers. Among her worries are the exposures associated with injuries to passengers. What ocean or inland marine policy form might best cover this exposure?

Answers to Assignment 6 Questions

NOTE: These answers are provided to give students a basic understanding of acceptable types of responses. They often are not the only valid answers and are not intended to provide an exhaustive response to the questions.

Educational Objective 1

1-1. In the early 1900s, U.S. insurers were restricted to writing one of the following three general kinds of insurance:

(1) Fire (insurance against fire and some other causes of property loss)

(2) Casualty (liability insurance and miscellaneous lines such as burglary, glass, and steam boilers)

(3) Marine (insurance for ships and their cargoes)

1-2. Early restrictions lead to the concept and terminology of "inland marine" because, in the early 1900s, fire insurers were not permitted to insure against most crime perils and were not interested in insuring property in transit or valuable property like jewelry. Marine insurers, accustomed to covering ocean cargoes against many different causes of loss, were thus more willing to provide like coverage (broad perils) on the type of property that fire insurers avoided. Typical properties insured included jewelry stores, property in inland transit, and even bridges. Hence, the insurance became known as inland marine insurance.

1-3. The Nationwide Marine Definition was written and adopted by the NAIC in 1933 to resolve the conflict from the perception that marine insurers were encroaching on the territory of fire insurers.

1-4. The Nationwide Marine Definition, or a similar updated definition, can be helpful to determine if the particular coverage that Sisterdale hopes to offer qualifies as inland marine insurance under the form and rate filing laws of the 14 states involved. Typically, commercial inland and ocean marine insurance are subject to less rate and form regulation than other lines of insurance, and thus Sisterdale might face fewer hurdles in getting the product to market. Under the Nationwide Marine Definition, coverage for electronic data processing equipment is classified as marine insurance.

Educational Objective 2

2-1. Commercial inland marine insurance coverage includes the following categories of property:
- Goods in domestic transit
- Property in the possession of bailees
- Movable equipment and unusual property
- Property of certain dealers (jewelers, furriers)
- Instrumentalities of communication and transportation

2-2. A common carrier is liable to a shipper for any damage other than that caused by the following:
- Acts of God
- Acts of a public enemy
- Acts of public authority
- The shipper's neglect or fault
- Inherent vice in the cargo itself

2-3. A contract carrier's liability is determined by the terms of the contract between the carrier and the shipper.

2-4. Terms of sale are important in evaluating the transit loss exposure of a shipper or receiver of sold goods because the terms of sale (such as F.O.B. Destination) determine the point at which ownership of the goods transfers from the seller to the buyer. When ownership shifts to the buyer, the loss exposure is also transferred to the buyer.

2-5. Many bailees want insurance that covers damage to customers' property regardless of whether the bailees are legally liable for the damage because bailees' customers expect to be compensated for any loss to their property that occurs while it is in the bailee's custody, not just those losses for which the bailee is legally liable. Accordingly, bailees want to be able to meet this expectation in the event of loss so that they will be able to satisfy and hold onto their customers.

2-6. The valuation methods used in inland marine insurance include replacement cost, actual cash value, agreed value, selling price, and invoice price.

2-7. Mickey's temporary possession of the personal property (fine wine) of others for a specific purpose (climate-controlled storage) constitutes a commercial bailment. In general, Mickey is responsible for damage to the wine that results from his negligence. Even if he is not negligent for the failure of the climate controls, the contract between Mickey and his customers, in which the value of the wine is declared, could stipulate Mickey's obligation and establish how the losses would be valued.

Educational Objective 3

3-1. Characteristics common to the filed classes of inland marine business are a large number of potential insureds and reasonably homogeneous loss exposures.

3-2. The nonfiled classes of inland marine business are characterized by a relatively small number of potential insureds, diverse loss exposures, or both.

3-3. Nonfiled classes of inland marine insurance are more flexible than the filed classes because the forms and rates used for the nonfiled classes of inland marine insurance do not have to be submitted to state insurance regulators for their approval. Thus, with the nonfiled classes, the insurer can tailor the form to fit the insured's particular situation and charge a rate that is appropriate for the particular exposure being insured. In contrast, with the filed classes, the insurer would be restricted to using the filed forms and rates.

3-4. Because the nonfiled classes do not need to be filed with state regulators, Callaway may be able to offer such coverages more quickly.

Educational Objective 4

4-1. Rental reimbursement coverage, often added by endorsement to contractors equipment floaters, pays the cost of renting equipment to substitute temporarily for covered equipment that is unusable because of damage by a covered cause of loss.

4-2. A typical inland marine builders risk policy covers building materials and supplies while at the building site, while in storage at other locations, or while in transit, in addition to the building under construction. The policy also covers temporary structures at the building site.

4-3. The coverage territory of an annual transit policy is often restricted to the continental United States, Alaska, and Canada, including airborne shipments between places within this territory. An ocean cargo policy is usually needed for cargo carried overseas by ship or plane.

4-4. The main reasons for buying a difference in conditions (DIC) policy are to cover flood and earthquake losses. A DIC policy can also be used to cover other exposures that are not covered by the policyholder's other property policies.

4-5. Coverage would be provided for the following loss exposures by the specified types of nonfiled inland marine insurance:
   a. The manufacturing company regularly using its own trucks to deliver finished products to customers would be covered by an annual transit policy.
   b. The construction company's owned mobile equipment at a construction site would be covered by a contractors equipment floater.
   c. The computer services company would be covered by an electronic data processing (EDP) equipment floater.
   d. Smith Warehouse's legal liability coverage for property of others would be covered by a warehouse operators legal liability policy.
   e. The dry cleaning business would be covered by a bailees' customers policy.

Educational Objective 5

5-1. The Physicians and Surgeons Equipment Coverage Form can be used to cover the insured's office furniture and fixtures and (if the insured is a tenant) the insured's interest in improvements and betterments to the building, in addition to the insured's medical instruments and equipment. By endorsement, coverage can be added for other items, such as money, personal effects, valuable papers and records, and extra expenses.

5-2. The signs form is used by many businesses because commercial property forms exclude or severely limit coverage for signs.

5-3. The Film Coverage Form covers exposed motion picture film and magnetic tapes or videotapes, including related soundtracks or sound records. The amount of insurance reflects—and the form covers—the cost of reshooting the film if it is lost or damaged.

5-4. Coverage is provided by the following inland marine coverage forms:
   a. The contents of the doctor's medical bag would be covered by the Physicians and Surgeons Equipment Coverage Form.
   b. The store owner's business record would be covered by the Accounts Receivable Coverage Form.
   c. The professional photographer's cameras and equipment would be covered by the Commercial Articles Coverage Form.

Educational Objective 6

6-1. The CLM contains rate factors, loadings, and credits. It does not contain rating methods for the traditionally nonfiled classes of inland marine insurance.

6-2. Judgment rating is often used in pricing nonfiled inland marine policies because inland marine risks are unusual, coverage terms are specialized, and insurers do not have enough previous loss information to develop a statistically accurate rate for these risks. Underwriters, therefore, develop judgment rates based on their knowledge and expertise.

6-3. Beyond the underwriter's judgment, market conditions can influence rates for the nonfiled classes of inland marine insurance.

6-4. Motor truck cargo liability insurance is a common form of inland marine coverage, with rates based on many years of loss experience. Insurers active in insuring truck shipments have developed their own manuals and rate schedules for this coverage. Russell can check with the insurers doing business with his agency to see which have developed rates for this nonfiled class of inland marine business.

Educational Objective 7

7-1. Overseas trade by oceangoing vessels creates the following loss exposures for cargo owners:
- Loss to the cargo while in the course of transit from point of origin to destination
- Loss of freight charges when freight is guaranteed by the shipper

7-2. Overseas trade by oceangoing vessels creates the following loss exposures for ship owners:
- Loss of or damage to the vessel
- Loss of freight if not guaranteed by the shipper
- Legal liability for damage to cargo; damage to other property; bodily injury to crew members, passengers, and others; and oil spill cleanup costs

7-3. Ocean marine exposures for Nathan's shipping business include the following:
- Damage to his vessel
- Loss of freight
- Legal liability for damage to cargo
- Legal liability for damage to other property (the other boat, the electronics)
- Legal liability for bodily injury to crew members
- Costs for cleaning up the spilled fertilizer

Educational Objective 8

8-1. A voyage policy covers cargo for a single trip described in the policy. An open cargo policy covers cargo for all trips during the term of the policy.

8-2. The coverage provided in a cargo policy is affected by the following clauses:
   a. Warehouse to warehouse clause—provides continuous coverage during the entire course of transit from the time the cargo leaves the point of shipment until it is delivered to its final destination, including inland transportation
   b. Sue and labor clause—provides coverage for expenses to protect covered property from further damage in the event of loss

8-3. General average is partial loss shared by all parties (cargo owners and shipowners) involved in a voyage. Particular average is partial loss borne by only one party involved in a voyage.

8-4. A hull insurance policy typically covers the following causes of loss:
- Perils of the seas
- Fire, lightning, earthquake
- Barratry
- All other like perils

If the policy includes the additional perils clause, it also covers several other perils, including electrical breakdown, bursting of boilers, breakage of shafts, latent defects, and negligence of the crew.

8-5. Under a hull policy, a vessel is normally insured for a value agreed on by the insurer and the insured. For a total loss, the insurer pays the agreed value. For a partial loss, the insurer pays the cost of repairs.

8-6. Collision liability coverage is a separate amount of insurance covering the insured's liability for collision damage to other vessels, their cargoes, resulting loss of freight charges, and the loss of use of the other owner's vessel. Liability for bodily injury from the collision is not covered. Defense costs are covered in addition to the limit of collision liability insurance.

8-7. Protection and indemnity insurance covers the following types of loss:
- Damage to bridges, piers, wharves, and other structures along waterways
- Injury to passengers, crew, and other persons on the ship
- Injury to persons on other ships
- Damage to cargo of others aboard the insured vessel

8-8. a. The hull policy will cover damage to the *Steamer*.
b. Damage to the *Piston* will be covered by the hull policy's collision liability clause.
c. The P&I policy will cover damage to the cargo owned by others aboard the *Steamer*.
d. Damage to the cargo aboard the *Piston* is covered under the collision liability clause of the hull policy.
e. The injuries to the crew members will be covered by the P&I policy.

8-9. P&I Insurance would cover injury to passengers, crew, and other persons on the *Malvern* and damage the *Malvern* causes to bridges, piers, wharves, and other structures along waterways.

Educational Objective 9

9-1. The best choice may be the inland marine Floor Plan Coverage Form, which covers merchandise being held for sale and that the dealer has financed under a floor plan. The Floor Plan Coverage Form may be used to insure (1) the interest of the dealer in floor-planned property, (2) the interest of the manufacturer or finance company, or (3) both interests.

9-2. Sandra might choose to insure this exposure under a nonfiled inland marine class of business. Property essential to transportation or communication can be insured under an inland marine policy. The major types of properties in this class are bridges, tunnels, pipelines, and radio and television broadcasting equipment.

9-3. Donna should find the coverage she needs with ocean marine P&I insurance, which covers shipowners against various liability claims due to operating the insured vessel, including injury to passengers, crew, and other persons on the ship.

Direct Your Learning

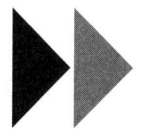

ASSIGNMENT 7

Commercial General Liability Insurance, Part I

Educational Objectives

After learning the content of this assignment, you should be able to:

1. Explain how each of the following can be the basis for legal liability:
   - Torts
   - Contracts
   - Statutes

2. Describe the following liability loss exposures that can be covered by commercial general liability (CGL) insurance:
   - Premises liability exposure
   - Operations liability exposure
   - Products liability exposure
   - Completed operations liability exposure
   - Other CGL exposures

3. Describe the insuring agreements, exclusions, and exceptions to exclusions under the following CGL coverages:
   - Coverage A—Bodily Injury and Property Damage Liability
   - Coverage B—Personal and Advertising Injury Liability
   - Coverage C—Medical Payments

4. Describe the supplementary payments provided by the CGL coverage form.

5. Explain whether, and for what amount, the CGL coverage form would cover a described loss.

6. Define or describe each of the Key Words and Phrases for this assignment.

Study Materials

Required Reading:
- Commercial Insurance
  - Chapter 8

Study Aids:
- SMART Online Practice Exams
- SMART Study Aids
  - Review Notes and Flash Cards—Assignment 7

Outline

- **Liability Loss Exposures**
    - A. Legal Liability
        1. Civil Law and Criminal Law
        2. Legal Liability Based on Torts
        3. Legal Liability Based on Contracts
        4. Legal Liability Based on Statutes
    - B. CGL Loss Exposures
        1. Premises Liability Exposure
        2. Operations Liability Exposure
        3. Products Liability Exposure
        4. Completed Operations Liability Exposure
        5. Other CGL Exposures
- **Overview of Commercial General Liability Insurance**
- **Coverage A—Bodily Injury and Property Damage Liability**
    - A. Coverage A Insuring Agreement
        1. Insurer's Duty to Pay Damages
        2. Insurer's Duty to Defend
    - B. Coverage A Exclusions
        1. Expected or Intended Injury
        2. Contractual Liability
        3. Liquor Liability
        4. Workers Compensation and Employers Liability
        5. Pollution
        6. Aircraft, Auto, or Watercraft
        7. Mobile Equipment
        8. War
        9. Damage to Property
        10. Insured's Products and Work
        11. Personal and Advertising Injury
        12. Electronic Data
        13. Fire Legal Liability Coverage
- **Coverage B—Personal and Advertising Injury Liability**
    - A. Coverage B Insuring Agreement
    - B. Coverage B Exclusions
        1. Knowing Violation of Rights of Another
        2. Material Published With Knowledge of Falsity
        3. Material Published Prior to Policy Period
        4. Criminal Acts
        5. Contractual Liability
        6. Breach of Contract
        7. Quality of Performance of Goods—Failure to Conform to Statements
        8. Wrong Description of Prices
        9. Infringement of Copyright, Patent, Trademark, or Trade Secret
        10. Insureds in Media and Internet Type Businesses
        11. Electronic Chatrooms or Bulletin Boards
        12. Unauthorized Use of Another's Name or Product
        13. Pollution
        14. Pollution-Related
        15. War
- **Supplementary Payments**
- **Coverage C—Medical Payments**
    - A. Coverage C Insuring Agreement
    - B. Coverage C Exclusions
- **Summary**

Study tips: Set aside a specific, realistic amount of time to study every day.

For each assignment, you should define or describe each of the Key Words and Phrases and answer each of the Review and Application Questions.

Educational Objective 1

Explain how each of the following can be the basis for legal liability:
- Torts
- Contracts
- Statutes

Key Words and Phrases

Commercial general liability (CGL) insurance (p. 8.3)

Liability loss (p. 8.3)

Legal liability (p. 8.4)

Civil law (p. 8.4)

Criminal law (p. 8.4)

Tort (p. 8.5)

Negligence (p. 8.5)

Intentional tort (p. 8.5)

Strict liability (or absolute liability) (p. 8.5)

Contract (p. 8.5)

Breach of contract (p. 8.6)

Hold-harmless agreement (or indemnity agreement) (p. 8.6)

Contractual liability (p. 8.6)

Statute (p. 8.6)

Review Questions

1-1. What costs, covered under general liability policies, might result from a liability claim? (p. 8.3)

1-2. Explain how a business can experience a liability loss even if it is found not to be legally liable. (p. 8.3)

1-3. Identify the elements of the tort of negligence. (p. 8.5)

1-4. Define and give an example of each of the following types of torts:

　　a. Intentional tort (p. 8.5)

　　b. Strict (absolute) liability (p. 8.5)

1-5. Give an example of each of the following:

　　a. Breach of contract (p. 8.6)

　　b. Hold-harmless agreement (p. 8.6)

Application Question

1-6. Agnes owns and operates an exotic pet store. Her most popular pets include varieties of poisonous spiders, scorpions, and snakes. Agnes is meticulous about stocking only legal pets and checking the background of buyers before every sale. One day, a scorpion that she sold to a customer escapes from the customer's home and injures a neighbor. For Agnes, on what type of tort might any potential liability be based?

Educational Objective 2

Describe the following liability loss exposures that can be covered by commercial general liability (CGL) insurance:

- Premises liability exposure
- Operations liability exposure
- Products liability exposure
- Completed operations liability exposure
- Other CGL exposures

Key Words and Phrases

Premises liability exposure (p. 8.7)

Operations liability exposure (p. 8.7)

Products liability exposure (p. 8.7)

Completed operations liability exposure (p. 8.8)

Review Questions

2-1. List the five broad categories of CGL loss exposures. (pp. 8.7–8.8)

2-2. Which kinds of businesses are typically associated with operations liability exposures? (p. 8.7)

2-3. What parties can have products liability exposure for a given product? (p. 8.7)

Application Questions

2-4. Fanny's Electrical Service sells and installs ceiling fans. Describe the nature of the loss exposure in the following scenarios:

   a. A service technician creates an electrical fire while preparing the wiring for a new fan installation in a customer's home.

b. Following the completion of a fan installation, the fan falls from the ceiling and damages the customer's floor and a coffee table.

2-5. Blithe Corporation is insured under a CGL coverage form. Would Blithe's CGL provide coverage in each of the following situations? Assume the amounts of all claims are within policy limits. Explain each of your answers.

   a. A visitor was injured during a visit to a building that Blithe leases from another company. Under the terms of the lease, Blithe assumed responsibility for all liability arising from its use of the building.

   b. Blithe Corporation spent $25,000 to withdraw a line of defective products from the market.

c. Blithe Corporation made untrue and disparaging statements about a competitor's products in an advertisement. Blithe's advertising copywriter did not realize the statements were false. A court ordered Blithe to pay damages to the competitor.

> ## Educational Objective 3
> Describe the insuring agreements, exclusions and exceptions to exclusions under the following CGL coverages:
>
> - Coverage A—Bodily Injury and Property Damage Liability
> - Coverage B—Personal and Advertising Injury Liability
> - Coverage C—Medical Payments

Key Words and Phrases

Occurrence coverage trigger (p. 8.12)

Auto (as defined in the CGL coverage form) (p. 8.16)

Mobile equipment (p. 8.18)

Fire legal liability coverage (p. 8.24)

Personal and advertising injury (p. 8.25)

Review Questions

3-1. Briefly describe the types of injury or damage that are covered by each of the following in a CGL coverage form:

   a. Coverage A (p. 8.9)

   b. Coverage B (p. 8.9)

   c. Coverage C (p. 8.9)

3-2. What is the coverage territory of a CGL coverage form? (p. 8.11)

3-3. Identify the types of contracts that are considered insured contracts in the CGL coverage form. (pp. 8.13–8.14)

3-4. Under what circumstances would an insured have coverage for liquor liability under the CGL coverage form? (pp. 8.14–8.15)

3-5. Briefly describe each of the following exclusions to Coverage A of the CGL coverage form:

a. Bodily injury to employee (exclusions *d* and *e*) (p. 8.15)

b. Pollution (exclusion *f*) (pp. 8.15–8.16)

c. Aircraft, auto, or watercraft (exclusion *g*) (pp. 8.16–8.17)

d. Mobile equipment (exclusion *h*) (p. 8.18)

e. War (exclusion *i*) (p. 8.20)

f. Damage to property (exclusion *j*) (pp. 8.20–8.21)

g. Insured's product (exclusion *k*) (pp. 8.21–8.22)

h. Insured's work (exclusion *l*) (p. 8.22)

i. Impaired property (exclusion *m*) (p. 8.22)

j. Recall of insured's product, work, or impaired property (exclusion *n*) (p. 8.23)

3-6. Give one example of loading or unloading that would not be covered by the CGL coverage form. (p. 8.17)

3-7. Give four examples of mobile equipment that would be insured under the CGL coverage form. (p. 8.19)

3-8. Give two examples of claims involving personal injury and advertising injury. (p. 8.25)

3-9. Identify three situations in which a person injured on the insured's premises or as a result of the insured's activities would *not* be covered under Coverage C—Medical Payments of the CGL coverage form. (p. 8.31)

Application Question

3-10. Power Wash, Inc. (PWI) operates a mobile power-washing service by which service trucks are dispatched to customer locations to clean building and deck exteriors. PWI is insured under a Commercial Package Policy that includes a Commercial General Liability Coverage Form (CGL). For each loss scenario, identify any exclusion(s) in PWI's CGL that would eliminate coverage for the described claim.

  a. A PWI employee damaged the stucco surface of a customer's building by using too much water pressure while power washing the building. All of this property damage occurred while PWI's operations were in progress. The customer sued PWI for damages because of this property damage.

  b. A PWI employee used the wrong cleaning solvent on a job, and, as a result, the customer's deck became cracked and discolored after the job was completed. All of this property damage occurred after PWI's operations had been completed. The customer sued PWI for damages because of this property damage.

c. A PWI employee fell from a ladder while washing the second floor of a building and suffered a broken leg. Because of the circumstances of the loss, the employee was permitted by the applicable laws in PWI's state to make a bodily injury liability claim against PWI, outside the workers compensation system, even though the employee's injury arose out of and in the course of employment by the insured.

Educational Objective 4
Describe the supplementary payments provided by the CGL coverage form.

Review Questions

4-1. Which CGL insuring agreements are supplemented by the supplementary payments section? (pp. 8.29–8.30)

4-2. Are the supplementary payments subject to the limits of insurance that apply to CGL coverage? (pp. 8.29–8.30)

4-3. Identify three supplementary payments included in the CGL coverage form. (p. 8.30)

Application Question

4-4. Amelia owns a tattoo parlor and insures her business with a CGL policy. Recently, Amelia was sued by a customer who developed a skin infection after receiving a new tattoo. The case went to court, and Amelia's insurer asked her to testify. Amelia missed three days of work for the trial and suffered lost income as a result. How much will Amelia's CGL policy compensate her, if at all, for loss of earnings?

Educational Objective 5
Explain whether, and for what amount, the CGL coverage form would cover a described loss.

Application Questions

5-1. Surewell Building Company, a general contractor, is insured under a CGL coverage form. Explain whether each of the following occurrences, which took place during the policy period, would be covered by Surewell's CGL:

   a. One of Surewell's employees became intoxicated at the annual company picnic while drinking beer that Surewell had provided. While driving home from the picnic, the intoxicated employee struck a pedestrian. The pedestrian is seeking damages from Surewell, alleging that the cause of the accident was Surewell's negligence in serving beer.

   b. A Surewell employee is suing Surewell, alleging that he was injured while operating a piece of earthmoving equipment that had been improperly maintained by Surewell.

c. While driving a mobile crane on a public road in order to move it to a new job site, a Surewell employee accidentally struck overhead power lines. As a result, Surewell was held liable not only for the physical damage to the power lines, but also for loss of business income incurred by several businesses that were left without power for several hours after the accident.

d. To perform repairs to a pier, Surewell rented a small work boat that was eighteen feet long. A Surewell employee's negligent operation of the work boat caused a collision with a sailboat. The owner of the sailboat sued Surewell for damage to her boat.

e. Surewell was the general contractor on a commercial building construction project that also involved several subcontractors. Shortly after the building was completed, an electrical subcontractor's defective work caused a fire that destroyed the entire building. The project owner sued Surewell for the cost of reconstructing the building.

5-2. Department Store is insured under a CGL coverage form. Would each of the following losses be covered by this policy? Justify each of your answers.

    a. A defective refrigerator recently purchased from Department Store caught fire and was destroyed. The owner of the refrigerator submitted a claim to Department Store for the cost to replace the refrigerator and for fire damage to his home.

    b. An employee was driving a truck owned by Department Store to make a delivery to a customer. The employee caused an accident in which the driver of a car was injured. The injured driver of the car was awarded damages in court.

    c. Insects destroyed several fur coats that had been placed in storage in Department Store. The owners of the fur coats submitted claims against Department Store for replacement of the coats.

Answers to Assignment 7 Questions

NOTE: These answers are provided to give students a basic understanding of acceptable types of responses. They often are not the only valid answers and are not intended to provide an exhaustive response to the questions.

Educational Objective 1

1-1. The costs of investigation and defense, as well as any damages for which the insured may be found liable, might result from a liability claim.

1-2. Even if found not legally liable, a business can have a liability loss because it has experienced the costs of investigating and defending against the suit.

1-3. The elements of the tort of negligence include all of the following:
- A duty owed to another person
- A breach of that duty
- A close causal connection between the negligent act (breach of duty) and the resulting harm
- The occurrence of actual loss or damage of a type recognized by law and measurable in monetary terms

1-4. a. An intentional tort is an act that a person can foresee (or should be able to foresee) that will harm another person, such as libel.

b. Strict liability is absolute liability for abnormally dangerous instrumentalities (for example, wild animals), ultra-hazardous activities (for example, blasting), and dangerously defective products. Strict liability is also imposed by statutes (for example, workers compensation laws).

1-5. a. An example of breach of contract—A store sells a bicycle with a defective frame, which breaks a week after it is sold. Jimmy buys this bicycle from the store and is injured while riding the bicycle. The store may be held legally liable for Jimmy's injuries. The seller has breached an implied warranty that the bicycle is fit for use and probably also an express warranty that the bicycle is free from defects.

b. An example of a hold-harmless agreement—A lease on an apartment building obligates Sue, a tenant, to hold the landlord harmless against liability claims made against the landlord by any person injured on the leased premises. With this lease, Sue is agreeing by contract to accept liability and pay any claims against the landlord for persons injured in her apartment.

1-6. Agnes may be liable under strict liability. Strict liability (or absolute liability) is liability that is imposed even though the defendant acted neither negligently nor with intent to cause harm.

Educational Objective 2

2-1. The five broad categories of CGL loss exposures are as follows:
- Premises liability exposure
- Operations liability exposure
- Products liability exposure
- Completed operations liability exposure
- Other CGL exposures

2-2. Operations liability exposure is generally associated with manufacturers, processors, or contractors.

2-3. Products liability can be imposed on a manufacturer, seller, or distributor of products under several different legal theories, including negligence, breach of warranty, and strict liability in tort.

2-4. a. When a service technician creates an electrical fire while preparing the wiring for a new fan installation in a customer's home, the event comes under Fanny's operations liability exposure.

b. When the fan falls from the ceiling and damages the customer's floor and a coffee table following the completion of installation, the event comes under Fanny's completed operations liability exposure.

2-5. A CGL coverage form would provide the following coverage:

a. A visitor injured during a visit to a leased building—Covered under the CGL. A lease of premises agreement is an insured contract.

b. Funds spent to withdraw a line of defective products—Not covered under the CGL. Exclusion n eliminates coverage for the cost or expense resulting from recall of impaired property.

c. The corporation made untrue statements about a competitor in an ad—Covered under Coverage B—personal and advertising injury liability of the CGL (slander, loss of reputation).

Educational Objective 3

3-1. A CGL coverage form provides the following coverages:

a. Coverage A—bodily injury and property damage

b. Coverage B—personal and advertising injury (libel, slander, and wrongful eviction; copyright infringement)

c. Coverage C—medical expenses and/or funeral expenses of persons injured on the insured's premises or injured from the insured's operations

3-2. The coverage territory that applies to most CGL claims is the United States (including its territories and possessions), Puerto Rico, and Canada. International waters and international airspace are included in the coverage territory if the injury or damage occurs in the course of travel or transportation between places included in the basic coverage territory. (The coverage territory can include the entire world for goods or products made or sold in the basic coverage territory and activities of a person residing in the basic coverage territory but pursuing the named insured's business outside the basic territory.)

3-3. The CGL coverage form considers the following as insured contracts:

- A lease of premises
- A railroad sidetrack agreement
- Any easement or license agreement, except in connection with construction or demolition within fifty feet of a railroad
- An obligation to indemnify a municipality if required by ordinance, excluding work performed for the municipality
- An elevator maintenance agreement
- Any other contract or agreement under which the insured's business assumes another's tort liability

3-4. An insured would have coverage for liquor liability under the CGL coverage form for the casual or occasional distribution of alcoholic beverages, such as the annual company picnic or holiday office party, as long as the insured is not in the alcoholic beverage business.

3-5. Exclusions to Coverage A of the CGL coverage form include the following:
    a. Bodily injury to employee—Eliminates coverage for obligations of the insured under any workers compensation, disability benefits, unemployment compensation, or similar law. Exclusion e eliminates coverage for bodily injury to any employee of the insured if the injury arises out of and in the course of employment.
    b. Pollution—Eliminates coverage for pollution liability claims related to the insured's premises and operations (claims for bodily injury, property damage resulting from pollution, and the cost or expense for cleanup of pollutants), subject to a few exceptions.
    c. Aircraft, auto, or watercraft—Eliminates coverage for bodily injury and property damage arising from the ownership, maintenance, or use of any aircraft, auto, or watercraft, subject to a few exceptions.
    d. Mobile equipment—Eliminates coverage for the transportation of mobile equipment by an auto owned, operated, rented, or borrowed by an insured and for the use of mobile equipment in a prearranged racing, speed, demolition contest, or stunting activity.
    e. War—Eliminates coverage for liability resulting from war, including undeclared or civil war; warlike action by a military force, by any government, sovereign or other authority; or insurrection, rebellion, revolution, usurped power, or action taken by governmental authority in hindering or defending against any of these.
    f. Damage to property—Eliminates coverage for damage to any of the following:
- Property owned, rented, or occupied by the named insured
- Premises the named insured has sold, given away, or abandoned if the damage arises out of any part of these premises
- Property loaned to the named insured
- Personal property in the care, custody, or control of an insured
- That particular part of any real property on which work is being performed by the named insured or any contractor or subcontractor working for the named insured if the damage arises from the work
- That particular part of any property that must be restored, repaired, or replaced because the named insured's work was incorrectly performed on it

    g. Insured's product—Eliminates coverage for damage to the insured's product if damage results from a defect in the product.
    h. Insured's work—Eliminates coverage for any property damage to the named insured's work arising out of the work or any part of it and included in the "products-completed operations hazard."
    i. Impaired property—Eliminates coverage for damage to impaired property or property that has not been physically injured if the damage arises from a defect in the insured's product or work or for failure of the insured or anyone acting on behalf of the insured to complete a contract or agreement according to its terms.

j. Recall of insured's product, work, or impaired property—Eliminates coverage for any loss, cost, or expense resulting from loss of use, withdrawal, recall, inspection, repair, replacement, adjustment, removal, or disposal of the insured's product, insured's work, or impaired property.

3-6. An example of loading or unloading that would not be covered by the CGL is a scenario in which employees of Appliance Store damaged wood trim and wallboard in a customer's house in the process of moving a freezer from Appliance Store's van to the delivery destination in the customer's house. (The CGL excludes the loading or unloading of autos by hand or by use of a hand truck.)

3-7. The CGL coverage form considers the following as mobile equipment:
- Bulldozers, farm machinery, forklifts, and other vehicles designed for off-road use
- Vehicles maintained for use on or next to premises owned or rented by the named insured
- Vehicles having crawler treads
- Vehicles providing mobility to permanently mounted power cranes, shovels, loaders, diggers, drills, or road construction or resurfacing equipment (graders, scrapers, or rollers)

3-8. The following are examples of claims involving personal and advertising injury:
- A building owner wrongfully evicts a tenant from a building.
- A business uses the advertising ideas of another business without permission.

3-9. Coverage C—medical payments of the CGL coverage form would not cover the following:
- Any insured (other than a volunteer worker of the named insured)
- Anyone hired to do work for an insured or for a tenant of an insured
- A person injured on a part of the named insured's premises normally occupied by this person
- A person entitled to workers compensation benefits for the injury
- A person injured while participating in athletics

3-10. a. Paragraph (5) of exclusion j., Damage to Property, would eliminate coverage for the building owner's suit against PWI. Paragraph (5) excludes property damage to "that particular part of real property on which you . . . are performing operations, if the 'property damage' arises out of those operations."

Paragraph (6) of exclusion j. could also be applied to this claim. Paragraph (6) excludes property damage to "that particular part of any property that must be restored, repaired or replaced because 'your work' was incorrectly performed on it."

(Exclusion l, Damage to Your Work, does not apply to this claim because that exclusion applies only to property damage that is included in the "products-completed operations hazard," and the property damage for which claim was made occurred before PWI's operations were completed.)

b. Exclusion l., Damage to Your Work, would eliminate coverage for the customer's claim against PWI. The Damage to Your Work exclusion applies to "'property damage' to 'your work' arising out of it or any part of it and included in the 'products-completed operations hazard.'" Because the property damage claimed against PWI occurred after PWI's operations were completed, this property damage was included in the products-completed operations hazard, as required by exclusion l.

(Exclusion j., Damage to Property, paragraphs (5) and (6) would not apply to this claim. Paragraph (5) applies to property damage to that particular part of real property on which the named insured or its contractors "are performing operations," thus applying only to property damage that occurs before the operations are completed. Paragraph (6) also does not apply, because exclusion j. contains the following statement: "Paragraph (6) of this exclusion does not apply to 'property damage' included in the 'products-completed operations hazard.'")

c. Exclusion e., Employer's Liability, would eliminate coverage for the employee's claim against PWI. This exclusion applies to bodily injury to an employee of the insured arising out of and in the course of employment by the insured.

(Exclusion d., Workers' Compensation and Similar Laws, would not apply to this claim because, as stated in the question, PWI did not have any obligation under a workers compensation law or any similar law.)

Educational Objective 4

4-1. CGL Coverage A and Coverage B are the insuring agreements supplemented by the supplementary payments section.

4-2. The supplementary payments are payable in addition to the limits of insurance that apply to CGL coverage. However, the insurer's obligation to pay these supplementary payments ends as soon as the applicable limit of insurance has been exhausted in paying damages for judgments or settlements.

4-3. The CGL coverage form includes the following supplementary payments:
- All expenses incurred by the insurer (fees for attorneys, witness fees, and cost of police reports).
- Up to $250 for the cost of bail bonds required because of accidents or traffic law violations involving any covered vehicle (typically mobile equipment).
- The cost of bonds to release any property of the insured's held by a plaintiff to ensure payment of any judgment that may be rendered against the insured. The insurer is not required to provide either of the bonds previously described; its only obligation is to pay the premium.
- Reasonable expenses incurred by the insured at the insurer's request including loss of earnings for missing work to testify, attend court, or assist in the defense.
- Court costs or other costs (excluding actual damages) assessed against the insured in a suit.

4-4. Supplementary payments coverage will pay reasonable expenses incurred by Amelia at the insurer's request, including loss of earnings (up to $250 a day) when she must miss work to testify, attend court, or otherwise assist in the defense.

Educational Objective 5

5-1. a. The claim would be covered by Surewell's CGL. The liquor liability exclusion applies only if an insured is in the business of manufacturing, selling, or otherwise furnishing alcoholic beverages. It does not apply to the casual or occasional distribution of alcoholic beverages, such as at Surewell's annual company picnic.

b. The employee's suit against Surewell would not be covered. The CGL excludes coverage for injuries to employees that arise out of and in the course of their employment.

c. Surewell's CGL would cover Surewell's liability for both the physical damage and the resulting loss of business income incurred by businesses that were left without power. A mobile crane qualifies as mobile equipment, even while it is being driven on a public road. And the CGL's definition of property damage includes both physical injury to tangible property and resulting loss of use (in this case, the loss of income experienced by the businesses that lost power).

d. Surewell's CGL insurer would defend Surewell against the sailboat owner's suit (and pay damages if awarded by the court). Although the CGL excludes liability arising out of the use of a watercraft, the exclusion does not apply to a watercraft that the named insured does not own if it is less than twenty-six feet long.

e. Surewell's CGL insurer would defend Surewell against the project owner's suit (and pay damages if awarded by the court). Although exclusion *l* eliminates coverage for damage to the named insured's completed work, the exclusion contains an exception: the exclusion does not apply if the damaged work or the work out of which the damage arises was performed on the named insured's behalf by a subcontractor. In Surewell's case, the damage to the building *did* arise out of work performed by a subcontractor. Consequently, the exclusion does not apply, and (subject to policy limits) Surewell's policy would cover the entire building loss if the court holds that Surewell is liable for the loss.

5-2. a. The CGL would not cover damage to the refrigerator because of exclusion *k* relating to damage to the named insured's own product. However, the CGL would cover the resulting fire damage to the buyer's home.

b. The CGL would not cover the damages awarded to the injured driver because exclusion *g* eliminates coverage for bodily injury caused by using any auto.

c. The fur coats damaged by the insects would not be covered because of the part of exclusion *j* relating to personal property in the care, custody, or control of the insured. (Department Store needed a bailees' customers policy to cover this exposure.)

Direct Your Learning

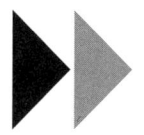

Assignment 8

Commercial General Liability Insurance, Part II

Educational Objectives

After learning the content of this assignment, you should be able to:

1. Identify the persons and organizations that may be insured by the Commercial General Liability (CGL) Coverage Form.

2. Explain how the following limits of insurance in the CGL coverage form are applied:
   - Each occurrence limit
   - Personal and advertising injury limit
   - "Damage to premises rented to you" limit
   - Medical expense limit
   - General aggregate limit
   - Products-completed operations aggregate limit

3. Summarize the CGL conditions.

4. Explain how the claims-made CGL form differs from the occurrence CGL form.

5. Describe the purposes that can be served by endorsements to the CGL coverage form.

6. Explain how the premium for CGL coverage is determined.

7. Describe the purpose of each of the following:
   - Liquor Liability Coverage Form
   - Products/Completed Operations Liability Coverage Form
   - Owners and Contractors Protective (OCP) Liability Coverage Form
   - Railroad Protective Liability Coverage Form

8. Explain whether, and for what amount, the CGL or other miscellaneous ISO liability coverage forms would cover a described loss.

9. Define or describe each of the Key Words and Phrases for this assignment.

Study Materials

Required Reading:
- Commercial Insurance
  - Chapter 9

Study Aids:
- SMART Online Practice Exams
- SMART Study Aids
  - Review Notes and Flash Cards—Assignment 8

Outline

- **Who Is an Insured?**
  - A. Named Insured and Related Parties
  - B. The Named Insured's Employees and Volunteer Workers
  - C. Other Persons and Organizations
    1. Real Estate Managers
    2. Legal Representatives
    3. Newly Acquired Organizations
    4. Mobile Equipment Operators
- **Limits of Insurance**
  - A. Each Occurrence Limit
  - B. Personal and Advertising Injury Limit
  - C. "Damage to Premises Rented to You" Limit
  - D. Medical Expense Limit
  - E. Aggregate Limits
  - F. Application of CGL Limits
- **CGL Conditions**
  - A. Bankruptcy
  - B. Duties in the Event of Occurrence, Offense, Claim, or Suit
  - C. Legal Action Against Us
  - D. Other Insurance
    1. When CGL Is Excess
    2. When CGL Is Primary
    3. Methods of Sharing
  - E. Premium Audit
  - F. Representations
  - G. Separation of Insureds
  - H. Transfer of Rights of Recovery Against Others to Us
  - I. When We Do Not Renew
- **Claims-Made CGL Coverage Form**
  - A. Claims-Made Trigger
  - B. Retroactive Date
  - C. Extended Reporting Periods
  - D. Non-ISO Claims-Made Forms
- **CGL Endorsements**
  - A. State Endorsements
  - B. Exclusion Endorsements
  - C. Classification Endorsements
  - D. Miscellaneous Endorsements
- **Certificates of Insurance**
- **Rating CGL Coverage**
  - A. Premium Base
  - B. Other Rating Considerations
- **Miscellaneous Liability Coverage Forms**
  - A. Liquor Liability Coverage Form
  - B. Products/Completed Operations Liability Coverage Form
  - C. Owners and Contractors Protective Liability Coverage Form
  - D. Railroad Protective Liability Coverage Form
  - E. Pollution Liability Coverage Forms
- **Summary**

study tips — Plan to take one week to complete each assignment in your course.

For each assignment, you should define or describe each of the Key Words and Phrases and answer each of the Review and Application Questions.

> ## Educational Objective 1
> Identify the persons and organizations that may be insured by the Commercial General Liability (CGL) Coverage Form.

Review Questions

1-1. Identify the persons who are automatically included as insureds if the named insured in the CGL declarations is one of the following:

   a. An individual (p. 9.3)

   b. A partnership or joint venture (p. 9.4)

   c. A limited liability company (p. 9.4)

   d. A corporation, municipality, or school district (p. 9.4)

e. A trust (p. 9.4)

1-2. Identify other persons or organizations who are insureds under the CGL. (p. 9.5)

1-3. The 2004 edition of the CGL does not provide coverage for injury to a passerby that may occur when an employee of the insured is operating a forklift that is subject to the state's motor vehicle laws. How can a business owner obtain insurance for that loss exposure? (pp. 9.5–9.6)

Application Question

1-4. One of the managers of a limited liability company (LLC) in Indiana took a prospective customer to a golf course. While there, the manager struck and injured a golfer on another fairway with an errant shot. The injured golfer sued the manager for her injuries. Would the company's CGL policy respond to the suit?

Educational Objective 2

Explain how the following limits of insurance in the CGL Coverage Form are applied:

- Each occurrence limit
- Personal and advertising injury limit
- "Damage to premises rented to you" limit
- Medical expense limit
- General aggregate limit
- Products-completed operations aggregate limit

Key Words and Phrases

Each occurrence limit (p. 9.7)

Personal and advertising injury limit (p. 9.7)

Damage to premises rented to you limit (p. 9.7)

Medical expense limit (p. 9.7)

Products-completed operations hazard (p. 9.7)

General aggregate limit (p. 9.8)

Products-completed operations aggregate limit (p. 9.8)

Review Questions

2-1. Identify all of the CGL limits of insurance that would apply to or be reduced by each of the following:

   a. A claim under Coverage A for bodily injury within the products-completed operations hazard (pp. 9.7–9.8)

   b. A claim under Coverage A for property damage not within the products-completed operations hazard (pp. 9.7–9.8)

   c. A claim under Coverage B for personal and advertising injury (p. 9.7)

   d. A claim under Coverage C for medical expenses (p. 9.7)

   e. A claim under Coverage A for fire damage to premises rented to the named insured (p. 9.7)

2-2. What determines whether a claim payment under Coverage A will reduce the general aggregate limit or the products-completed operations aggregate limit? (p. 9.8)

Application Question

2-3. Sandy operates a sporting goods store in a building that she leases from General Leasing Company. Sandy has a CGL policy with the following limits:

General aggregate	$1,000,000
Products-completed operations aggregate	$1,000,000
Personal and advertising injury	$500,000
Each occurrence	$500,000
Damage to premises rented to you	$100,000
Medical payments	$5,000

What dollar amount, if any, will Sandy's CGL insurer pay for each of the following losses that occurred during the same policy period? If a loss is not covered, or not fully covered, explain why.

a. A fire in the building, caused by the negligence of one of Sandy's employees, caused $120,000 damage to the building.

b. A display case collapsed and injured two of Sandy's customers. One customer incurred medical expenses of $3,500, and the other had medical expenses of $4,900. Both customers made claims for medical payments coverage under Sandy's CGL policy.

c. A customer who bought a weight bench from Sandy was injured when the bench collapsed while the customer was exercising at home. The customer, who claimed the weight bench was defective, sued Sandy and was awarded $600,000 in court.

Educational Objective 3
Summarize the CGL conditions.

Key Words and Phrases

Contribution by equal shares (p. 9.12)

Contribution by limits (p. 9.13)

Review Questions

3-1. What are the insured's duties in the event of an occurrence, a claim, or a suit under a CGL coverage form? (pp. 9.10–9.11)

3-2. According to the CGL conditions, under what circumstances can the insured bring legal action against the insurer? (p. 9.11)

3-3. Explain how loss payment under two or more CGL policies would be shared using the following:

   a. Contribution by equal shares (p. 9.12)

   b. Contribution by limits (p. 9.13)

3-4. Summarize each of the following CGL conditions:

   a. Premium audit (p. 9.13)

   b. Representations (pp. 9.13–9.14)

   c. Separation of insureds (p. 9.14)

   d. Transfer of right of recovery against others (p. 9.14)

Application Question

3-5. A manufacturing company is insured under two CGL policies. The each occurrence limit under Policy A is $500,000. Under Policy B, the each occurrence limit is $1,000,000. The company was held to be legally liable for $300,000 in damages arising from one occurrence.

   a. What dollar amount would be payable under each policy if loss payment is based on contribution by limits? Show your calculations.

   b. What dollar amount would be payable under each policy if loss payment is based on contribution by equal shares?

Educational Objective 4
Explain how the claims-made CGL form differs from the occurrence CGL form.

Key Words and Phrases

Claims-made coverage trigger (p. 9.15)

Retroactive date (p. 9.16)

Extended reporting period (p. 9.16)

Review Questions

4-1. Why do insurers offer claims-made coverage? (p. 9.15)

4-2. Describe the coverage trigger in claims-made CGL coverage. (pp. 9.15–9.16)

4-3. How does the occurrence CGL form differ from the claims-made CGL form? (p. 9.15)

4-4. Identify the three options regarding retroactive dates for claims-made policies. (p. 9.15)

4-5. Explain how coverage is affected in a claims-made policy that has a retroactive date. (p. 9.16)

4-6. Explain how coverage is affected in a claims-made policy that does *not* have a retroactive date. (p. 9.16)

4-7. Describe the extended reporting period aspect of claims-made coverage. (pp. 9.16–9.17)

4-8. Describe the two conditions that must be met in order for claims made within the basic extended reporting period to be covered. (p. 9.17)

4-9. Describe two features of a supplemental extended reporting period. (pp. 9.16–9.17)

Application Questions

4-10. Jolton, Inc., is a meat packing company specializing in canned hams and frozen pork products. Jolton's insurer offered a renewal of Jolton's CGL policy only on a claims-made basis with a retroactive date the same as the date of the renewal, January 1 of this year. Jolton's previous CGL policies were written on an occurrence basis. For the following losses, determine whether coverage is provided. If coverage is provided, determine whether it will be covered by Jolton's previous occurrence-based CGL policies, or by the current claims made policy.

   a. A claim involving contaminated canned ham occurred last November 15, but was not reported until March 15 of this year.

   b. A claim involving contaminated frozen pork occurred February 20 of this year, and was reported March 1 of this year.

   c. A claim involving allergies due to additives to pork products occurred two years ago, but was not reported until April of this year.

4-11. Zelles Tanks, Inc., manufactures composite-material tanks that are used at commercial facilities to store fuel for emergency generators. Zelles is merging with another organization and discontinuing the manufacture of tanks. Zelles's insurance agent has suggested that the company purchase a supplemental extended reporting period. Explain why the insurance agent would have made this recommendation.

Educational Objective 5
Describe the purposes that can be served by endorsements to the CGL coverage form.

Key Word or Phrase
Certificate of insurance (p. 9.21)

Review Questions

5-1. Describe the purpose of each of the following categories of CGL endorsements:

a. State endorsements (p. 9.19)

b. Exclusion endorsements (p. 9.19)

c. Classification endorsements (pp. 9.19–9.20)

5-2. Briefly describe the overall purposes of miscellaneous CGL endorsements. (pp. 9.20–9.21)

5-3. Describe the following miscellaneous endorsements that can be used to add coverages, deductibles, or insureds to a CGL policy:

a. Boats endorsement (p. 9.20)

b. Deductible Liability Insurance endorsement (p. 9.20)

c. Additional Insured—Vendors endorsement (p. 9.20)

5-4. Describe a certificate of insurance and why it is needed.
(p. 9.21)

Application Question

5-5. JKL Corporation is a pharmaceutical firm conducting pioneering research in immunization techniques that are based on products derived from human and animal blood. What type of endorsement should JKL consider if it wants to eliminate coverage for a particular new product it is developing? Explain.

Educational Objective 6
Explain how the premium for CGL coverage is determined.

Key Words and Phrases
Premium base (p. 9.23)

Class code (p. 9.23)

Review Questions

6-1. What is the formula used to determine the premium for CGL coverage? (p. 9.23)

6-2. Differentiate between rate and exposure. (p. 9.23)

6-3. Explain why two rates are used for most businesses when determining the premium for CGL coverage. (p. 9.23)

6-4. What premium base is normally used in rating CGL coverage for each of the following?

   a. Mercantile businesses (p. 9.23)

   b. Contracting businesses (p. 9.23)

c. Special events (p. 9.23)

Application Question

6-5. A building contractor received a bill following the expiration of his first year of coverage with the ABC Insurance Company. The bill resulted from an audit performed on his CGL policy, and he was charged an additional premium. Considering the premium base used for contractors, explain why the additional charge was made as a result of the audit.

Educational Objective 7

Describe the purpose of each of the following:

- Liquor Liability Coverage Form
- Products/Completed Operations Liability Coverage Form
- Owners and Contractors Protective (OCP) Liability Coverage Form
- Railroad Protective Liability Coverage Form

Key Words and Phrases

Liquor Liability Coverage Form (p. 9.25)

Products/Completed Operations Liability Coverage Form (p. 9.25)

Owners and Contractors Protective Liability Coverage Form (p. 9.25)

Railroad Protective Liability Coverage Form (p. 9.26)

Review Questions

7-1. What is the purpose of miscellaneous liability coverage forms? (p. 9.25)

7-2. Describe the circumstances under which each of the following is typically purchased:

   a. Liquor Liability Coverage Form (p. 9.25)

   b. Products/Completed Operations Liability Coverage Form (p. 9.25)

c. Owners and Contractors Protective Liability Coverage Form (pp. 9.25–9.26)

d. Railroad Protective Liability Coverage Form (p. 9.26)

7-3. When does the Owners and Contractors Protective Liability Coverage Form terminate? (pp. 9.25–9.26)

Application Question

7-4. A microbrewery serves its own beer with sandwiches and chicken wings for lunch and dinner. Explain why it would seek liability coverage through a Liquor Liability Coverage Form.

Educational Objective 8

Explain whether, and for what amount, the CGL or other miscellaneous ISO liability coverage forms would cover a described loss.

Application Questions

8-1. A discount store is insured under a CGL policy. Indicate whether the products-completed operations aggregate limit in the store's CGL policy would be reduced by each of the following claims. (Make sure that you fully understand the policy definition of "products-completed operations hazard" before answering.)

    a. A man was injured by a defective power drill while making bookcases in his basement. The man sued the store and won damages for his injury.

    b. A young girl was injured by a defective toy only minutes after her parents had bought the toy. The injury occurred on the store's premises. The girl's parents sued the store and won damages for their daughter's injury.

8-2. A construction company is insured under a CGL policy with a $1,000,000 general aggregate limit, a $1,000,000 products-completed operations aggregate limit, and a $500,000 each occurrence limit. The company was sued separately by two bystanders who were injured in the same accident at one of the company's construction sites. The court awarded $200,000 to the first bystander, and the second bystander was awarded $250,000. The total cost of defending the company in these two lawsuits was $80,000. To what extent, if any, will these amounts be paid by the company's CGL insurer? Explain.

8-3. Radley Corporation, a manufacturer of small home appliances, is insured under a CGL policy written on an occurrence basis. The following limits of insurance apply:

General aggregate	$2,000,000
Products-completed operations aggregate	$2,000,000
Personal and advertising injury	$1,000,000
Each occurrence	$1,000,000
Damage to premises rented to you	$100,000
Medical expense	$10,000

What dollar amount, if any, will Radley's CGL insurer pay for each of the following losses that occurred during the policy period? If a loss is not covered, or not fully covered, explain why. Assume that each loss would be paid in the order presented.

a. Radley Corporation placed an advertisement in a national magazine that made inaccurate and unfavorable statements about a competitor's product. The competitor sued Radley for libel and was awarded $1,500,000 in court.

b. A warehouse leased to Radley was destroyed by a fire that resulted from Radley's negligence. Radley was legally liable for the resulting $250,000 in damage.

c. A defective Radley product caused serious injury to a consumer, who was awarded $400,000 by the court. The injury occurred after the customer took the product to her home.

d. Radley hosted a holiday party for its employees. An employee who became intoxicated at the party struck and killed a pedestrian while driving home. A court ordered Radley to pay $2,100,000 to the pedestrian's surviving family members.

8-4. Gallon Pharmaceuticals is a developer and manufacturer of drugs made specifically to treat expectant mothers. Due to the potential long-tail losses that can occur with such drugs, Gallon has been able to find only claims-made CGL coverage. In addition, the insurer is willing to renew coverage only if the retroactive date is reset to the effective date of each renewal. Explain why this coverage would not protect Gallon from potential long-tail losses from its products.

# Answers to Assignment 8 Questions

NOTE: These answers are provided to give students a basic understanding of acceptable types of responses. They often are not the only valid answers and are not intended to provide an exhaustive response to the questions.

Educational Objective 1

1-1. Individuals are automatically included as insureds if the named insured in the CGL declaration is one of the following:

   a. An individual—If the named insured is an individual, the named insured's spouse is also an insured.

   b. A partnership or joint venture—If the named insured is a partnership or joint venture, all partners or members and their spouses are also insureds.

   c. A limited liability company—If the named insured is a limited liability company, all members and managers of the company are also insureds.

   d. A corporation, municipality, or school district—All executive officers, directors, and stockholders of the organization are also insureds.

   e. A trust—If the named insured is a trust (a legal entity created for the benefit of designated beneficiaries), the named trust is an insured. The named insured's trustees are also insureds, but only with respect to their duties as trustees.

1-2. Other than the named insured, the following are insureds under the CGL:
   - Employees and volunteer workers of the named insured
   - Real estate managers
   - Legal representatives
   - Newly acquired organizations (ninety days maximum)
   - Mobile equipment operators (for CGL versions predating 2004)

1-3. A business owner can obtain insurance for injury to a passerby that may occur when an employee is operating a forklift that is subject to the state's motor vehicle laws through a commercial automobile insurance policy.

1-4. The test for whether the manager qualifies as an insured in this incident is whether he was acting within his duties as a manager for the LLC. Because he was entertaining a potential new customer, it does seem that he qualifies as an insured, and the CGL would respond.

Educational Objective 2

2-1. CGL limits of insurance would apply to or be reduced by the following:

   a. A claim under Coverage A for bodily injury within the products-completed operations hazard would be subject to the each occurrence limit and the products-completed operations aggregate limit.

   b. A claim under Coverage A for property damage not within the products-completed operations hazard would be subject to the each occurrence limit and the general aggregate limit.

   c. A claim under Coverage B for personal and advertising injury would be subject to the personal and advertising injury liability limit and the general aggregate limit.

d. A claim under Coverage C for medical expenses would be subject to the medical expense limit and the general aggregate limit.

e. A claim under Coverage A for fire damage to premises rented to the named insured would be subject to the damages to premises rented to you limit and the general aggregate limit.

2-2. If the injury or damage is within the "products-completed operations hazard" as defined in the CGL, any claim payment will reduce the products-completed operations aggregate limit. If the injury is not within the products-completed operations hazard, any claim payment will reduce the general aggregate limit.

2-3. Sandy's CGL policy will cover the following losses that occurred during the policy period:

a. $100,000—the "damage to premises rented to you" limit.

b. $3,500 for the first customer and $4,900 for the second customer, for a total of $8,400. The medical expense limit applies separately to each person.

c. $500,000—the each occurrence limit.

Educational Objective 3

3-1. The insured's duties in the event of an occurrence, a claim, or a suit under a CGL coverage form include the following:

- Provide notice of how, when, and where the occurrence or offense happened.
- Provide the name and addresses of any injured persons and any witnesses.
- Describe the nature and location of any damage or injury resulting from the occurrence or offense
- Immediately record the details of the claim or suit and the date received.
- Notify the insurer in writing as soon as practicable.
- Immediately forward the insurer copies of any legal papers related to the suit.
- Authorize the insurer to obtain any legal records or other documents.
- Cooperate with the insurer in the investigation or settlement of the claim or in the insurer's defense against the suit.
- Assist the insurer in any action against any third party that may be liable to the insured because of the injuries or damage for which claim is made.
- Refrain from making voluntary payments, assuming obligations, or incurring any expenses without the insurer's consent.

3-2. According to CGL conditions, the insured can sue the insurer to get the insurer to pay a third-party claim only if the insured has fully complied with all policy conditions.

3-3. Loss payment under two or more CGL policies would be shared as follows:

a. Contribution by equal shares—Each insurer contributes an equal amount to the payment of the claim until the claim is fully paid or until each insurer exhausts its limit of insurance, whichever occurs first.

b. Contribution by limits—Each insurer pays that proportion of the claim that its limit bears to the total of all applicable insurance, but no insurer will pay more than its applicable limit of insurance.

3-4. a. The premium audit CGL condition requires the named insured to keep adequate records to permit correct calculation of the premium and to make these records available to the insurer.

b. The representations CGL condition states that, by accepting the policy, the named insured agrees to the following:
- The statements in the declarations are accurate and complete.
- The statements in the declarations are based on representations made by the named insured to the insurer.
- The insurer has issued the policy in reliance on the named insured's representations. This condition encourages the insured to read the policy declarations and make sure that the representations made in the policy are accurate.

c. The separation of insureds CGL condition states that the insurance provided by the policy applies separately to each person insured. This condition can provide coverage for one insured sued by another insured.

d. If the insured has any right to recover from a third party all or any part of a claim paid by the insurer, the insured must transfer that right to the insurer. The insurer is subrogated to the rights of the insured to recover the amount paid.

3-5. a. The dollar amounts payable under each policy if loss payment is based on contribution by limits are as follows:

Policy A: $500,000/$1,500,000 × $300,000 = $100,000.

Policy B: $1,000,000/$1,500,000 × $300,000 = $200,000.

b. If loss payment is based on contribution by equal shares, Policy A pays $150,000 and Policy B pays $150,000.

Educational Objective 4

4-1. Insurers offer claims-made coverage because the long-tail nature of claims often makes it difficult for insurers to accurately predict the ultimate cost of claims. The claims-made CGL coverage form addresses this problem.

4-2. Under the coverage trigger in claims-made CGL coverage, the claim for bodily injury, property damage, or personal and advertising injury must be first made against any insured during either the policy period or an extended reporting period provided by the policy.

4-3. Under the occurrence form, damage is covered only if it occurs during the policy period, regardless of when the claim is made. In claims-made CGL coverage, damage is covered for claims first made against the insurer during either the policy period or an extended reporting period provided by the policy.

4-4. Three options regarding retroactive dates for claims-made policies are as follows:

(1) A claims-made policy might not contain a retroactive date.

(2) A claims-made policy might contain a retroactive date that is the same as the policy inception date.

(3) A claims-made policy might contain a retroactive date that is before the policy inception date.

4-5. If a claims-made policy has a retroactive date (shown in the CGL declarations), the policy will not cover claims for (1) bodily injury or property damage that occurred before the retroactive date or (2) personal and advertising injury offenses committed before the retroactive date, even if claim is first made during the policy period.

4-6. If a claims-made policy has no retroactive date, it will cover claims first made during its policy period, regardless of when the bodily injury or property damage occurred or when the personal and advertising injury offense was committed.

4-7. An extended reporting period is a time period following the termination date of a claims-made policy during which claims may be reported for injuries that occurred after the retroactive date and before the policy expiration date. If such claims are first made within the extended reporting period, they will be covered under the expired claims-made policy.

4-8. Claims made within the basic extended reporting period are covered only if both of the following two conditions are met:
   (1) The injury occurred (or the offense was committed) on or after the retroactive date, if any, and before the policy expiration date.
   (2) The insured reported the occurrence to the insurer within sixty days after the policy expired.

4-9. Two features of a supplemental extended reporting period are as follows:
   (1) It lasts indefinitely and does not require that the occurrence be reported within sixty days after policy expiration.
   (2) It restores the expiring policy's aggregate limits to their original levels, but only for claims first received and recorded during the supplemental extended reporting period.

4-10. a. A claim involving contaminated canned ham that occurred last November 15, but was not reported until March 15 of this year would be covered by the previous occurrence-based policy.
   b. A claim involving contaminated frozen pork that occurred February 20 of this year and was reported March 1 of this year would be covered by the current claims-made policy.
   c. A claim involving allergies due to additives to pork products occurred two years ago but that was not reported until April of this year would be covered under the occurrence-based policy in force at the time of the occurrence.

4-11. The extended reporting period that is provided automatically on claims-made policies extends the reporting period of a claims-made policy for five years. Claims that occur during the policy period are covered as long as they are reported within five years. The supplemental extended reporting period extends that period of time indefinitely. Because losses might occur with the storage tanks as a result of errors in manufacturing that occurred during the policy period, the extension will allow those losses to be reported for an indefinite period of time and coverage will still be provided.

Educational Objective 5

5-1. a. State endorsements modify the basic CGL form to conform to the laws or regulations (such as cancellation laws) of a particular state in which the insured has operations.
   b. Exclusion endorsements modify the CGL form to exclude particular types of claims (such as personal or advertising injury) or categories of insureds (such as employees and volunteer workers).

c. Classification endorsements restrict or expand coverage under the CGL form in order to make it appropriate for insuring particular types of organizations (excluding, for example, professional liability of a blood bank).

5-2. The overall purposes of miscellaneous CGL endorsements are as follows:
- To amend certain coverages or the limits of insurance and to modify the claims-made CGL form.
- To provide supplemental extended reporting periods or to exclude specified locations, products, or work.

5-3. a. The Boats endorsement extends CGL coverage to any watercraft described in the endorsement and owned or used by or rented to the insured.
   b. The Deductible Liability Insurance endorsement enables the insured to apply deductibles to the bodily injury and property damage liability coverages, either separately or combined. The deductibles can be on either a per claim or a per occurrence basis.
   c. In the Additional Insured—Vendors endorsement, the vendor is covered for bodily injury or property damage liability arising from distributing or selling any of the named insured's products listed in the endorsement.

5-4. A certificate of insurance is a brief outline of the coverage in force when the certificate is issued; a certificate of insurance is *not* an endorsement to the policy. Many organizations demand that firms with whom they do business provide evidence of insurance. Furthermore, rating rules for both workers compensation and general liability insurance require that the insured either obtain proof of insurance from contractors or subcontractors that they employ or pay a higher premium. The customary method of providing such evidence is a certificate of insurance.

5-5. JKL should consider the Exclusion—Designated Product endorsement. This endorsement excludes liability arising out of specified products of the insured.

Educational Objective 6

6-1. The following formula is used to determine the premium for CGL coverage:

Rate × exposure = premium.

6-2. The rate depends on the nature of the insured organization and its susceptibility to liability losses. The exposure reflects the size of business operations insured, not the type of losses to which the business is susceptible.

6-3. Two rates are used for most businesses when determining the premium for CGL coverage because one rate applies to the exposure for premises operations, and another rate applies to the exposure for products-completed operations.

6-4. a. The premium base used for mercantile businesses is gross sales.
   b. The premium base used for contracting businesses is payroll.
   c. The premium base used for special events is number of admissions.

6-5. Contracting businesses are generally rated on the basis of payroll for CGL coverage. Because the exact amount of payroll can only be estimated at the beginning of the year, the building contractor was charged an additional premium based on a comparison of the estimated and actual payroll. Evidently, payroll was higher than initially estimated.

Educational Objective 7

7-1. The purpose of miscellaneous liability coverage forms is to cover significant loss exposures the CGL forms exclude.

7-2. a. The Liquor Liability Coverage Form is used when an organization that is in the business of manufacturing, selling, serving, or distributing alcoholic beverages wishes to insure against liquor liability arising out of those activities.

b. The Products/Completed Operations Liability Coverage Form is used to provide products and completed operations liability coverage separately from the regular CGL form. That situation might arise when an insured sells hazardous products and the insurer writing the insured's commercial package policy adds an exclusion of products and completed operations to the CGL form. The insured might then purchase products liability insurance from a separate insurer that specializes in high-risk products liability exposures.

c. The Owners and Contractors Protective Liability coverage form is ordinarily purchased by an independent contractor that will be performing operations for a property owner that has requested the contractor to buy this type of coverage. The coverage protects the property owner against liability arising out of the contractor's operations on behalf of the property owner or arising out of the property owner's general supervision of the contractor's work.

d. The Railroad Protective Liability Coverage Form is purchased by an independent contractor at the request of a railroad when the contractor will be performing operations on or near railroad property. The coverage protects the railroad against losses arising out of the contractor's operations.

7-3. The Owners and Contractors Protective Liability Coverage Form terminates as soon as the contractor's work is completed or put to its intended use.

7-4. The Liquor Liability Coverage Form can be used to provide liquor liability for insureds that are in the business of manufacturing and serving alcoholic beverages. Coverage is provided for bodily injury and property damage resulting from selling or serving alcohol. Such a loss might occur if a patron overindulges and exhibits alcohol poisoning or injures a third party. Liquor liability is excluded in the CGL policy.

Educational Objective 8

8-1. a. This claim would reduce the products-completed operations aggregate limit because the circumstances of the injury meet the policy definition of "products-completed operations hazard": the injury occurred away from the named insured's premises and arose out of the named insured's product.

b. This claim would not reduce the products-completed operations aggregate limit. Although the injury arose out of the named insured's product, the injury did not occur away from the named insured's premises and thus was not within the "products-completed operations hazard." The claim would reduce the general aggregate limit.

8-2. The insurer will pay all the damages awarded to both bystanders because the total ($450,000) is less than the each occurrence limit. The insurer will also pay the $80,000 in defense costs in full because defense costs are payable in addition to the policy limits.

8-3. Radley's CGL insurer will pay the following dollar amounts:
  a. $1,000,000—the personal and advertising injury limit
  b. $100,000—the damage to premises rented to you limit
  c. $400,000
  d. $900,000—general aggregate limit reached after payment of the claims in parts (a) and (b).

  (The $400,000 paid in part (c) reduces the products-completed operations aggregate limit, not the general aggregate limit.)

8-4. If the retroactive date is reset at each renewal, liability losses will be covered only if the claims were made during the policy period and the claims did not occur before the retroactive date, which is the effective date. If any losses occurred prior to the effective date of the renewal, there would be no coverage. Considering the time that would be required for any injuries resulting from the drugs to be discovered as the children of the expectant mothers are born and mature, Gallon would not be covered for the potentially catastrophic liability losses that would be discovered years after the manufacture of the drugs.

SEGMENT C

Assignment 9   Commercial Auto Insurance

Assignment 10   Businessowners Policies and Farm Insurance

Assignment 11   Workers Compensation and Employers Liability Insurance

Assignment 12   Miscellaneous Coverages

Segment C is the third of three segments in the INS 23 course. These segments are designed to help structure your study.

Direct Your Learning

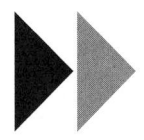

ASSIGNMENT 9

Commercial Auto Insurance

Educational Objectives

After learning the content of this assignment, you should be able to:

1. Describe the property, liability, and personal loss exposures that arise from the ownership, maintenance, and use of commercial autos.
2. Describe the symbols and the symbol system used to activate coverage under the Business Auto Coverage Form.
3. Describe what is covered and what is excluded by the liability and physical damage coverages of the Business Auto Coverage Form.
4. Describe the conditions contained in the Business Auto Coverage Form.
5. Describe the following coverages that may be added by endorsement to the Business Auto Coverage Form:
    - Medical payments
    - Personal injury protection and added personal injury protection
    - Uninsured and underinsured motorists
6. Explain how the symbols used in the Garage Coverage Form differ from the symbols used in the Business Auto Coverage Form.
7. Describe what is covered and what is excluded by each of the following coverages of the Garage Coverage Form:
    - Liability
    - Garagekeepers
    - Physical damage
8. Explain how the Motor Carrier Coverage Form differs from the Business Auto Coverage Form in each of the following ways:
    - Covered autos
    - Coverage for owner-operators
    - Trailer interchange coverage
    - Physical damage exclusion of trailer interchange
9. Explain how the following are rated for commercial auto coverage:
    - Private passenger vehicles
    - Trucks, tractors, and trailers
10. Explain whether, and for how much, the Business Auto Coverage Form and applicable endorsements would cover a described claim.
11. Define or describe each of the Key Words and Phrases for this assignment.

Study Materials

Required Reading:
- Commercial Insurance
  - Chapter 10

Study Aids:
- SMART Online Practice Exams
- SMART Study Aids
  - Review Notes and Flash Cards—Assignment 9

Outline

- **Commercial Auto Loss Exposures**
  - A. Property Exposures
  - B. Liability Exposures
    1. Owned Autos
    2. Hired and Borrowed Autos
    3. Liability Assumed Under Contract
    4. Employers Nonownership Liability
    5. Bailee Loss Exposures
  - C. Personal Loss Exposures
- **Business Auto Coverage Form**
  - A. Section I—Covered Autos
    1. Symbol 1—Any Auto
    2. Symbol 2—Owned Autos Only
    3. Symbol 3—Owned Private Passenger Autos Only
    4. Symbol 4—Owned Autos Other Than Private Passenger Autos
    5. Symbol 5—Owned Autos Subject to No-Fault
    6. Symbol 6—Owned Autos Subject to a Compulsory Uninsured Motorists Law
    7. Symbol 7—Specifically Described Autos
    8. Symbol 8—Hired Autos Only
    9. Symbol 9—Nonowned Autos Only
    10. Symbol 19—Mobile Equipment Subject to Compulsory or Financial Responsibility or Other Motor Vehicle Insurance Law Only
    11. Coverage for Newly Acquired Autos
    12. Other Covered Items
  - B. Section II—Liability Coverage
    1. Coverage Agreement
    2. Who Is an Insured
    3. Coverage Extensions
    4. Exclusions
    5. Limit of Insurance
  - C. Section III—Physical Damage Coverage
    1. Available Coverages
    2. Exclusions
    3. Limit of Insurance
    4. Deductible
  - D. Section IV—Business Auto Conditions
    1. Appraisal for Physical Damage Losses
    2. Duties in the Event of Accident, Claim, Suit, or Loss
    3. Legal Action Against the Insurer
    4. Loss Payment—Physical Damage Coverages
    5. Transfer of Rights Against Others
    6. Bankruptcy
    7. Concealment, Misrepresentation, or Fraud
    8. Liberalization
    9. No Benefit to Bailee—Physical Damage Insurance Only
    10. Other Insurance
    11. Premium Audit
    12. Policy Period, Coverage Territory
    13. Two or More Coverage Forms or Policies Issued by the Insurer
  - E. Coverages Added by Endorsement
    1. Medical Payments
    2. Personal Injury Protection and Added Personal Injury Protection
    3. Uninsured and Underinsured Motorists Insurance
- **Garage Coverage Form**
  - A. Section I—Covered Autos
  - B. Section II—Liability Coverage
  - C. Section III—Garagekeepers Coverage
  - D. Section IV—Physical Damage Coverage
    1. Dealers' Autos
    2. Exclusions
  - E. Section V—Garage Conditions
  - F. Section VI—Definitions
- **Motor Carrier Coverage Form**
  - A. Eligibility
  - B. Motor Carrier Coverage Form Compared With Business Auto Form
    1. Section I—Covered Autos
    2. Coverage for Owner-Operators
    3. Trailer Interchange Coverage
    4. Physical Damage Exclusion
- **Rating Commercial Auto Insurance**
  - A. Private Passenger Vehicles
  - B. Trucks, Tractors, and Trailers
    1. Primary Factor
    2. Premium Computation
- **Summary**

For each assignment, you should define or describe each of the Key Words and Phrases and answer each of the Review and Application Questions.

Educational Objective 1

Describe the property, liability, and personal loss exposures that arise from the ownership, maintenance, and use of commercial autos.

Key Word or Phrase

Employers nonownership liability (p. 10.5)

Review Questions

1-1. What property loss exposures are associated with commercial automobiles? (p. 10.3)

1-2. Explain how auto liability can result from each of the following:

a. Ownership of autos (p. 10.4)

b. Use of autos that are not owned (pp. 10.4–10.5)

1-3. What is a personal loss exposure? (p. 10.6)

1-4. Describe the commercial automobile coverages designed to respond to the personal loss exposures that arise from auto accidents. (p. 10.6)

Application Question

1-5. The Spring Insurance Company has 500 employees at its home office. Spring's executives, marketing representatives, and field claim representatives have company private passenger vehicles. The maintenance team has use of a pickup truck and a box truck that belongs to Spring. In addition, the mail room staff has use of a company van. Other employees who require transportation for company business rent cars or use their own vehicles and are reimbursed for their mileage. Describe Spring's commercial automobile loss exposures.

Educational Objective 2

Describe the symbols and the symbol system used to activate coverage under the Business Auto Coverage Form.

Key Words and Phrases

Business Auto Coverage Form (p. 10.6)

Coverage symbols (p. 10.7)

Review Questions

2-1. Explain how the Business Auto Coverage Form definition of "mobile equipment" compares to the definition of "mobile equipment" in the CGL. (p. 10.7)

2-2. Explain the numerical symbol system used to indicate the covered autos for the various coverages available under the Business Auto Coverage Form. (p. 10.7)

2-3. Contrast the coverage for newly acquired autos provided by symbols 1 through 6 or 19 with that provided by symbol 7 in the Business Auto Coverage Form. (pp. 10.9–10.10)

Application Question

2-4. Howard is a local beverage distributor who owns four delivery trucks. In ordinary circumstances, these four vehicles handle all of his business needs. On occasion, when one vehicle is out of service, Howard's employees will use their own cars to make small deliveries. For liability coverage in his Business Auto Coverage Form, what symbol or symbols are appropriate for Howard's business?

Educational Objective 3

Describe what is covered and what is excluded by the liability and physical damage coverages of the Business Auto Coverage Form.

Key Words and Phrases

Collision coverage (p. 10.19)

Comprehensive coverage (p. 10.19)

Specified causes of loss coverage (p. 10.20)

Towing and labor coverage (p. 10.20)

Transportation expenses (p. 10.20)

Loss of use expenses (p. 10.20)

Review Questions

3-1. What three basic duties are imposed upon the insurer in Section II of the Business Auto Coverage Form? (p. 10.12)

3-2. Other than the named insured, who is an insured under the Business Auto Coverage Form? (p. 10.14)

3-3. Describe the out-of-state extensions applicable to Section II of the Business Auto Coverage Form. (p. 10.15)

3-4. Identify the Section II exclusions of the Business Auto Coverage Form. (pp. 10.15–10.19)

3-5. Briefly describe the three principal physical damage coverages available under Section III of the Business Auto Coverage Form. (p. 10.19)

Application Question

3-6. Lois insures six trucks and vans under the Business Auto Coverage Form for her family-run business. A person files a lawsuit against Lois, alleging that he was struck as a pedestrian by one of Lois's red vans. For many years, all of Lois's vehicles have been painted in the blue and yellow colors of her company logo. After a few months, it is proved that the suit is fraudulent. Meanwhile, Lois's insurer has been defending Lois in this suit and incurring thousands of dollars in legal costs. How much of these costs will Lois ultimately bear?

Educational Objective 4

Describe the conditions contained in the Business Auto Coverage Form.

Review Questions

4-1. Describe the insured's duties after a loss. (pp. 10.22–10.23)

4-2. What are the insurer's loss payment options with regard to damaged or stolen property under the Business Auto Coverage Form? (p. 10.23)

4-3. Describe the insurer's right known as subrogation. (p. 10.23)

Application Question

4-4. Hector runs a cheese shop in a large city. One of his trucks is involved in a liability claim, and two primary Business Auto policies apply to the claim. Policy A has a $300,000 liability limit, and Policy B has a $500,000 liability limit. The covered amount of the claim is determined to be $160,000. Using the Other Insurance provision of the Business Auto conditions, how much coverage, if any, is provided to Hector by Policy A and by Policy B?

Educational Objective 5

Describe the following coverages that may be added by endorsement to the Business Auto Coverage Form:

- Medical payments
- Personal injury protection and added personal injury protection
- Uninsured and underinsured motorists

Key Words and Phrases

Auto medical payments coverage (p. 10.26)

Auto no-fault laws (p. 10.26)

Personal injury protection (PIP) coverage (p. 10.27)

Uninsured and underinsured motorists laws (p. 10.28)

Uninsured motorists coverage (p. 10.28)

Review Questions

5-1. a. Describe the coverage provided by the auto medical payments insurance available by endorsement to the Business Auto Coverage Form. (p. 10.26)

b. Identify the persons covered by auto medical payments insurance in the Business Auto Coverage Form. (p. 10.26)

5-2. Describe the benefits provided by a typical PIP endorsement to a Business Auto Coverage Form. (pp. 10.26–10.27)

5-3. Describe the coverage provided by uninsured motorists insurance in the Business Auto Coverage Form. (p. 10.28)

Application Questions

5-4. Lorena owns an electrical repair service and insures her service vehicles under the Business Auto Coverage Form. She lives and works in a state that has enacted a no-fault law. Her business auto policy includes liability, PIP, UM ($300,000 limit), and UIM ($300,000 limit) coverages. She is injured in an accident involving the service truck she was driving. In court, the other party is found to be 100 percent responsible for the accident, and Lorena is awarded $100,000 for her pain and suffering. The negligent party carried auto liability limits of $25,000. Lorena also incurs $150,000 of medical expenses. What coverage, if any, from Lorena's business auto policy will apply?

Educational Objective 6

Explain how the symbols used in the Garage Coverage Form differ from the symbols used in the Business Auto Coverage Form.

Key Word or Phrase

Garage Coverage Form (p. 10.29)

Review Questions

6-1. Compare Garage Coverage Form symbols 21 through 29 with the Business Auto Coverage Form symbols. (p. 10.30)

6-2. Describe the purpose of Garage Coverage Form symbol 30. (p. 10.30)

6-3. Describe the purpose of Garage Coverage Form symbol 31. (p. 10.30)

Educational Objective 7

Describe what is covered and what is excluded by each of the following coverages of the Garage Coverage Form:

- Liability
- Garagekeepers
- Physical damage

Key Words and Phrases

Garagekeepers insurance (p. 10.32)

Garagekeepers direct excess option (p. 10.33)

Garagekeepers direct primary option (p. 10.33)

Review Questions

7-1. Briefly describe each of the following coverages under the Garage Coverage Form:

 a. Liability coverage (pp. 10.30–10.32)

 b. Garagekeepers coverage (pp. 10.32–10.33)

 c. Physical damage coverage (pp. 10.33–10.34)

7-2. Describe the coverage eliminated under the false pretense exclusion. (p. 10.34)

7-3. Explain why insurers are reluctant to include collision coverage for any covered auto, under the Garage Coverage Form, while it is being driven or transported from the point of purchase to its destination if such points are more than fifty road miles apart. (p. 10.34)

Application Question

7-4. Auto Dealer is insured under a Garage Coverage Form. Identify the specific coverage, if any, that is available under the Garage Coverage Form for covering each of the following losses:

a. A tow truck owned by Auto Dealer was involved in a head-on collision with a car. The tow truck was damaged, and Auto Dealer was sued by the driver of the car.

b. A hailstorm damaged most of the cars being held for sale on Auto Dealer's lot.

c. An elderly customer slipped on an oil slick in Auto Dealer's parking lot. The fall resulted in a broken hip, and the customer made claim against Auto Dealer for damages.

d. A fire in Auto Dealer's service area destroyed five customers' autos that Auto Dealer was repairing.

e. One of Auto Dealer's mechanics performed a defective brake job on a customer's car. As a result of the defective work, the customer was involved in an accident. Auto Dealer was held liable for all damages resulting from its mechanic's defective work.

Educational Objective 8

Explain how the Motor Carrier Coverage Form differs from the Business Auto Coverage Form in each of the following ways:

- Covered autos
- Coverage for owner-operators
- Trailer interchange coverage
- Physical damage exclusion of trailer interchange

Key Words and Phrases

Motor Carrier Coverage Form (p. 10.35)

Owner-operators (p. 10.36)

Bobtail and deadhead coverage (p. 10.36)

Trailer interchange agreement (p. 10.36)

Trailer interchange coverage (p. 10.37)

Review Questions

8-1. Briefly describe the provisions that make coverage under the Motor Carrier Coverage Form different from coverage under the Business Auto Coverage Form. (pp. 10.35–10.37)

8-2. Describe the conditions under which a lessor is considered an insured under the Motor Carrier Coverage Form. (p. 10.36)

8-3. Explain why a motor carrier might need to purchase trailer interchange coverage. (pp. 10.36–10.37)

Application Question

8-4. Conglomerate Gravel Haulers was a small operation that owned its own gravel pit and sold sand and gravel. It used its own dump trucks to transport the sand and gravel. Conglomerate expanded its business to include hauling for other companies and added twenty more trucks and trailers. When it does not have enough trucks and trailers for a large road-construction contract, it hires owner-operators to haul construction materials, such as a reinforcement bar and culverts, to the job sites. With the expansion in its business, Conglomerate's insurance carrier is requiring Conglomerate to change from a Business Auto Coverage Form to a Motor Carrier Coverage Form.

Explain the benefits the Motor Carrier Coverage Form will provide to Conglomerate that the Business Auto Coverage Form does not.

> ## Educational Objective 9
> Explain how the following are rated for commercial auto coverage:
> - Private passenger vehicles
> - Trucks, tractors, and trailers

Key Word or Phrase

Zone rated vehicles (p. 10.39)

Review Questions

9-1. Describe the three components of the primary factor used in rating trucks, tractors, and trailers for business auto insurance. (p. 10.38)

9-2. Explain how base liability premiums and base physical damage coverage premiums are determined for non-zone rated vehicles. (p. 10.39)

9-3. Explain how base premiums and base physical damage premiums are determined for zone rated vehicles. (p. 10.39)

Application Question

9-4. Worthley Grocery has a small chain of grocery stores in five states. It maintains six trucks and trailers to purchase organic produce from wholesalers and carry the produce to its stores. Worthley entered into agreements with other organic grocers with whom it shares the produce distribution within a five-state area so that its trucks and trailers were only transporting produce in a 175-mile radius. However, due to the demand for fresh produce in the winter, Worthley is regularly sending some trucks with trailers 700 miles to warmer states for produce.

Explain how Worthley's insurer will determine the rates for the vehicles that are now traveling the longer distances.

Educational Objective 10
Explain whether, and for how much, the Business Auto Coverage Form and applicable endorsements would cover a described claim.

Application Questions

10-1. Foreway Transport Company is insured under a Business Auto Coverage Form that provides liability coverage for "any auto" with a single limit of $500,000 and comprehensive and collision coverage for "owned autos only" with a $2,500 deductible for each coverage. What dollar amount, if any, will be paid under Foreway's business auto form for each of the following losses? If a loss is not covered, or not fully covered, explain why.

   a. A truck valued at $60,000 was stolen from the parking area at Foreway's headquarters. The truck was never recovered.

b. Two of Foreway's trucks collided with each other on the highway.

   (1) Each truck suffered $7,000 in damage.

   (2) One of the drivers was injured and incurred medical expenses of $2,300.

10-2. Road Construction Company (RCC) has purchased liability coverage for "owned autos only" under a Business Auto Coverage Form with a $300,000 single limit of liability. The policy also provides comprehensive and collision coverage for "owned autos only" with a $500 deductible for each coverage. What dollar amount, if any, will be paid under RCC's policy for each of the following losses? If a loss is not covered, or not fully covered, explain why.

   a. While a supervisor was driving to a construction site in a truck owned by RCC, he caused an accident in which the driver of the other auto was injured. The injured driver sued the supervisor, and the court awarded the driver damages of $150,000.

b. An RCC employee was using her own auto to run an errand for RCC. While on this errand, the employee caused an auto accident that injured another motorist. The injured motorist made a liability claim against both the employee and RCC.

c. A truck owned by RCC was hauling lumber to a work site. While en route, the truck overturned, resulting in the destruction of both the truck and the load of lumber.

10-3. Marie owns a fleet of limousines and operates Marie's Limousine Company (MLC). MLC is insured under an unendorsed Business Auto Coverage Form that provides liability coverage for "owned autos only" with a single limit of $500,000. The policy also provides collision and comprehensive coverage for "owned autos only" with a $1,000 deductible for each coverage.

a. Marie's son, who is not an employee of MLC, borrowed one of Marie's limousines for his personal use. Marie's son caused an accident that resulted in $7,000 damage to the limousine and medical expenses of $3,750 for Marie's son. What dollar amount, if any, will be paid under this policy for each of these losses? If a loss will not be covered, explain why.

b. Because of a recently enacted state law, Marie has decided to purchase an endorsement for personal injury protection (PIP) coverage. Describe two of the benefits likely to be provided by this endorsement.

10-4. Transport Company has a Business Auto Coverage Form providing $500,000 single limit liability coverage on "any auto," $500,000 single limit uninsured motorists coverage on "owned autos only," and comprehensive and collision coverage with a $1,000 deductible on "owned autos only." Transport operates in a state that does not have a no-fault law. For each of the following losses, what dollar amount, if any, would Transport's business auto policy pay? Explain your answers. (Treat each loss separately.)

a. As the result of an accident involving a Transport Company truck and a car occupied by the Smith family, a court ordered Transport to pay damages of $150,000 to Mr. Smith, $200,000 to Mrs. Smith, and $250,000 to the Smiths' daughter.

b. A cargo ship sank while transporting a truck owned by Transport Company from Alaska to San Francisco. The truck had an actual cash value of $28,000.

c. A brick thrown by a person on an overpass went through the windshield of a Transport Company truck passing underneath. As a result of this incident, the Transport employee driving the truck incurred medical expenses of $3,000 and lost wages of $1,500. The cost to replace the broken windshield and replace damaged components inside the truck's cab was $2,500.

Answers to Assignment 9 Questions

NOTE: These answers are provided to give students a basic understanding of acceptable types of responses. They often are not the only valid answers and are not intended to provide an exhaustive response to the questions.

Educational Objective 1

1-1. The following property loss exposures are associated with commercial autos:
- Decrease in or loss of the auto's value
- Loss of use of the auto until it can be repaired or replaced

1-2. Auto liability can result from the following occurrences:
  a. Ownership of autos—Liability is placed on the employer when, within the scope of employment, an employee of the business operates an auto owned by the business and negligently injures other persons or damages their property.
  b. Use of autos that are not owned—A business can become liable for injury or damage to others resulting from the use of autos it does not own. A business could rent or borrow an auto, or employees could use their own autos for business purposes. The business could be held legally responsible for an accident in any of these circumstances.

1-3. Personal loss exposure describes the possibility of financial loss that results from injury, sickness, or death. Anyone who could suffer injury in an auto accident—either while occupying an auto or as a pedestrian—has a personal loss exposure.

1-4. Commercial auto coverages that respond to the personal loss exposures that arise from auto accidents include the following:
- Auto medical payments coverage
- Personal injury protection (PIP) coverage
- Uninsured motorists (UIM) coverage

1-5. Spring's commercial automobile loss exposures are as follows:
- Property exposures to the owned vehicles
- Loss of use of the owned vehicles
- Liability exposures from the owned vehicles
- Liability exposures from employee's vehicles used for company business (employers non-ownership liability)
- Liability exposures assumed under contract when vehicles are rented by employees for company business
- Personal loss exposures to the employees using the vehicles

Educational Objective 2

2-1. The Business Auto Coverage Form definition of "mobile equipment" is the same as the CGL coverage form's. Consequently, mobile equipment (generally covered under the CGL coverage form) is excluded under the business auto form unless it is subject to motor vehicle or financial responsibility laws.

2-2. The Business Auto Coverage Form uses the following numerical symbols to indicate covered autos:
- Symbol 1—Any Auto
- Symbol 2—Owned Autos Only
- Symbol 3—Owned Private Passenger Autos Only
- Symbol 4—Owned Autos Other Than Private Passenger Autos
- Symbol 5—Owned Autos Subject To No-Fault
- Symbol 6—Owned Autos Subject To A Compulsory Uninsured Motorists Law
- Symbol 7—Specifically Described Autos
- Symbol 8—Hired Autos Only
- Symbol 9—Nonowned Autos Only
- Symbol 19—Mobile Equipment Subject to Compulsory or Financial Responsibility or Other Motor Vehicle Insurance Law Only

One or more of these numerical symbols is entered beside each coverage listed in the policy schedule to indicate which types of autos are covered.

2-3. If symbols 1 through 6 or 19 are used, newly acquired autos are automatically covered. The insurer will learn of newly acquired autos at the end of the policy period (during the audit), and the insured will pay the additional premium.

If symbol 7 is used, newly acquired autos are covered from the time of acquisition only if both of the following conditions are met:
- The insurer insures all autos owned by the named insured, or the newly acquired auto replaces a covered auto.
- The named insured asks the insurer to cover the newly acquired auto within thirty days after the acquisition.

2-4. Howard will have coverage for any auto, owned or nonowned, if symbol 1 is entered for liability coverage. Because vehicles used in the business are limited to owned vehicles and those of his employees, he can alternatively use symbols 2 and 9.

Educational Objective 3

3-1. Section II of the Business Auto Coverage Form imposes the following three basic duties on the insurer:
(1) A duty to pay damages
(2) A duty to pay "covered pollution cost or expense"
(3) A duty to defend the insured

3-2. An insured under the Business Auto Coverage Form includes anyone having the named insured's permission to use a covered auto owned, hired, or borrowed by the named insured, except for the following:
- The owner or someone from whom the named insured hires or borrows a vehicle
- An employee of the named insured who is operating his or her own vehicle
- A person while working in an auto business (example: a mechanic test-driving the car) unless it is the named insured's business

- Anyone who is not an employee, a partner, or a lessee or borrower of a covered auto or their employees, while moving property to or from a covered auto
- A partner, with respect to the partner's own car or one from the partner's household

Any person or organization liable for the conduct of an "insured" is also insured.

3-3. Section II of the Business Auto Coverage Form provides the following out-of-state extensions: If a covered auto is outside the state in which it is licensed, the limit of insurance is, if necessary, increased on that auto to the minimum required by the outside jurisdiction in which the auto is being operated. Also, if the outside jurisdiction requires a different type of coverage, the policy provides such coverage automatically.

3-4. Section II of the Business Auto Coverage Form excludes loss resulting from the following:
- Expected or intended injury
- Contractual liability
- Workers compensation
- Employee indemnification and employers liability
- Fellow employee
- Care, custody, or control
- Handling of property
- Movement of property by mechanical device
- Operations
- Completed operations
- Pollution
- War
- Racing

3-5. Section III of the Business Auto Coverage Form can include the following three physical damage coverages:
(1) Collision coverage—loss to a covered auto caused by collision with another object or by overturn
(2) Comprehensive coverage—loss to a covered auto by any peril except collision or overturn or a specifically excluded peril
(3) Specified causes of loss coverage (an alternative to comprehensive)—loss to a covered auto caused by fire, lightning, explosion, theft, windstorm, hail, earthquake, flood, mischief, vandalism, or the sinking, burning, collision, or derailment of a conveyance transporting the covered auto

3-6. Even though it is discovered that there are no covered damages, the insurer has the right and the duty to defend any insured against any claim or suit alleging damages that would be covered under the policy. The claim or suit only needs to *allege* damages that would be covered. Hence, the insurer must defend against even false or fraudulent claims or suits as long as they allege covered damages. Lois is not responsible for any of the defense costs.

Educational Objective 4

4-1. The insured's duties after a loss are essentially the same as those imposed by the CGL policy. The named insured must give prompt notice of accident or loss to the insurer or its agent and assist the insurer in obtaining the names of injured persons or witnesses. Also, both the named insured and any other person who seeks liability coverage under the policy (for example, the driver of an insured vehicle) must do the following:

- Cooperate with the insurer in its investigation and defense of the accident or loss
- Immediately send to the insurer copies of any notices or legal papers received in connection with the accident or loss
- Submit to physical examinations by physicians selected and paid by the insurer as often as the insurer may reasonably request
- Authorize the insurer to obtain medical reports and other medical information

4-2. The insurer has the following loss payment options for damaged or stolen property under the Business Auto Coverage Form:

- Pay to repair or replace the property
- Return the property at the expense of the insurer and repair any damage caused by theft
- Keep all of the property and pay an agreed or appraised value

4-3. Subrogation entails the insured's right to recover a loss from some other party, usually because the other party caused the loss. If the insurer pays the loss, it is entitled, under this condition, to take over the insured's right of recovery from the other party.

4-4. Policy A, which has three-eighths of the total limits ($300,000/$800,000), would pay $60,000 ($160,000 × 3/8), and Policy B, which has five-eighths of the total limits ($500,000/$800,000), would pay $100,000 ($160,000 × 5/8).

Educational Objective 5

5-1. Medical payments coverage applies regardless of fault or liability to the following parties:

　a. Reasonable and necessary medical and funeral expenses incurred by a person injured by an auto accident

　b. Persons injured by an accident while "occupying" (entering into, riding in, or alighting from) a covered auto and, if the named insured is an individual proprietorship, the named insured and members of his or her family while occupying any auto or if struck by an auto while a pedestrian

5-2. The benefits provided by a typical PIP endorsement are payable for expenses resulting from bodily injury to occupants of a covered auto because of an auto accident, and consist of the following:

- Medical and rehabilitation expenses
- Income loss benefit
- Substitute services benefit
- Death benefits to survivors

5-3. Uninsured motorists insurance covers any person injured by a legally liable uninsured motorist while riding in an auto insured under the policy for uninsured motorists coverage. Benefits are paid to the injured person by his or her own insurer.

5-4. Lorena's PIP coverage pays medical benefits regardless of fault. Hence, Lorena's business auto policy will pay her medical expenses (subject to her PIP limit). Lorena's UIM coverage can be applied to all damages resulting from bodily injury in an auto accident (including medical expenses that may exceed her PIP limit). Unlike PIP coverage, Lorena may find compensation under UIM for her noneconomic losses (pain and suffering) related to injuries sustained in the auto accident. The UIM coverage will pay the $75,000 portion of her pain and suffering award (the amount that exceeds the $25,000 provided by the negligent party's insurer).

Educational Objective 6

6-1. Symbols 21 through 29 correspond in most respects to business auto symbols 1 through 9.

6-2. Symbol 30 indicates garagekeepers coverage on customers' autos left with the named insured for service, repair, storage, or safekeeping.

6-3. Symbol 31 indicates dealers' autos and autos held for sale by nondealers or trailer dealers.

Educational Objective 7

7-1. Coverage provided under the Garage Coverage Form includes the following:
   a. Liability coverage—This broad insuring agreement provides bodily injury and property damage liability coverage comparable to that provided by the CGL form (occurrence version) and the business auto form. The insurer agrees to pay "all sums the insured legally must pay as damages because of bodily injury or property damage…caused by an accident and resulting from *garage operations*."
   b. Garagekeepers coverage—Garagekeepers insurance covers the insured's liability for damage by a covered cause of loss to autos left in the insured's care while the insured is attending, servicing, repairing, parking, or storing the autos in the garage operation.
   c. Physical damage coverage—Garage physical damage insurance provides the collision and comprehensive or specified causes of loss coverages available under the business auto form. In most ways, garage physical damage insurance is subject to the same provisions as business auto physical damage insurance.

7-2. The false pretense exclusion eliminates coverage for loss to a covered auto resulting from someone causing the named insured to *voluntarily* part with the auto by trick, scheme, or other false pretense. The exclusion also eliminates coverage for an auto the insured has acquired from a seller who did not have legal title.

7-3. Insurers are reluctant to provide collision coverage for any covered auto under the Garage Coverage Form while being driven or transported from the point of purchase or distribution to its destination if such points are more than fifty road miles apart. Because the "driveaway" exposure can be significant, insurers do not want to cover it without being able to assess the risk and charge an appropriate additional premium.

7-4. The following coverages of the Garage Coverage Form are available to cover the losses experienced by Auto Dealer:
   a. Collision coverage is available under the physical damage section of the garage form to cover damage to Auto Dealer's tow truck. Auto liability coverage is available under the liability section of the garage form to cover Auto Dealer's liability for the auto accident.

b. Damage to autos being held for sale by Auto Dealer can be covered (on an aggregate basis, subject to a single overall limit) under the physical damage section of the garage form.
c. The liability section of the garage form covers liability arising out of "garage operations," including the slip-and-fall type of claim described. (The liability coverage of the garage form is comparable to that provided by the CGL form.)
d. Damage to customers' autos being worked on by the insured can be covered under the garagekeepers coverage section of the garage form. (There is no coverage under the garage form for fire damage to any of the insured's own property other than physical damage coverage on owned autos.)
e. All of the damages (other than the work actually performed by the insured) resulting from the defective work (which qualifies as "garage operations") are covered under the liability coverage section of the garage form. (The coverage provided for this claim is comparable to the completed operations coverage of a CGL policy.)

Educational Objective 8

8-1. The Motor Carrier Form contains some provisions that address specific characteristics of the trucking business, including the following:
- Section I – Covered Autos—This section parallels Section I of the business auto form. The symbols used with the Motor Carrier Coverage Form are 61 through 71 and 79.
- Coverage for owner-operator—Coverage for owner-operators while using their own trucks to haul property for the insured motor carrier.
- Trailer interchange coverage—Coverage for damage to trailers in a motor carrier's possession under written trailer interchange agreements.
- Physical damage exclusion—Eliminates loss to a covered auto while in someone else's possession under a trailer interchange agreement. This exclusion can be eliminated by showing the appropriate coverage symbol.

8-2. A lessor is considered an insured under the Motor Carrier Coverage Form only while the auto is being used in the named insured's business as a motor carrier.

8-3. A motor carrier might need to purchase trailer interchange coverage because trucking carriers commonly swap trailers and agree to indemnify each other for any damage to the trailer in the borrower's possession. Trailer interchange coverage can cover this liability.

8-4. The benefits the Motor Carrier Coverage Form will provide are as follows:
- If Conglomerate enters into trailer interchange agreements, coverage for damage to trailers in Conglomerate's possession will be covered under trailer interchange coverage.
- If Conglomerate's own trailers are being used by another carrier that is providing coverage for damage to those trailers, Conglomerate can exclude physical damage coverage for those trailers.

Educational Objective 9

9-1. The three components of the primary factor for rating business auto insurance are as follows:
(1) Size class determined by the vehicle's gross vehicle weight (GVW) or gross combination weight (GCW) and two size classes for truck-tractors
- Trucks (GVW)—light, medium, heavy, or extra-heavy
- Truck-tractors (GCW)—heavy or extra-heavy

(2) Business use
- Service—carrying workers, equipment, and supplies to or from job sites
- Retail—pickup and delivery of property to or from individual households
- Commercial—neither service nor retail use

(3) Radius class for the area within which the vehicle is operated
- Local—within 50 miles
- Intermediate—between 51 and 200 miles
- Long distance—beyond 200 miles

9-2. The base premiums for liability and physical damage coverage for non-zone rated vehicles are multiplied by the combined factors (sum of primary and secondary factors). Base liability premiums are determined on the basis of the policy limit and the territory in which the auto is principally garaged. Base physical damage premiums are determined on the basis of the vehicle's age and its cost new.

9-3. After the primary factor has been determined for the zone rated vehicle, its physical damage and liability premiums are calculated by applying the primary factor to base premiums. Secondary factors are not used for zone rated autos.

Base premiums for zone rated vehicles are affected by the various geographical zones in which the vehicles are operated because liability and collision losses are more likely in metropolitan areas than on the open road. Base physical damage premiums depend on the vehicle's cost new, the current age of the vehicle, the type of vehicle (with respect to collision coverage), and the chosen deductible.

9-4. The trucks and trailers that are now traveling a 700-mile radius will be zone rated. The primary rating factors will not change. However, the zone rating for these vehicles, which will apply to the collision and liability premiums, will be based on the geographical zones in which the vehicles are operated.

Educational Objective 10

10-1. The following amounts will be paid under Foreway's Business Auto Coverage Form:
   a. Stolen truck—$57,500 ($60,000 loss minus $2,500 deductible)
   b. Foreway-owned truck collision on the highway—
      (1) $9,000 total—$2,500 deductible applies to each truck ($14,000 total loss minus $5,000 in deductibles)
      (2) $0—employers liability/workers compensation exclusions

10-2. The following amounts will be paid by RCC's business auto coverage:
   a. $150,000 (plus defense costs) would be paid by RCC's business auto insurer.
   b. RCC's policy will not cover RCC for this loss because the policy covers owned autos only (for liability coverage). RCC needed either symbol 1 (any auto) or symbol 9 (nonowned autos) to cover the employee's auto. Even if RCC had had symbol 1 or 9 for liability coverage, only RCC would have been covered because the business auto form does not include employees as insureds while operating their own autos.

c. RCC's collision coverage would cover the damage to RCC's truck because the policy defines "collision" to include overturn. RCC's policy would not cover the loss of the lumber, because auto physical damage coverage insures only the covered auto and its equipment. RCC needed cargo insurance to cover the lumber.

10-3. a. The following amounts will be paid by MLC's unendorsed Business Auto Coverage Form:
(1) The policy will pay $6,000 for damage to the limousine—$7,000 loss minus $1,000 deductible.
(2) The policy will pay $0 for Marie's son's medical expenses because the policy does not have a medical payments coverage endorsement.

b. Two of the benefits likely to be provided by the PIP endorsement are first-party medical and rehabilitation expenses and an income loss benefit to an injured insured. These expenses would be paid without regard to fault or negligence.

10-4. The following amounts would be paid by Transport's business auto policy:
a. The most that Transport Company's policy will pay in total for all three of the injured Smith family members (whose combined damages equal $600,000) is the policy limit of $500,000. (The court would direct how the insurance recovery is to be distributed among the three claimants.)
b. The policy will pay $27,000 ($28,000 – $1,000) under the comprehensive coverage because the truck was between two United States ports, which is in the policy territory.
c. The business auto policy will not cover the driver due to the employers liability and workers compensation exclusions.

The policy will pay $1,500 for damage to the truck ($2,500–$1,000 deductible = $1,500) under comprehensive coverage.

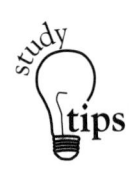

study tips Try to establish a study area away from any distractions, to be used only for studying.

Direct Your Learning

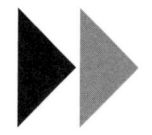

ASSIGNMENT 10

Businessowners Policies and Farm Insurance

Educational Objectives

After learning the content of this assignment, you should be able to:

1. Identify the kinds of businesses that are generally eligible for coverage under a businessowners policy (BOP).

2. Compare the property coverages typically contained in a BOP with the direct damage and business income/extra expense coverages available under an Insurance Services Office (ISO) commercial property coverage part.

3. Describe the property coverages, in addition to those of the ISO commercial property coverage part, that are commonly included in BOPs.

4. Compare the liability coverage typically provided by a BOP with the Commercial General Liability (CGL) Coverage Form.

5. Explain how BOPs are rated and why that approach to rating is less complicated than rating comparable coverages in a commercial package policy.

6. Describe the purpose of each of the insuring agreements of the ISO farm program.

7. Compare the causes of loss that can be insured under the ISO farm program with those that can be insured under the ISO causes of loss forms for commercial property.

8. Describe the agricultural coverages that farmers may need in addition to those provided by farmowners policies.

9. Define or describe each of the Key Words and Phrases for this assignment.

Study Materials

Required Reading:
- Commercial Insurance
  - Chapter 11

Study Aids:
- SMART Online Practice Exams
- SMART Study Aids
  - Review Notes and Flash Cards—Assignment 10

Outline

- **Businessowners Policies**
  - A. Eligibility for BOPs
    1. Retail, Wholesale, Service, or Processing Risks
    2. Apartment Buildings
    3. Office Buildings
    4. Contractors
    5. Restaurants
    6. Other Eligible Occupancies
    7. Ineligible Operations
  - B. BOP Forms
    1. Property Coverage Differences
    2. Businessowners Property Loss Example
    3. Liability Coverage Differences
    4. Industry-Specific Endorsements
  - C. Rating BOP Coverage
- **Farm Insurance**
  - A. ISO Farm Forms
    1. Farm Property—Farm Dwellings, Appurtenant Structures and Household Personal Property Coverage Form
    2. Farm Property—Farm Personal Property Coverage Form
    3. Farm Property—Barns, Outbuildings and Other Farm Structures Coverage Form
    4. Extra Expense and Business Income Coverage
    5. Causes of Loss Form
    6. Farm Inland Marine Coverage Forms
    7. Farm Liability Coverage Form
    8. Endorsements
  - B. Specialty Farm Coverages
    1. Crop-Hail Insurance
    2. Federal Crop Insurance
    3. Animal Mortality Insurance
- **Summary**

study tips: Writing notes as you read your materials will help you remember key pieces of information.

For each assignment, you should define or describe each of the Key Words and Phrases and answer each of the Review and Application Questions.

Educational Objective 1

Identify the kinds of businesses that are generally eligible for coverage under a businessowners policy (BOP).

Key Word or Phrase

Businessowners policy (BOP) (p. 11.3)

Review Questions

1-1. Why do businessowners policies (BOPs) reduce handling costs for insurers? (p. 11.3)

1-2. What advantage(s) do BOPs bring for policyholders? (pp. 11.3–11.4)

1-3. How do insurers typically define the size limit for eligible risks in the following categories?

   a. Retail, wholesale, service, or processing (p. 11.5)

b. Apartment buildings (p. 11.5)

c. Office buildings (p. 11.5)

1-4. What limitations are often placed on BOP eligibility of the following?

a. Contractors (pp. 11.5–11.6)

b. Restaurants (p. 11.6)

1-5. Identify six categories of operations that are generally not eligible for BOPs. (p. 11.6)

Application Question

1-6. Which of the following businesses would probably be eligible for a typical businessowners policy program?

   a. A steel mill

   b. A carpenter with gross receipts of $150,000 per year

   c. A single-location book store

   d. A fifty-story office tower

   e. The office contents of a tenant occupying part of one floor in the fifty-story office tower

f. A sandwich shop

g. A computer factory

h. A nightclub whose main business is serving alcohol

i. A two-story apartment building

Businessowners Policies and Farm Insurance 10.7

Educational Objective 2

Compare the property coverages typically contained in a BOP with the direct damage and business income/extra expense coverages available under an ISO commercial property coverage part.

Key Word or Phrase

Seasonal increase provision (pp. 11.8–11.9)

Review Questions

2-1. How are business income coverage, employee dishonesty coverages, and equipment breakdown coverage typically incorporated in a BOP? (p. 11.10)

2-2. How does a typical BOP differ from the basic Building and Personal Property Coverage Form (BPP) with regard to each of the following?

   a. Valuation of covered property (p. 11.7)

   b. Insurance-to-value requirements (p. 11.7)

c. Property not covered (p. 11.7)

2-3. Explain why each of the following coverage options is generally not available under BOPs:

a. Manufacturer's selling price clause (p. 11.8)

b. Blanket insurance for separate locations (p. 11.8)

Application Question

2-4. A clothing shop is insured under a BOP that includes a personal property limit of $400,000 and a seasonal increase provision. The policy does not have a coinsurance clause or any other insurance-to-value requirement. When the shop suffered a total loss by fire during a peak season, the amount of the personal property loss was $550,000. Disregarding deductibles, how much would the shop be able to recover for its personal property loss if each of the following were true?

a. For the twelve months preceding the loss, the shop's average monthly personal property value was $425,000.

b. For the twelve months preceding the loss, the shop's average monthly personal property value was $390,000.

Educational Objective 3

Describe the property coverages, in addition to those of the ISO commercial property coverage part, that are commonly included in BOPs.

Review Questions

3-1. Explain how insureds collect full replacement cost on their BOP forms under ISO's insurance-to-value provision. (p. 11.8)

3-2. How does the business income and extra expense coverage that is included in a BOP typically differ from the coverage provided by the Business Income (and Extra Expense) Coverage Form with regard to each of the following?

   a. Coinsurance requirements (p. 11.8)

   b. Limits of insurance (p. 11.10)

3-3. Identify the coverages that would require separate policies or separate coverage parts in the commercial package program, but which are frequently either included as part of the BOP or available as options. (p. 11.10)

Application Question

3-4. Jeff and Chris started their own small business on the Florida waterways—J&C's Tours. Jeff and Chris offer wildlife tours via four-passenger jet boats, which they operate. J&C's Tours is operated from a 500-square-foot office adjacent to a floating dock. J&C owns both the building and the dock. Assuming that J&C Tours is eligible for a BOP policy, what advantages would the BOP offer in providing property coverage that the ISO commercial property coverage part would not?

Educational Objective 4
Compare the liability coverage typically provided by a BOP with the Commercial General Liability (CGL) coverage form.

Review Questions

4-1. In what ways does businessowners liability coverage typically differ from the standard, occurrence-basis CGL coverage form? (p. 11.13)

4-2. Explain why the availability of hired and nonowned auto coverage under the BOP offers an advantage to small insureds who own no automobiles. (p. 11.14)

4-3. What is the value to the insured of the ISO or AAIS BOP endorsement adding employee benefit liability coverage and employment practice liability? (p. 11.14)

Application Question

4-4. A law firm is shopping for a new insurance program. The firm owns a 10,000-square-foot building, its office contents, five cars driven by the firm's partners, and an aircraft used for business transportation. Attorneys professional liability insurance is one of the firm's biggest insurance concerns. Employee dishonesty is another concern because the firm recently lost over $100,000 to a dishonest employee, and its policy had only a $10,000 limit for employee dishonesty. The firm is also interested in having business income and extra expense insurance plus coverage against robbery and burglary.

If this law firm were insured under a typical businessowners policy, what additional policies, if any, would the firm probably need to obtain to cover all of the exposures noted above?

Educational Objective 5
Explain how BOPs are rated and why that approach to rating is less complicated than rating comparable coverages in a commercial package policy.

Review Questions

5-1. How is the ISO BOP rated? (p. 11.15)

5-2. Explain how insurers who offer BOP-type policies for contractors rate liability coverage. (p. 11.16)

5-3. Identify the variables insurers consider in BOP rating. (p. 11.16)

Application Question

5-4. Atley Insurance has designed a BOP specifically for computer sales and repair shops. Atley has established a Web site that allows prospective applicants to enter data about businesses to obtain a quotation for the BOP. Explain why this type of quotation would be possible for a BOP but not for a commercial package policy.

Educational Objective 6
Describe the purpose of each of the insuring agreements of the ISO farm program.

Key Word or Phrase
Farmowners policy (p. 11.16)

Review Questions

6-1. What property and liability coverages are available in a farm policy to parallel the coverages of a homeowners policy? (p. 11.17)

6-2. Identify the difference in coinsurance between scheduled (Coverage E) and unscheduled (Coverage F) farm personal property. (pp. 11.18–11.19)

6-3. What property and liability coverages are available in a farm policy to cover farming, other-than-residential exposures? (p. 11.19)

Application Question

6-4. A 1,000-acre sod farm has twenty deep wells to supply water to the irrigation systems that service the farm. The pump for each well is housed in a concrete-block building. Ten tractors with mowing decks are housed in a long shed connected to the office building. Also stored in the shed are five flat-bed trucks used to haul the sod to customers and three fork lifts used to load the trucks. The office building includes a showroom, offices for sales staff, and a lounge and facilities for the field workers. Under which insuring agreements (A through G) of the ISO farm policy will the sod farm's property be covered?

Educational Objective 7

Compare the causes of loss that can be insured under the ISO farm program with those that can be insured under the ISO causes of loss forms for commercial property.

Review Questions

7-1. Identify the three aspects of the collision peril found on a farm policy's basic causes-of-loss form. (p. 11.20)

7-2. In addition to the usual broad-form perils, what causes of loss to livestock can be insured under the ISO farm program? (p. 11.20)

7-3. Explain how the exclusions in the Special Causes of Loss Form for the ISO farm program differ from those found in the commercial property special form. (p. 11.20)

Application Question

7-4. The 1,000-acre sod farm has changed coverages from a basic causes of loss ISO commercial property form to a basic causes of loss ISO farm policy. Considering the following property owned by the farm, what advantages are provided by the farm policy that are not provided by the commercial property form?

- Twenty deep wells with pumps and pump houses
- A shed covering ten tractors with mowing decks, five flatbed trucks, and three forklifts
- An office building

Educational Objective 8
Describe the agricultural coverages that farmers may need in addition to those provided by farmowners policies.

Key Words and Phrases

Crop-hail insurance (p. 11.22)

Multiple Peril Crop Insurance (MPCI) (p. 11.22)

Animal mortality insurance (p. 11.22)

Review Questions

8-1. Identify the perils, other than crop loss resulting from hail, frequently covered by crop-hail insurance. (p. 11.22)

8-2. Identify the exclusions to the Multiple Peril Crop Insurance (MPCI) plan. (p. 11.22)

8-3. Why might a farm family want to buy animal mortality insurance instead of simply using the livestock coverage under its farm policy? (p. 11.22)

Application Question

8-4. On a fifty-acre farm dedicated to producing organic goat milk for infants with milk allergies, the goats are housed in concrete block sheds on the property and brought into a sanitary milking facility on the farm twice daily. The farm keeps prize-winning border collies that protect and herd the goats from the fields of Ramon foliage that is specially grown for the goats to graze on. Describe the agricultural coverages that this farm might need in addition to a farmowners policy.

Answers to Assignment 10 Questions

NOTE: These answers are provided to give students a basic understanding of acceptable types of responses. They often are not the only valid answers and are not intended to provide an exhaustive response to the questions.

Educational Objective 1

1-1. BOPs reduce insurers' handling costs because they entail a reduced number of coverage options and simplified rating procedures, and they are underwritten using automated systems instead of individually.

1-2. To the advantage of policyholders, a BOP provides the convenience of one policy that meets most of their needs (and may even include coverages they would otherwise overlook) at a reduced cost.

1-3 Insurers typically define the size limit for eligible risks in the following categories:
   a. Retail, wholesale, service, or processing—By maximum floor area, such as 25,000 square feet.
   b. Apartment buildings—Some insurers restrict eligibility to apartment buildings of not more than a certain number of stories or apartments (such as six stories or sixty apartments).
   c. Office buildings—By maximum floor area or by height of the building (such as six stories).

1-4 The following limitations are often placed on BOP eligibility:
   a. Eligibility of contractors for BOPs is usually limited to those having less than a stated amount of annual receipts and payroll (such as not more than $3 million in annual receipts and annual payroll not exceeding $500,000).
   b. Eligibility of restaurants for BOPs may be limited to fast-food restaurants and restaurants with limited cooking facilities (such as a sandwich shop). Some insurers offer broader eligibility for restaurants. The AAIS BOP program, for example, can include full service (not just fast food) restaurants.

1-5. Six categories of operations that are generally not eligible for BOPs include the following:
   (1) Automobile businesses
   (2) Bars and, in most cases, full-service restaurants
   (3) Most manufacturing firms
   (4) One- or two-family dwellings other than multiple-unit garden apartment complexes
   (5) Amusement parks and similar risks
   (6) Financial institutions

1-6. The eligibility for the businesses listed would be as follows:
   a. A steel mill would not be eligible for a typical businessowners policy program.
   b. A carpenter with gross receipts of $150,000 per year would be eligible for a typical businessowners policy program.
   c. A single-location bookstore would be eligible for a typical businessowners policy program.
   d. A fifty-story office tower would not be eligible for a typical businessowners policy.
   e. The office contents of a tenant occupying part of one floor in the fifty-story office tower would be eligible for a typical businessowners policy.

f. A sandwich shop would be eligible for a typical businessowners policy.
g. A computer factory would not be eligible for a typical businessowners policy.
h. A nightclub whose main business is serving alcohol would not be eligible for a typical businessowners policy.
i. A two-story apartment building would be eligible for a typical businessowners policy.

Educational Objective 2

2-1. Business income coverage, employee dishonesty coverages, and equipment breakdown coverage are typically provided as part of the BOP coverage form or available as preprinted options in the coverage form; they are not usually added by separate coverage forms as in a commercial package policy.

2-2. A typical BOP differs from the basic Building and Personal Property Coverage Form (BPP) regarding the following:
   a. Valuation of covered property—Most BOPs provide replacement cost coverage, whereas the BPP uses actual cash value (ACV) valuation unless the insured selects the replacement cost option.
   b. Insurance-to-value requirements—Most BOPs have no coinsurance requirement, whereas the BPP contains a coinsurance clause. Some BOPs, following the ISO model, have a clause that requires the insured to insure to at least 80 percent of the insurable value of covered property in order to collect full replacement cost.
   c. Property not covered—The list of property not covered in most BOPs is much shorter than the list of property not covered in the BPP.

2-3. The following coverage options are generally not available under BOPs:
   a. The manufacturer's selling price clause is not included because manufacturers generally are not eligible for a BOP.
   b. Blanket coverage for multiple locations is not permitted under most BOP programs because insureds that need such coverage do not fit well into the class-rated, simplified-underwriting structure of the BOP.

2-4. The clothing shop would be able to recover the following amounts:
   a. $400,000—The clothing shop would not be eligible for the additional 25 percent of the personal property limit under the seasonal increase provision, because the average monthly value ($425,000) over the 12 months exceeded the property limit ($400,000).
   b. $500,000—In this case, the clothing shop qualifies for the additional 25 percent of the personal property limit under the seasonal increase provision, because the average monthly value ($390,000) over the 12 months did not exceed the property limit ($400,000). Thus, the clothing shop can collect the $400,000 limit plus an additional $100,000.

Educational Objective 3

3-1. Insureds collect full replacement cost on their BOP forms under ISO's insurance-to-value provision by carrying insurance equal to at least 80 percent of the insurable value of the covered property. Otherwise, recovery is limited to (1) actual cash value or (2) a proportion of the loss equal to the amount of insurance carried divided by 80 percent of the insurable value, whichever is greater.

3-2. The business income and extra expense coverage that is included in a BOP typically differs from the coverage provided by the Business Income (and Extra Expense) Coverage Form regarding the following:
   a. Coinsurance requirement—The business income and extra expense coverage under the BOP is usually not subject to coinsurance, monthly limitation, or even a total dollar limit. In contrast, the business income forms used in CPPs are usually subject to coinsurance or (if no coinsurance applies) the maximum period of indemnity option, the monthly limit of indemnity option, or the agreed amount option.
   b. Limits of insurance—The business income and extra expense coverage in BOPs is normally subject to a one-year limit, which is not found in the business income forms used with the CPP. Under a typical BOP, business income loss and extra expenses are payable for up to twelve consecutive months following the occurrence of the direct physical damage. Some BOPs limit ordinary payroll coverage to ninety days. Many BOPs impose no monetary limit on the amount that the insured can collect during the one-year coverage period. However, some BOPs have added a monetary limit to the one-year limitation.

3-3. Coverages that would require separate policies or separate coverage parts in the commercial package program, but which are frequently either included as part of the BOP or available as options include the following:
   - Employee dishonesty
   - Money and securities, when special-form property coverage applies; or burglary and robbery, when named-perils property coverage applies
   - Forgery
   - Interior and exterior glass (if not included as part of the building and personal property coverage)
   - Outdoor signs
   - Mechanical breakdown
   - Money orders and counterfeit paper currency
   - Computer coverage
   - Accounts receivable
   - Valuable papers and records

3-4.
   - Wharves and docks are not excluded by the BOP. Therefore, J&C's dock would be covered.
   - Business income and extra expense coverage is automatically included. If the office or the dock is damaged by a covered peril, J&C would have extra expense to lease other office and dock space. This could be especially important during a busy tourist season.

Educational Objective 4

4-1. The following differences may exist between businessowners liability insurance and regular CGL coverage:
   - The BOP generally allows fewer options regarding the amount of limits.
   - The BOP often may be endorsed to provide professional liability coverage for various occupations such as barbers, beauticians, funeral directors, veterinarians, optical and hearing aid stores, pharmacies, and printers.

- The BOP often may include, or be endorsed, to provide hired and nonowned autos liability coverage.

4-2. The availability of hired and nonowned auto coverage under the BOP offers an advantage to small insureds who own no automobiles because the BOP eliminates the need to obtain a separate business auto policy. If small insureds do not own any autos, they often overlook the need for, or cannot obtain, a separate policy covering hired and nonowned autos liability. Yet, almost every business at some time or another uses rented, leased, borrowed, or employee-owned autos.

4-3. The value to the insured of the ISO or AAIS BOP endorsement adding employee benefit liability coverage and employment practice liability is that it is a cost-effective option that enables smaller insureds to avoid the higher minimum premiums that usually apply to stand-alone policies.

4-4. The firm would need to obtain, in addition to a businessowners policy, an automobile policy, an aircraft policy, and an attorneys professional liability policy. (Although some insurers provide professional liability endorsements to the businessowners policies, these endorsements usually do not include attorneys professional liability insurance.) Moreover, the firm might want a higher limit for employee dishonesty insurance than the businessowner's insurer is willing to provide. In that case, the firm could purchase a separate employee dishonesty (or theft) policy. Most BOPs provide business income and extra expense coverage and various crime coverage options that meet the needs of most eligible insureds, so the firm probably would not need additional policies to cover those loss exposures.

Educational Objective 5

5-1. BOP rating resembles homeowners insurance rating. BOPs are class rated; specific rates are not used. When originally developed, rating procedures for a BOP were based on the amounts of coverage provided for building and personal property. Rates included both the property and liability coverage. No separate rating calculations were needed for liability coverage. The ISO BOP now requires separate liability rating for all classes of business. In calculating the BOP liability premium for most classifications, the liability rate is applied to the property insurance amount rather than to the rating basis that would be used to rate CGL coverage. For example, under the ISO BOP, the liability premium for an apartment house is based on the amount of building insurance; under the CGL, the number of apartment units is used to determine the rate. AAIS and most independent insurers use separate rating for only certain classes of business.

5-2. Most insurers who offer BOP-type policies for contractors rate the liability coverage for eligible contracts separately from the property coverages by applying a separate liability rate to the insured's payroll, receipts, or number of full- and part-time employees.

5-3. Insurers' BOP rating considers the following variables:
- Territory (theft losses are higher in metropolitan areas, etc.)
- Type of construction (such as frame, joisted masonry, and so forth)
- Public fire protection
- Building occupancy
- Presence of sprinklers
- Deductible applicable (standard deductible for most insurers is $250 or $500 per loss)

5-4. Rating a BOP is much less complicated than rating comparable coverages provided by a commercial package policy. Loadings for business income, liability coverage, and additional coverages are automatically included in the BOP rates. It would be feasible to build a simple Web site to provide a quotation for a BOP. It would be difficult (if not impossible) to build a Web site to provide a quotation on a commercial package policy due to the many possible variations in exposures and coverages.

Educational Objective 6

6-1. A farm policy can cover the insured's dwelling, structures appurtenant to the dwelling (such as a garage), household personal property (excluding farm personal property), loss of use of the foregoing, and personal liability coverage.

6-2. To discourage underinsurance, unscheduled farm personal property is subject to an 80 percent coinsurance clause. Scheduled farm personal property is not subject to a coinsurance requirement.

6-3. A farm policy can cover farm personal property (excluding household personal property) on either a scheduled or an unscheduled basis; farm structures (such as barns and silos); farm income and extra expense; farm inland marine coverages, such as agricultural machinery and livestock; and the commercial liability exposures of farming. Numerous endorsements are also available, to cover a variety of exposures including crop dusting and pollution liability.

6-4. The sod farm's property will be covered as follows:
- The irrigation equipment and pumps could be insured under Coverage F—Unscheduled Farm Personal Property.
- The tractors and forklifts could be insured under Coverage E—Scheduled Farm Personal Property.
- The pump houses, office, and shed could be included under Coverage G—Barns, Outbuildings, and Other Farm Structures.
- The trucks used for road use would be covered by a separate business automobile policy.

Educational Objective 7

7-1. The collision peril found on a farm policy's basic causes-of-loss form includes the following three aspects:
(1) Collision damage to covered farm machinery
(2) Death of covered livestock resulting from contact with vehicles
(3) Collision damage to other farm personal property

7-2. In addition to the usual broad-form perils, the ISO farm program can be used to insure livestock against death resulting from the following perils:
- Earthquake
- Flood
- Electrocution
- Drowning
- Accidental shooting
- Attacks by dogs or wild animals
- Loading/unloading accidents

7-3. Exclusions in the ISO farm program Special Causes of Loss Form differ from those found in the commercial property special form in that some are modified either to address the particular exposures of farms or to emulate homeowners special-form coverage.

7-4. The basic causes of loss farm policy includes theft and collision damage to farm machinery as well as collision damage to other farm property. These perils are not covered by the basic causes of loss commercial property form. These coverages could be especially important to the sod farm. Their equipment is housed in one location. It is susceptible to collision damage and theft.

Educational Objective 8

8-1. Crop-hail insurance is frequently extended to cover perils such as fire, windstorm, accompanying hail, damage caused by livestock, and vehicles. Such policies might also cover harvested crops against named perils while being transported to the first place of storage.

8-2. The exclusions to the Multiple Peril Crop Insurance (MPCI) plan are losses resulting from neglect, poor farming practices, or theft.

8-3. A farm family might prefer animal mortality insurance for the following reasons:
- It can be used to provide adequate limits on valuable animals that are worth more than the relatively low per-head livestock limits in farm policies.
- It covers loss of covered animals by any fortuitous cause, including illness or disease, whereas farm policies only cover death resulting from specified accidental losses.

8-4. The agricultural coverages that the organic goat milk farm might need are as follows:
- Crop-hail insurance for the specialty crop grown for the goats
- Animal mortality insurance for the more expensive goats used for breeding and the border collies

Direct Your Learning

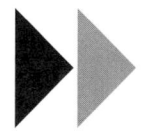

Assignment 11

Workers Compensation and Employers Liability Insurance

Educational Objectives

After learning the content of this assignment, you should be able to:

1. Describe the following aspects of workers compensation statutes:
   - Employers' loss exposures created by statutes
   - Requirements for benefits
   - Benefits provided
   - Benefit administration
   - Persons and employments covered
   - Extraterritorial provisions
   - Federal jurisdiction
   - Methods for meeting the employer's obligation
2. Explain how Part One of the Workers Compensation and Employers Liability (WC&EL) Insurance Policy provides the benefits required by state workers compensation laws.
3. Explain why employers liability insurance is needed and how Part Two of the WC&EL policy addresses this need.
4. Describe the purpose and operation of Part Three—Other States Insurance in the WC&EL policy.
5. Describe the need for and the coverage provided by each of the following endorsements:
   - Voluntary Compensation and Employers' Liability Coverage Endorsement
   - Longshore and Harbor Workers' Compensation Act Coverage Endorsement
6. Explain how premium bases, classifications, and premium adjustments affect the rating of WC&EL policies.
7. Explain whether, and for what amount, the WC&EL policy would cover a described employee injury or illness.
8. Define or describe each of the Key Words and Phrases for this assignment.

Study Materials

Required Reading:
- Commercial Insurance
  - Chapter 12

Study Aids:
- SMART Online Practice Exams
- SMART Study Aids
  - Review Notes and Flash Cards—Assignment 11

Outline

- **Workers Compensation Statutes**
  - A. Requirements for Benefits
  - B. Benefits Provided
    1. Medical Benefits
    2. Disability Income Benefits
    3. Rehabilitation Benefits
    4. Death Benefits
  - C. Benefit Administration
  - D. Persons and Employments Covered
    1. Employee or Independent Contractor?
    2. Leased Employees and Temporary Employees
  - E. Extraterritorial Provisions
    1. Application of Laws Out of State
    2. Application of Laws in Foreign Countries
  - F. Federal Jurisdiction
  - G. Methods for Meeting the Employer's Obligation
    1. Voluntary Insurance
    2. Assigned Risk Plans
    3. State Funds and Employers Mutuals
    4. Qualified Self-Insurance Plans
    5. Self-Insured Groups
- **The Workers Compensation and Employers Liability Policy**
  - A. Information Page
  - B. General Section
  - C. Part One—Workers Compensation Insurance
  - D. Part Two—Employers Liability Insurance
    1. Employers Liability Insuring Agreement
    2. Employers Liability Exclusions
    3. Limits of Liability
  - E. Part Three—Other States Insurance
  - F. Part Four—Your Duties If Injury Occurs
  - G. Part Five—Premium
  - H. Part Six—Conditions
    1. Inspection
    2. Long-Term Policy
    3. Transfer of Insured's Rights and Duties
    4. Cancellation
    5. Sole Representative
  - I. Endorsements
    1. Voluntary Compensation and Employers Liability Coverage Endorsement
    2. LHWCA Coverage Endorsement
- **Rating Workers Compensation Insurance**
  - A. Basis of Premium
  - B. Classifications
    1. Governing Classification
    2. Standard Exception Classifications
  - C. Premium Adjustments
    1. Experience Rating
    2. Retrospective Rating
    3. Premium Discount
    4. Merit or Schedule Rating Factors
    5. Rate Deviations
    6. Expense Constant
    7. Deductible Plans
    8. Dividend Plans
- **Summary**

study tips

Before starting a new assignment, briefly review the Educational Objectives of those preceding it.

For each assignment, you should define or describe each of the Key Words and Phrases and answer each of the Review and Application Questions.

Educational Objective 1

Describe the following aspects of workers compensation statutes:

- Employers' loss exposures created by statutes
- Requirements for benefits
- Benefits provided
- Benefit administration
- Persons and employments covered
- Extraterritorial provisions
- Federal jurisdiction
- Methods for meeting the employer's obligation

Key Words and Phrases

Workers compensation statute (p. 12.3)

Occupational disease (p. 12.4)

Temporary partial disability (p. 12.5)

Temporary total disability (p. 12.5)

Permanent partial disability (p. 12.5)

Permanent total disability (p. 12.5)

Employee (p. 12.8)

Independent contractor (p. 12.8)

United States Longshore and Harbor Workers' Compensation Act (LHWCA) (p. 12.11)

Jones Act (p. 12.11)

Competitive state fund (p. 12.13)

Monopolistic state fund (p. 12.13)

Employers mutual insurance company (p. 12.13)

Aggregate excess insurance (stop loss excess) (p. 12.14)

Specific excess insurance (p. 12.14)

Review Questions

1-1. Describe the trade-off, for both employers and for injured workers, that is established by workers compensation statutes. (p. 12.3)

1-2. Explain the basic requirements for an injury or a disease to be covered for workers compensation benefits. (p. 12.4)

1-3. Briefly explain the types of benefits included under the following categories:

   a. Medical benefits (p. 12.5)

   b. Disability income benefits (pp. 12.5–12.6)

   c. Rehabilitation benefits (p. 12.6)

d. Death benefits (pp. 12.6–12.7)

1-4. Explain the procedure a worker should follow if a workers compensation claim is contested by the employer. (p. 12.7)

1-5. What is the purpose of a second-injury fund? (p. 12.7)

1-6. Identify the employees and the types of employment that are frequently excluded from state workers compensation statutes. (p. 12.8)

1-7. Why is it important for a principal to verify that its independent contractors carry valid workers compensation insurance on their employees? (p. 12.8)

1-8. A traveling sales representative is injured on the job while away from the state where she usually works. In what three jurisdictions might she be able to file a workers compensation claim? (p. 12.9)

1-9. Aside from the Jones Act, identify two additional remedies available to injured crew members of vessels. (p. 12.11)

1-10. How do employers mutual insurance companies differ from other mutual insurance companies? (pp. 12.12–12.13)

1-11. What must an employer do to qualify as a self-insurer for workers compensation? (p. 12.13)

Application Questions

1-12. Corp-Right Corporation has branch offices in twenty-five states. Management trainees and data processing specialists employed by Corp-Right are often given temporary assignments in branch offices outside their home states.

A Corp-Right Corporation employee who is injured while on temporary assignment may be eligible for workers compensation benefits in more than one state. Identify two of the factors that may determine the jurisdiction(s) in which the injured worker is eligible for workers compensation benefits.

1-13. A large fireworks manufacturer with 400 employees cannot obtain private insurance in the voluntary market because it does not meet any insurer's underwriting criteria. How can it demonstrate the financial ability to pay any claims that may arise?

Educational Objective 2
Explain how Part One of the Workers Compensation and Employers Liability Insurance Policy (WC&EL Policy) provides the benefits required by state workers compensation laws.

Key Words and Phrases
Workers compensation and employers liability insurance (p. 12.15)

Workers Compensation and Employers Liability Insurance Policy
(WC&EL policy) (p. 12.15)

Review Questions

2-1. Explain why it is possible to use the same workers compensation policy containing uniform provisions even though benefits vary by state. (p. 12.15)

2-2. Explain an insurer's payment obligations and legal requirements under Part One of the WC&EL policy. (pp. 12.18–12.19)

2-3. Name four instances that would require an insured to reimburse an insurer for penalties required under a workers compensation law. (p. 12.19)

Application Question

2-4. Joanne is a chemical engineer who works at a large experimental facility that creates ways to improve the stability of plastic explosives, making them safer to transport. One day, Joanne used a mislabeled liquid solution that acted like acid when mixed with the other chemicals in her test tube. As a result, the solution exploded, leaving Joanne with third-degree burns over most of her body. The CEO of the facility withheld the information from the company's insurer, hoping that Joanne would accept his offer to "settle things quietly" to protect the company from an unfavorable public image. A few days later, Joanne died as a result of her injuries. Explain how Part One of the WC&EL policy will protect Joanne's dependents, regardless of the facility's misconduct.

Educational Objective 3

Explain why employers liability insurance is needed and how Part Two of the WC&EL policy addresses this need.

Review Questions

3-1. Contrast workers compensation coverage with employers liability coverage. (p. 12.19)

3-2 Explain why employers need employers liability insurance in addition to workers compensation insurance. (p. 12.19)

3-3. Describe the three limits of liability that apply to employers liability coverage. (p. 12.21)

Application Question

3-4 John is a car mechanic who works in a state listed in Item 3.A. of the WC&EL Information Page. He drives to an unlisted state to buy the supplies he needs until his out-of-stock supplies are delivered. John is injured in an auto accident while in the unlisted state. Explain whether Part Two of the WC&EL policy will cover John's injuries.

Educational Objective 4
Describe the purpose and operation of Part Three—Other States Insurance in the WC&EL policy.

Key Words and Phrases
Other states insurance (p. 12.22)

Stopgap coverage (p. 12.22)

Review Questions

4-1. When an insurer is adding the appropriate wording to Item 3.A., what states should be specifically excluded? (p. 12.22)

4-2. If an insurer is licensed to write workers compensation insurance in all states, explain how the following Item 3.C. wording protects the insured: "All states except those listed in Item 3.A. and ND, OH, WA, WV, and WY." (p. 12.22)

4-3. Describe the audit provision contained in the WC&EL policy. (p. 12.23)

Application Question

4-4. The owners of a bottled water distributor located and insured in a state listed in Item 3.A. are considering expanding operations into three unlisted states. Explain their responsibilities if they decide to expand operations on the effective date of the policy, and how the insurer differentiates between listing the states in Item 3.A. or Item 3.C.

Educational Objective 5

Describe the need for and the coverage provided by each of the following endorsements:

- Voluntary Compensation and Employers' Liability Coverage Endorsement
- Longshore and Harbor Workers' Compensation Act Coverage Endorsement

Key Words and Phrases

Voluntary Compensation and Employers Liability Endorsement (p. 12.25)

United States Longshore and Harbor Workers' Compensation Act Endorsement (p. 12.26)

Review Questions

5-1. Identify occupations and situations commonly exempted from statutory workers compensation insurance. (pp. 12.27–12.28)

5-2. Explain an insurer's obligations regarding compensation with a Voluntary Compensation and Employers Liability Endorsement. (p. 12.25)

5-3. Explain how the LHWCA endorsement amends the definition of workers compensation law. (p. 12.26)

Application Question

5-4. Eriq and Liliana own Appleberry Farm. To protect their employees in the event of illness or injury, Eriq and Liliana purchased a Voluntary Compensation and Employers Liability Endorsement. John, a farmhand, was injured on the tractor while harvesting crops. John sued Appleberry Farm, stating that his complaints about the tractor's faulty emergency brake were ignored by Eriq and Liliana. Explain how the Voluntary Compensation and Employers Liability Endorsement will affect John's lawsuit.

Educational Objective 6
Explain how premium bases, classifications, and premium adjustments affect the rating of WC&EL policies.

Key Words and Phrases

Experience rating plan (p. 12.29)

Experience modification (p. 12.29)

Retrospective rating plan (p. 12.29)

Expense constant (p. 12.30)

Large deductible plan (p. 12.30)

Review Questions

6-1. Explain why payroll is an effective premium base for workers compensation insurance. (p. 12.26)

6-2. What is the purpose of the workers compensation classification system? (p. 12.27)

6-3. Briefly explain how premium determined by applying the rates to the exposures (payroll) can be modified by the following WC&EL premium adjustments:

a. Premium discount (p. 12.29)

b. Merit or schedule rating factors (p. 12.30)

c. Rate deviations (p. 12.30)

d. Dividend plans (p. 12.31)

Application Question

6-4. The owner of West Coast Widget, a small manufacturing company, asked her insurance agent to explain several aspects of West Coast's workers compensation insurance.

  a. West Coast Widget received one rating classification for all of its employees, although the work of some employees is more hazardous than that of others. Explain the classification system used in rating workers compensation insurance.

b. How would experience rating affect West Coast Widget's workers compensation insurance premium?

c. West Coast's owner is considering self-insurance of its workers compensation exposure. Is West Coast Widget a good candidate for self-insurance? Explain.

Educational Objective 7

Explain whether, and for what amount, the WC&EL policy would cover a described employee injury or illness.

Review Questions

7-1. Mike suffered a severe allergic reaction to the dyes used at the carpet store in which he worked and was unable to work for several weeks. Explain whether Mike is eligible for benefits under the carpet store's standard WC&EL policy.

7-2. A dock worker fell into a shrimp boat's open hatch and broke his leg. What endorsement would his employer need in order to cover this worker's claim?

7-3. John buys his lobsters from lobster boat operators who use their own methods and judgment for supplying the lobsters to John. Would these boat operators be considered John's employees? Explain.

Application Question

7-4. Duane's Dirt Bike Shop has incurred four workers compensation claims in the past year. Because Duane's workers compensation premiums have reached certain levels, they are subject to experience rating modification. Suppose that the basic calculation for Duane's WC&EL policy is $40,000 and that he has an experience modification factor of 1.10. Calculate Duane's premium.

Answers to Assignment 11 Questions

NOTE: These answers are provided to give students a basic understanding of acceptable types of responses. They often are not the only valid answers and are not intended to provide an exhaustive response to the questions.

Educational Objective 1

1-1. The trade-off for employees established by workers compensation statutes is that workers receive no-fault protection for workplace injuries, while losing the right to sue the employer for injury. The trade-off for employers is that they are obligated to provide compensation to insured employees even when there is no negligence on the part of the employer; in return, the employer's liability is limited by statute.

1-2. To be covered under a workers compensation statute, an injury or a disease must (in most states) arise out of and in the course of employment. The injury or disease must be causally related to the employment and occur while the employee is engaged in work-related activities.

1-3. The following benefits are included in workers compensation:
   a. Medical benefits—full and unlimited medical expense benefits for a covered injury or disease (medical, hospital, surgical, and other related medical care costs)
   b. Disability income benefits—compensation for wage loss for a temporary partial disability, a temporary total disability, a permanent partial disability, or a permanent total disability (subject to a waiting period deductible), and limited to a percentage of the employee's average weekly wage at the time of disability; also subject to maximum and minimum weekly benefit amounts, depending on state law
   c. Rehabilitation benefits—payment of expenses for complete medical treatment and rehabilitation
   d. Death benefits—a flat amount for burial expense and partial replacement of the worker's former weekly wage

1-4. If an employer contests a workers compensation claim, an officer of the workers compensation board in that state can provide a hearing, and the employee can appeal the decision to the workers compensation board and then to the appropriate court.

1-5. Second-injury funds were established to encourage employers to hire partially impaired workers. Should additional injury occur to an already impaired worker that results in a total or near total impairment, the second-injury fund will pay a portion of the claim.

1-6. State workers compensation statutes generally exclude the following employees and types of employment:
   - Employees working for employers with fewer than a minimum number of employees
   - Farm labor
   - Domestic workers
   - Casual employees (unskilled workers paid daily for a day's work)
   - Independent contractors
   - Federal government workers
   - Maritime workers
   - Interstate railroad workers

1-7. It is important for a principal to verify that its independent contractors carry valid workers compensation insurance on their employees because if an independent contractor does not carry workers compensation insurance on its employees, the principal for whom the independent contractor is working may be held responsible for providing workers compensation to employees of the independent contractor.

1-8. The traveling sales representative injured on the job while away from the state where she usually works could file a workers compensation claim in any one of the following jurisdictions, according to the laws of many states. She will probably choose the one where the workers compensation law provides the most generous benefits:
- State where she was hired
- State where she was injured
- State where she usually works

1-9. Aside from the Jones Act, two additional remedies available to injured crew members of vessels include:
- A lawsuit against the employer for injury resulting from unseaworthiness of the vessel
- An injured crew member's right to "maintenance" (food and shelter) and "cure" (medical attention), regardless of whether the employer was at fault

1-10. Employers mutual insurance companies closely resemble any other mutual insurance company except that they are typically required by their charters to provide workers compensation insurance to any qualified employer in the state.

1-11. To qualify as a self-insurer for workers compensation, an employer must post a surety bond with the workers compensation administrative agency of the state to guarantee the security of benefit payments. In addition, most states require evidence of an ability to administer the benefit payments and services mandated by law.

1-12. The factors that may determine the jurisdiction(s) in which the injured worker is eligible for workers compensation benefits are the following:
- Place of employment
- Place where the employee was hired
- The employee's place of residence
- The state in which the employer is domiciled

1-13. Because the fireworks manufacturer cannot obtain private insurance in the voluntary market, the following options may be available (varies by state) to allow it to demonstrate financial ability to pay any claims that may arise:
- Insurance through assigned risk plans—It can apply to the assigned risk plan in the appropriate state to obtain coverage. In a typical assigned risk plan, the state will "assign" each applicant (rejected first by the voluntary market) to be insured by a private insurer. The private insurers are compelled to accept assigned risk policies in a quantity that is proportionate to their share of the voluntary market.
- Insurance through state funds or employers mutual insurance companies—accept any good faith applicant for insurance in the state, and no assigned risk plan is necessary. In most jurisdictions, the fund competes with private insurers. In a few other jurisdictions, the state fund is the sole provider of workers compensation coverage. The legislatures in a handful of states

have created employers mutual insurance companies that also accept virtually all applicants but, unlike state funds, are not controlled by the state.

- Qualified self-insurance plans—Almost all states allow employers to retain (self-insure) the risk of workers compensation losses if they demonstrate the financial capacity to do so by meeting certain requirements. Because the company has a large number of employees, self-insurance would be a practical alternative.

Note: Self-insured groups—Self-insured groups consist of employers in the same industry that jointly (as a whole) and severally (individually) guarantee payments of workers compensation benefits to the employees of the group's members. Because of this company's unique product (manufacturing fireworks), it is unlikely it would find similar companies with which it could form a self-insured group. As a result, this insurance might not be practical.

Educational Objective 2

2-1. It is possible to use the same workers compensation policy in various states because the applicable workers compensation laws are incorporated by reference in the policy. Thus, the covered workers compensation benefits are not itemized in the policy. The benefits specified in the applicable statute govern the types and amounts of benefits payable by the insurer.

2-2. The coverage provided by Part One obligates the insurer to pay all compensation and other benefits required of the insured by the workers compensation law or occupational disease law of any state listed in Item 3.A. of the Information Page. The policy also recognizes the legal requirements that directly obligate the insurer to pay workers compensation benefits to any injured employee or, in the event of death, to the employee's dependents.

2-3. The policy provides that the insured will reimburse the insurer for any penalties required under a workers compensation law in the following four instances:

(1) Employer's willful misconduct

(2) Employer's knowingly employing anyone illegally

(3) Employer's failure to comply with health and safety laws and regulations

(4) Employer's discrimination against employees who claim workers compensation benefits

2-4. For the protection of the employee, the WC&EL policy provides that the obligations of the insurer will not be affected by the failure of the employer to comply with the policy requirements. The company's insurer will pay workers compensation benefits to Joanne's dependents. Since the contract is made primarily for the benefit of employees and their dependents, they have a direct right of action against the insurer.

Educational Objective 3

3-1. In contrast with workers compensation coverage, which covers an employer's *statutory* liability under workers compensation laws for occupational injury to employees, employers liability insurance covers an employer against its *common-law* liability for occupational injury to employees. In addition, unlike workers compensation coverage, employers liability coverage is subject to monetary limits of liability stated in the policy.

3-2. Employers need employers liability insurance in addition to workers compensation insurance because, depending on the laws of the particular state, an employer can still be held liable under the common law as the result of employee injuries, such as third-party claims or claims for care and loss of services.

3-3. The three limits of liability that apply to employers liability coverage are as follows:
   (1) The bodily injury by accident limit is the most that the insurer will pay for bodily injury resulting from any one accident, regardless of the number of employees injured.
   (2) The bodily injury by disease—policy limit is the most that the insurer will pay for bodily injury by disease, regardless of the number of employees who sustain disease.
   (3) The bodily injury by disease—each employee limit is the most that the insurer will pay for bodily injury by disease to any one employee.

3-4. While Part Two requires that the employment out of which the injury arises be necessary or incidental to the insured's work in a state or territory listed in Item 3.A. of the Information Page, it is not a requirement that the injury must *occur* in one of the states or territories listed. Even though John's injuries occurred outside of the listed state, the injury still arose out of employment that was necessary or incidental to the insured's work in a listed state. Therefore, Part Two of the WC&EL policy will cover John's injuries.

Educational Objective 4

4-1. When an insurer is filling in Item 3.A., it should exclude the monopolistic fund states; any other states in which the insurer is not licensed to sell workers compensation insurance; and any other states in which the insurer does not wish to provide coverage for underwriting reasons.

4-2. If an insurer is licensed to write workers compensation insurance in all states, the wording used in Item 3.C. often reads: "All states except those listed in Item 3.A. and ND, OH, WA, WV, and WY." This protects the insured if it commences operations in any state other than those listed in Item 3.A., which are already covered, or in any state other than the five monopolistic fund states, where it would be illegal for the insurer to provide workers compensation insurance.

4-3. The audit provision in the WC&EL policy explains the following:
   - Insurer's right to examine and audit the insured's books and records
   - Why the final and estimated premiums might be different
   - How premiums will be determined if the policy is canceled

4-4. If the distributor has operations in a particular state on the effective date of the policy but that state is not listed in Item 3.A., the owners must notify the insurer within thirty days or else no coverage will apply for that state. Thus, when operations are *known* to exist in a particular state, the insurer lists that state in Item 3.A. When operations do not currently take place in additional states but could be extended into those states, the insurer lists those states in Item 3.C.

Educational Objective 5

5-1. The occupations and situations most commonly exempted from statutory workers compensation insurance are farm labor, domestic employment, and casual labor. In some cases, the law does not apply to employers with fewer than a certain minimum number of employees. In addition, the workers compensation laws of some states do not apply to partners, sole proprietors, or executive officers.

5-2. The Voluntary Compensation and Employers Liability Endorsement, called "voluntary compensation," obligates the insurer to pay, on behalf of the insured, an amount equal to the compensation benefits that would be payable to such employees if they were subject to the workers compensation law designated in the endorsement.

5-3. The LHWCA endorsement amends the definition of workers compensation law to include the LHWCA with respect to operations in any state designated in the endorsement's schedule.

5-4. The voluntary compensation endorsement states that if an employee entitled to payment under the endorsement brings a suit under the common law, the coverage provided by the endorsement reverts to employers liability insurance. The insurer will defend the insured against the employee's suit and pay any settlement awarded, subject to the stipulated limits of liability.

Educational Objective 6

6-1. Payroll is an effective premium base for workers compensation insurance because it varies directly with the exposure covered by the insurance, it is easy to determine and verify from available records, and it is not easily manipulated by the insured.

6-2. The purpose of the workers compensation classification system is to identify groups of similar employments whose experience is then combined for the purpose of establishing appropriate rates.

6-3. Premium determined by applying the rates to the exposures (payroll) can be modified by the following WC&EL premium adjustment in these ways:

   a. Premium discount—Many of the expenses of providing workers compensation insurance do not increase proportionately with increases in premium. For example, the costs of policy issuance and premium collection generally do not increase with the size of the premium. Also, the percentage paid to producers as a commission is usually reduced as the premium increases. In recognition of these lowered expenses, the premium discount plan provides an increasing credit for premiums in excess of a certain minimum.

   b. Merit or schedule rating factors—In many states, the premium can also be modified by a merit or schedule rating factor to give the insured credit for conditions that are more favorable than those normally expected, such as superior housekeeping (standards that foster workplace safety), excellent employee training, and on-site medical facilities.

   c. Rate deviations—In some states, insurers are permitted to apply a rate deviation factor (for example, 10 percent) to the premium as calculated by the rating manual. Insurers generally reserve these credits for better risks, although competitive pressures sometimes result in average risks receiving a rate deviation.

   d. Dividend plans—For policies written on a dividend plan, the cost of the insurance can be reduced by dividends declared by the insurer. Dividends are, essentially, a return to the insured of a portion of the premiums paid for an expiring policy term. Two general types of dividend plans are available: a flat-dividend plan and a sliding-scale dividend plan. Under a flat-dividend plan, all eligible policies receive the same percentage of their premium as a dividend regardless of their individual loss experience. Under a sliding-scale dividend plan, the size of the dividend varies with the insured's own experience; the lower the insured's loss ratio, the higher the dividend percentage. In sliding-scale dividend plans, no dividend is paid when the loss ratio for the expiring year exceeds a certain percentage, usually 45 to 60 percent.

6-4. West Coast's workers compensation insurance has the following characteristics:

   a. The classification system used in rating workers compensation insurance identifies groups of similar employments and combines their experience to establish rates. The insurer must determine the basic classification that best describes West Coast's business within the state. Then West Coast's exposure base and loss experience can be pooled with similar businesses.

b. With experience rating, West Coast's premium for workers compensation insurance would be adjusted for a future period based on West Coast's loss experience for a recent period. For example, West Coast's premium for 2008 might be adjusted based on West Coast's loss experience for 2004, 2005, and 2006. The premium for 2008 would be reduced if West Coast's losses for 2004, 2005, and 2006 were less than the average for the class and increased if West Coast's losses were higher.

c. No, West Coast Widget is not a candidate for workers compensation self-insurance. Self-insurance is practical only for large employers. To retain the risk of losses and guarantee the security of benefit payments, Widget would need to post a surety bond with the workers compensation administrative agency. A small business like Widget would not have the necessary resources to post this bond or to administer the benefits and services mandated by law.

Educational Objective 7

7-1. Yes, Mike is eligible for benefits under MCC's WC&EL policy. Most states provide coverage for occupational diseases attributed to the work or occupational exposure. Since Mike's condition arose out of and in the course of employment, he should receive medical benefits as well as disability income.

7-2. The dock worker's employer would need the U.S. Longshore and Harbor Workers' Compensation Act (LHWCA) Endorsement to cover the dock worker's injury.

7-3. No, the boat operators would probably be considered independent contractors and not employees. An independent contractor is not subject to direction and control regarding the details of the work. John does not tell the boat operators where to drop their traps or which lobsters to keep.

7-4. If the experience modification (or mod) is less than 1.00, the premium is reduced; if the mod is greater than 1.00, the premium is increased. Because Duane's mod rate is greater than 1.00, his premium will increase, calculated as $40,000 × 1.10 = $44,000.

Direct Your Learning

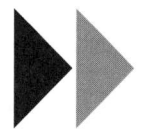

ASSIGNMENT 12

Miscellaneous Coverages

Educational Objectives

After learning the content of this assignment, you should be able to:

1. Explain how three characteristics of liability insurance create the need for excess or umbrella liability coverage.
2. Describe the three basic types of excess liability insurance policies.
3. Explain how umbrella liability insurance differs from ordinary excess liability insurance.
4. Describe the following aspects of umbrella liability insurance: drop-down coverage, required underlying coverages, aggregate umbrella limits, insuring agreement, coverage triggers, exclusions, and conditions.
5. Given a case about a covered liability loss, determine amounts payable under primary insurance and excess or umbrella liability insurance.
6. Explain how the requirements of providing professional liability coverage and the exclusions required by the Insurance Services Office *Commercial Lines Manual* (CLM) create a need for separate professional liability and management liability insurance.
7. Describe the major differences between professional liability and management liability insurance and commercial general liability insurance.
8. Describe the loss exposures insured by the following management liability coverages:
   - Directors and officers liability insurance
   - Employment practices liability insurance
   - Employee benefits liability insurance
   - Fiduciary liability insurance
9. Describe aircraft-related exposures and the coverages that can be included in an aircraft insurance policy.
10. Explain how an organization domiciled in the United States can insure foreign loss exposures that would not be covered under standard property and liability insurance policies.
11. Describe the characteristics of surety bonds, including how surety bonds contrast with insurance.
12. Describe the circumstances that create the need for surety bonds and the guarantees provided by the various types of contract bonds and commercial surety bonds.
13. Define or describe each of the Key Words and Phrases for this assignment.

Study Materials

Required Reading:
- Commercial Insurance
  - Chapter 13

Study Aids:
- SMART Online Practice Exams
- SMART Study Aids
  - Review Notes and Flash Cards—Assignment 12

Outline

- **Excess and Umbrella Liability Insurance**
  A. Need for Excess or Umbrella Liability Coverage
     1. Probable Maximum Loss
     2. Layering of Liability Coverages
     3. Effect of Aggregate Limits
  B. Insurance Treatment
  C. Excess Liability Insurance
  D. Umbrella Liability Insurance
     1. Drop-Down Coverage
     2. Required Underlying Coverages
     3. Aggregate Umbrella Limits
     4. Insuring Agreement
     5. Occurrence and Claims-Made Coverage Triggers
     6. Exclusions
     7. Conditions
- **Professional Liability and Management Liability Insurance**
  A. Distinguishing Between Professional and Management Liability
  B. Need for Professional and Management Liability Insurance
  C. Professional and Management Liability Contrasted With CGL
     1. Claims-Made Trigger
     2. Consent to Settle
     3. Duty to Defend and Selection of Defense Counsel
     4. Deductibles
- **Professional Liability Exposures and Policy Forms**
  A. Physicians Professional Liability
  B. Insurance Agents and Brokers Errors and Omissions Liability
  C. Conflicts and Overlaps With the CGL Policy
- **Management Liability Exposures and Policy Forms**
  A. Directors and Officers Liability
     1. Insuring Agreements
     2. Exclusions
     3. Deductibles
     4. Entity Coverage
     5. D&O Coverage for Smaller Corporations and Not-for-Profits
  B. Employment Practices Liability
  C. Employee Benefits Liability
  D. Fiduciary Liability Insurance
- **Aircraft Insurance**
  A. Aircraft Liability Coverage
  B. Aircraft Hull Coverage
  C. Other Aircraft Coverages
- **Coverage for Foreign Operations**
- **Surety Bonds**
  A. Surety Bonds Contrasted With Insurance
     1. Three Parties
     2. Principal Liable to Surety
     3. Surety Expects No Losses
     4. Indefinite Coverage Period
  B. Other Characteristics of Surety Bonds
     1. Statutory Nature of Bonds
     2. Bond Limit
  C. Types of Surety Bonds
     1. Contract Bonds
     2. License and Permit Bonds
     3. Public Official Bonds
     4. Court Bonds
     5. Miscellaneous Bonds
- **Summary**

Perform a final review before your exam, but don't cram. Give yourself between two and four hours to go over the course work.

For each assignment, you should define or describe each of the Key Words and Phrases and answer each of the Review and Application Questions.

> ## Educational Objective 1
> Explain how three characteristics of liability insurance create the need for excess or umbrella liability coverage.

Key Words and Phrases

Excess liability policy (p. 13.4)

Umbrella liability policy (p. 13.4)

Review Questions

1-1. Identify three characteristics of liability insurance that are not shared by property insurance. (p. 13.3)

1-2. Explain why it is difficult to estimate probable maximum loss for liability losses. (p. 13.3)

1-3. Explain the difference in how property and liability insurers provide high limits of coverage. (p. 13.4)

Application Question

1-4. Company A has CGL coverage with a $1,000,000 each occurrence limit, a $2,000,000 general aggregate limit, and a $2,000,000 aggregate limit for products and completed operations. If Company A has five products liability losses for $500,000 each, for a total of $2,500,000 in losses during the policy period, how much will the policy pay for the losses?

Educational Objective 2

Describe the three basic types of excess liability insurance policies.

Review Questions

2-1. List the three basic forms an excess liability policy may take. (p. 13.5)

2-2. Describe the following types of excess liability policies:

   a. Following-form excess policy (p. 13.5)

   b. Self-contained excess policy (p. 13.6)

2-3. Explain why a self-contained excess policy might not cover a liability injury claim even though the underlying policy provides coverage. (p. 13.6)

Application Question

2-4. EFG Company has a commercial auto policy with a $1 million per accident limit for liability coverage. EFG also has a following form excess liability policy with a $5 million limit. An EFG employee causes an auto accident, and EFG is held liable for a bodily injury claim of $3 million. Assuming that the claim is covered under EFG's commercial auto policy, how much will each of EFG's policies pay for this claim?

Educational Objective 3
Explain how umbrella liability insurance differs from ordinary excess liability insurance.

Review Questions

3-1. What are two functions performed by both umbrella liability policies and ordinary excess liability policies? (p. 13.6)

3-2. What is one additional function performed by umbrella liability policies but not by ordinary excess liability policies? (p. 13.6)

3-3. Explain how an insurer might restrict coverage provided by an umbrella policy. (p. 13.6)

Application Question

3-4. The directors and officers of Mammoth Corporation are covered by a directors and officers (D&O) liability insurance policy with a $1 million limit of liability, a $50,000 deductible, and a 5 percent participation rate. A group of Mammoth Corporation stockholders sued the board of directors and was awarded damages of $750,000 in court. Assuming this loss is covered, determine how much Mammoth's D&O insurer will pay toward this amount. Show your calculations.

Educational Objective 4

Describe the following aspects of umbrella liability insurance: drop-down coverage, required underlying coverages, aggregate umbrella limits, insuring agreement, coverage triggers, exclusions, and conditions.

Key Words and Phrases

Drop-down coverage (p. 13.6)

Self-insured retention (SIR) (p. 13.7)

Maintenance of underlying insurance condition (p. 13.11)

Review Questions

4-1. Explain when the self-insured retention applies to claims payable by umbrella liability insurance. (p. 13.7)

4-2. What underlying coverages are usually required by an umbrella liability insurer? (p. 13.8)

4-3. What types of limits usually apply to an umbrella liability policy? (p. 13.9)

4-4. What basic types of injury or damage are usually covered by the insuring agreement of an umbrella liability policy? (p. 13.10)

Application Question

4-5. For each of the following loss exposures, identify a type of policy that could be purchased to cover the exposure:

   a. XYZ Corporation knows it might need to lay off some workers, but it is concerned about possible employee suits for wrongful termination.

   b. Jones Enterprises provides group health insurance for all of its employees. The company is worried that its human resources department might neglect to add a new employee to the plan and that Jones might thus become liable for medical claims for such an employee.

c. The owners of a corporation are responsible for investing funds accumulated for their employee retirement plan. They are concerned about their responsibility if they make negligent investment decisions.

Educational Objective 5

Given a case about a covered liability loss, determine amounts payable under primary insurance and excess or umbrella liability insurance.

Application Question

5-1. The Brownwell Company has an umbrella liability policy with a limit of $1,000,000 and an SIR of $10,000. It also carries a business auto policy with a limit of $500,000. What dollar amount will Brownwell's umbrella insurer be obligated to pay for each of the following claims? Explain your answers.

a. One of Brownwell's employees has caused an accident that is covered under both Brownwell's auto and umbrella policies. The injured party has been awarded $700,000 in damages from Brownwell.

b. One of Brownwell's employees committed a personal injury offense that was not covered by any of Brownwell's primary liability policies but was covered by Brownwell's umbrella policy. Brownwell was held liable for $160,000 in damages because of the personal injury.

Educational Objective 6

Explain how the requirements of providing professional liability coverage and the exclusions required by the Insurance Services Office *Commercial Lines Manual* (CLM) create a need for separate professional liability and management liability insurance.

Key Words and Phrases

Professional liability insurance (p. 13.12)

Management liability insurance (p. 13.13)

Review Questions

6-1. Distinguish between the malpractice liability and errors and omissions professional liability. (pp. 13.12–13.13)

6-2. Identify the coverages commonly included in management liability insurance. (p. 13.13)

6-3. Explain why most insurers do not want to include professional liability coverage as part of the CGL coverage. (p. 13.14)

Educational Objective 7

Describe the major differences between professional liability and management liability insurance and commercial general liability insurance.

Review Questions

7-1. Briefly explain how professional liability and management policies commonly differ from CGL policies with regard to each of the following points:

    a. Claims-made triggers (p. 13.14)

    b. Consent to settle requirements (p. 13.15)

    c. Selection of defense counsel (p. 13.15)

    d. Use of deductibles (p. 13.16)

7-2. What is the typical period of time for a negligence lawsuit to be filed, after which claims are barred? (p. 13.17)

7-3. Describe the professional liability policy provision known as the "hammer clause." (p. 13.15)

7-4. Identify two categories of errors and/or omissions for which physicians may be held liable. (p. 13.17)

7-5. Explain how an insurance agent or broker can be held liable to both clients and the insurer represented. (p. 13.18)

7-6. Describe the provisions of a typical insurance agent's errors and omissions policy in terms of the following:

a. The liability exposure covered (p. 13.18)

b. Exclusions (p. 13.18)

Educational Objective 8

Describe the loss exposures insured by the following management liability coverages:

- Directors and officers liability insurance
- Employment practices liability insurance
- Employee benefits liability insurance
- Fiduciary liability insurance

Key Words and Phrases

Directors and officers (D&O) liability insurance (p. 13.20)

Entity coverage (p. 13.21)

Employment practices liability (EPL) insurance (p. 13.22)

Employee benefits liability insurance (p. 13.24)

Fiduciary liability insurance (p. 13.25)

Review Questions

8-1. Describe how directors and officers are typically selected by an organization. (p. 13.19)

8-2. Explain why even corporations with no public stockholders need D&O liability insurance. (p. 13.20)

8-3. Describe the following insuring agreements contained in a typical D&O policy:

a. Coverage A (p. 13.20)

b. Coverage B (p. 13.20)

8-4. Describe the loss exposures covered by each of the two insuring agreements normally included in a directors and officers liability policy. (p. 13.20)

8-5. In addition to paying a dollar deductible, how might a D&O policyholder be required to participate in a covered loss? (p. 13.21)

8-6. Give four examples of wrongful acts that are usually covered under employment practices liability insurance. (pp. 13.20–13.21)

8-7. Describe, and distinguish between, the loss exposures covered under each of the following:

a. Employee benefits liability insurance (p. 13.24)

b. Fiduciary liability insurance (p. 13.25)

Application Questions

8-8. Dee, a physician, is insured under a professional liability policy. Describe two types of errors or omissions that are likely to be covered by her professional liability policy.

8-9. Bill, a fifty-five-year-old employee of Ace Company, is fired even though his performance reviews have been outstanding. Bill believes he has been discriminated against because of his age and sues the directors of Ace Company. Describe the type of insurance policy that Ace Company would need to provide coverage for this type of lawsuit.

Educational Objective 9
Describe aircraft-related exposures and the coverages that can be included in an aircraft insurance policy.

Key Word or Phrase
Aircraft insurance (p. 13.26)

Review Questions

9-1. Describe the two most common aircraft hull coverages. (p. 13.28)

9-2. Identify the limits that usually apply to aircraft liability insurance. (p. 13.27)

9-3. In addition to liability and physical damage, what other coverages are often included in aircraft insurance policies? (p. 13.28)

Application Question

9-4. Vicki and Associates has purchased a single-engine high-performance aircraft. Vicki flies the plane as she travels for her consulting business. She keeps the plane in a hangar at a private runway owned by an association of professionals in her community. Describe the exposures that Vicki and Associates faces from the aircraft and the coverage available to address those loss exposures.

Educational Objective 10

Explain how an organization domiciled in the United States can insure foreign loss exposures that would not be covered under standard property and liability insurance policies.

Review Questions

10-1. What feature of standard commercial insurance policies leaves U.S. businesses exposed to potentially serious losses involving foreign loss exposures? (p. 13.29)

10-2. List some of the specialized coverages that insurers offer to firms with foreign loss exposures. (p. 13.30)

10-3. What unique coverage is offered by many foreign voluntary workers compensation policies? (p. 13.30)

Application Question

10-4. Julia flew from her company's corporate headquarters in New York to Mexico City and rented a car to visit one of her company's suppliers. After her visit and dinner, the car Julia was driving hit and injured a pedestrian while she was en route to her hotel. Julia was found to be intoxicated and charged with the injuries to the pedestrian. Explain how Julia's company's business auto policy and its foreign supplemental and excess auto policy will respond to this loss.

Educational Objective 11
Describe the characteristics of surety bonds, including how surety bonds contrast with insurance.

Key Words and Phrases
Surety bond (p. 13.30)

Principal (p. 13.31)

Obligee (p. 13.31)

Surety (p. 13.31)

Review Questions

11-1. What are four characteristics of surety bonds that distinguish them from most insurance policies? (p. 13.31)

11-2. Describe the statutory nature of surety bonds. (p. 13.32)

11-3. What does the "penalty" mean in reference to surety bonds? (p. 13.32)

Application Question

11-4. Charlie is a contractor who has agreed to construct a building for Big Business, Inc. (BBI). BBI has required that Charlie purchase a performance bond for this project. Identify the three parties to this bond using the terminology that is generally associated with surety bonds.

Educational Objective 12

Describe the circumstances that create the need for surety bonds and the guarantees provided by the various types of contract bonds and commercial surety bonds.

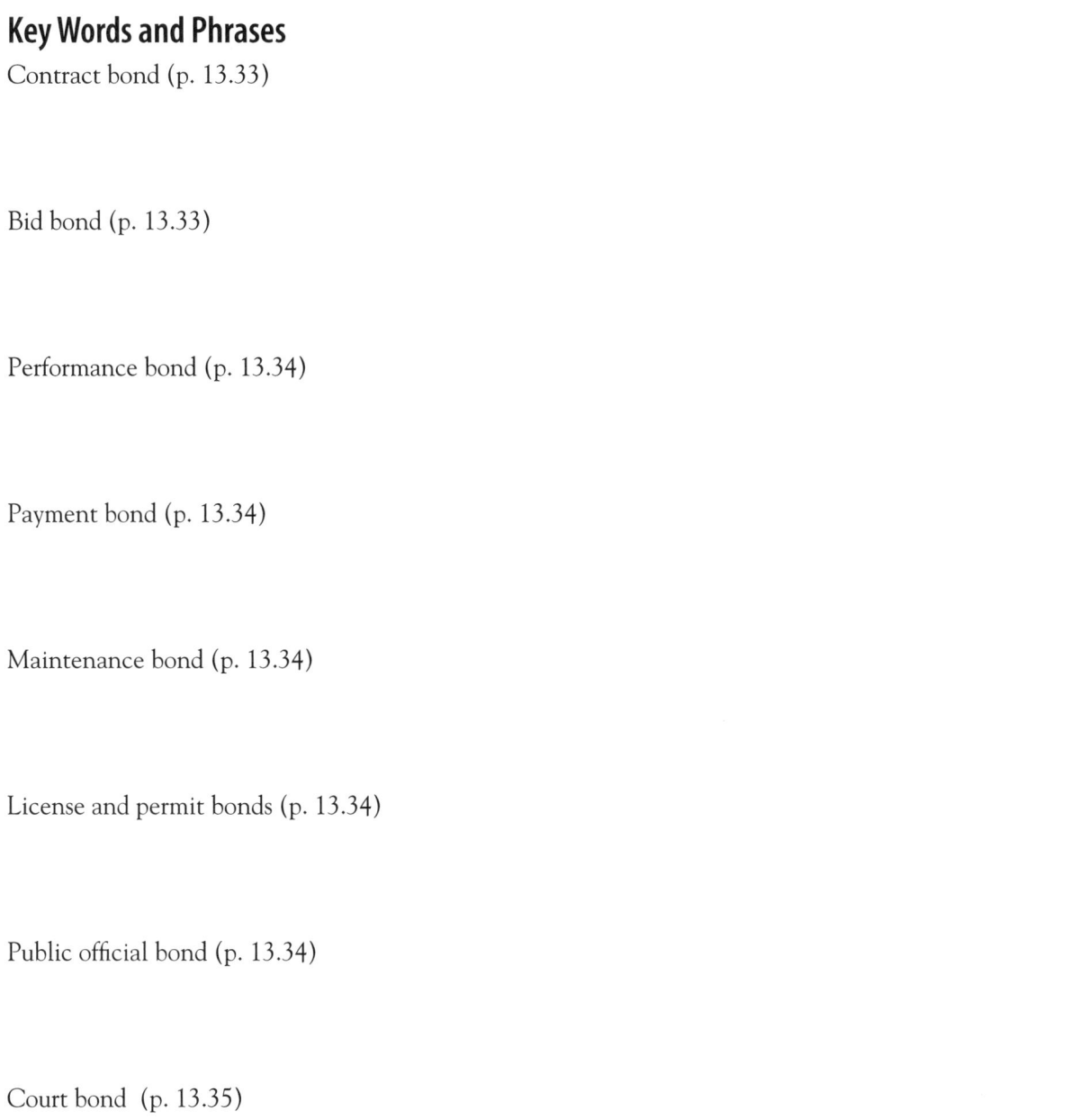

Key Words and Phrases

Contract bond (p. 13.33)

Bid bond (p. 13.33)

Performance bond (p. 13.34)

Payment bond (p. 13.34)

Maintenance bond (p. 13.34)

License and permit bonds (p. 13.34)

Public official bond (p. 13.34)

Court bond (p. 13.35)

Judicial bond (p. 13.35)

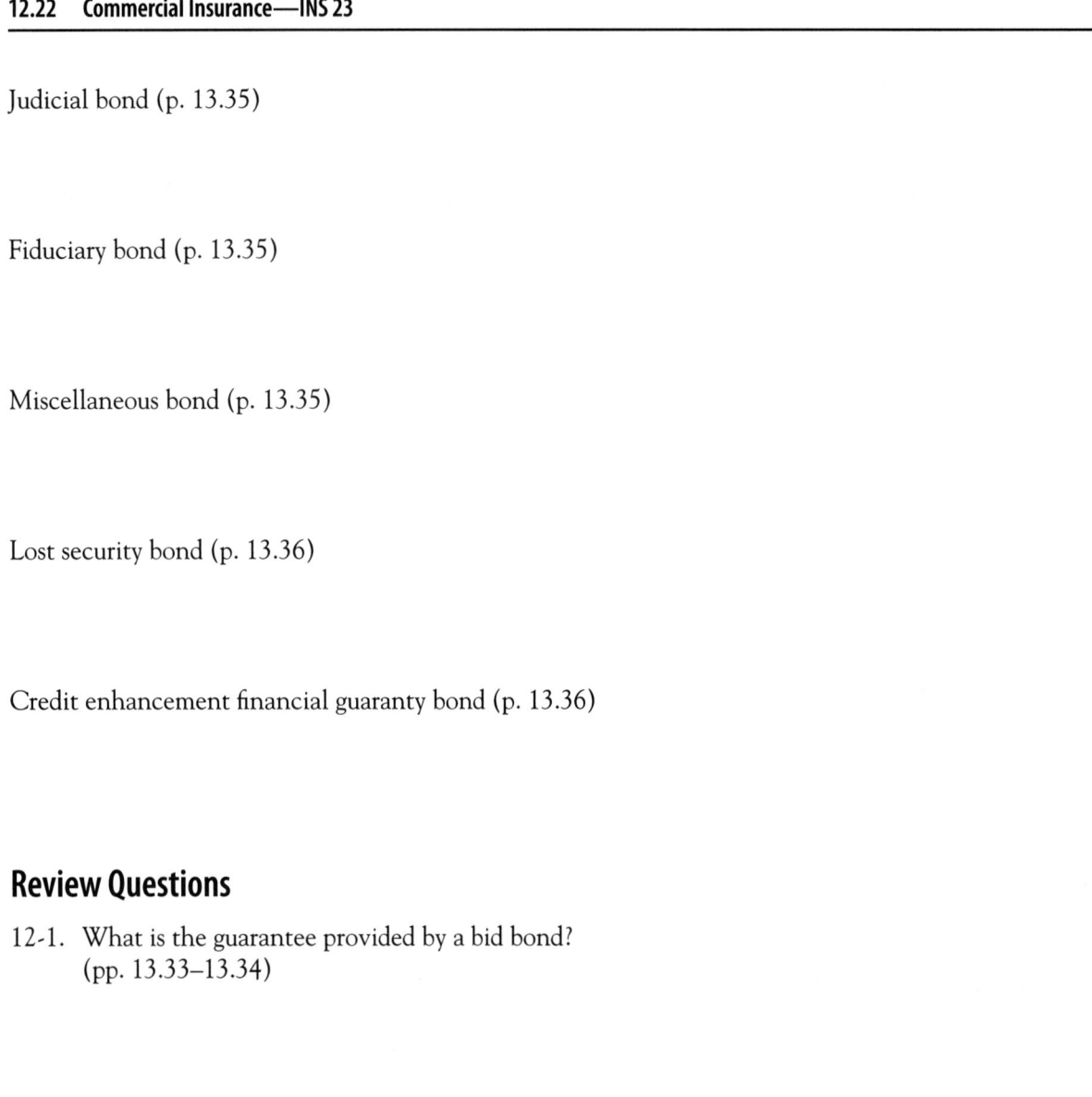

Fiduciary bond (p. 13.35)

Miscellaneous bond (p. 13.35)

Lost security bond (p. 13.36)

Credit enhancement financial guaranty bond (p. 13.36)

Review Questions

12-1. What is the guarantee provided by a bid bond? (pp. 13.33–13.34)

12-2. What is the guarantee provided by a payment bond? (p. 13.34)

12-3. What is the guarantee provided by a maintenance bond? (p. 13.34)

12-4. What is the guarantee provided by a court bond? (p. 13.35)

Application Question

12-5. Identify the type of surety bond that would be most appropriate in each of the following situations:

a. A building contractor needs a bond guaranteeing that it will complete a project in accordance with the contract.

b. A liquor store needs a bond guaranteeing to a local government that it will not sell liquor in violation of alcoholic beverage control laws.

c. A city treasurer needs a bond guaranteeing that she will perform her duties faithfully and honestly.

d. The administrator of a deceased person's estate needs a bond guaranteeing that he will faithfully perform all duties as prescribed by law or as specified by the probate court having jurisdiction.

Answers to Assignment 12 Questions

NOTE: These answers are provided to give students a basic understanding of acceptable types of responses. They often are not the only valid answers and are not intended to provide an exhaustive response to the questions.

Educational Objective 1

1-1. Three characteristics of liability insurance that are not shared by property insurance include the following:
   (1) Difficulty in estimating probable maximum loss for liability exposures
   (2) Layering of liability coverages
   (3) Effect of aggregate limits

1-2. It is difficult to estimate probable maximum loss for liability losses because both awards to injured persons and property damage claims can reach enormous amounts.

1-3. If several insurers participate on a property risk, they often do so on a pro rata basis, with each insurer sharing proportionately in all losses. High limits liability insurance is generally arranged in two or more layers, in which the primary insurer must totally exhaust coverage before the next layer of insurance makes a payment.

1-4. Company A's policy will pay only up to the aggregate limit, $2,000,000.

Educational Objective 2

2-1. An excess liability policy may take the following three basic forms:
   (1) Following form policy
   (2) Self-contained policy
   (3) A combination of following form and self-contained forms

2-2. The types of excess liability policies are described as follows:
   a. Following-form excess policy—Subject to the same terms as the underlying policy
   b. Self-contained excess policy—Subject only to its own terms

2-3. A self-contained excess policy might not cover a liability injury claim even though the underlying policy provides coverage because the loss might not be covered under the terms of the excess policy.

2-4. EFG's auto policy will pay its per accident limit of $1 million. EFG's excess liability policy will pay the remaining $2 million of the claim.

Educational Objective 3

3-1. Two functions performed by both umbrella liability policies and ordinary excess liability policies are to provide additional limits above the each occurrence limits of the insured's primary policies, and to take the place of the primary insurance when primary aggregate limits are reduced or exhausted.

3-2. An additional function performed by umbrella liability policies is to cover some claims that are not covered by the insured's primary policies.

3-3. An insurer might restrict coverage provided by an umbrella policy by attaching a following form endorsement.

3-4. Mammoth's D&O insurer will pay $665,000 for the covered loss, calculated as follows:
$750,000 − $50,000 = $700,000.
$700,000 × 0.05 = $35,000.
$700,000 − $35,000 = $665,000.

Educational Objective 4

4-1. The self-insured retention applies to claims payable by umbrella liability insurance only when a claim covered by the umbrella policy is not also covered, at least in part, by a primary policy. The umbrella policy will pay the part of the claim exceeding the insured's retention and will generally cover defense costs in full.

4-2. The underlying coverages usually required for a commercial umbrella policy are CGL, business auto liability, and employer's liability.

4-3. An umbrella liability policy is usually subject to an each occurrence limit and an aggregate limit. (In many policies, these limits are set at the same amount.)

4-4. The insuring agreement of a commercial umbrella liability policy usually covers bodily injury, property damage, personal injury, or advertising injury.

4-5. The following policies could be purchased by XYZ Corporation to cover the specified exposure:
   a. Employment practices liability (EPL) insurance
   b. Employee benefits liability insurance
   c. Fiduciary liability insurance

Educational Objective 5

5-1. a. Brownwell's umbrella policy will pay $200,000. After the business auto policy pays its limit of $500,000, the umbrella policy will pay the amount of the claim in excess of $500,000. Because primary coverage applies, the SIR is not applicable to this claim.
   b. Brownwell's umbrella policy will pay $150,000. In this case, the SIR is deducted from the amount of the claim because the claim was not covered by any of Brownwell's primary policies.

Educational Objective 6

6-1. Malpractice liability is used to describe liability associated with occupations that involve contact with the human body. Errors and omissions liability is used to describe professional liability for occupations such as accounting, insurance production, law, and engineering.

6-2. Coverages commonly included in management liability insurance are directors and officers liability, employment practices liability, employee benefits liability, and fiduciary liability.

6-3. Most insurers do not want to include professional liability coverage as part of the CGL coverage because professional liability requires different underwriting, rating, and claim handling skills.

Educational Objective 7

7-1. Professional liability policies commonly differ from CGL policies in the following ways:

   a. Claims-made triggers—Professional liability policies are usually written on a claims-made basis, whereas CGL policies are usually written on an occurrence basis. When compared to the claims-made CGL form, most professional liability policies are less generous in the granting of extended reporting periods. Many professional liability policies provide an extended reporting period only if the insured requests it and pays an additional premium. In contrast, the CGL claims-made form automatically provides a five-year extended reporting period, with the option for buying an unlimited one. When an insured obtains an extended reporting period under a professional liability policy, it commonly lasts for one to three years.

   b. Consent to settle—Many professional liability policies contain a consent-to-settle clause. This requires the insurer to obtain the insured's consent before settling a claim. The CGL policy allows the insurer to settle claims without obtaining the insured's consent.

   c. Selection of defense counsel—Some professional liability policies allow the insured to select defense counsel. In contrast, the CGL policy leaves this decision to the insurer.

   d. Deductibles—Professional liability policies are usually subject to a significant deductible. In contrast, CGL policies are often not subject to any deductible.

7-2. In most states, a statute of limitations provides that negligence claims are unenforceable unless suit is begun within two years of the date of the injury.

7-3. The professional liability provision known as the "hammer clause" states that if the insured does not agree to a proposed settlement, the insured must take over the defense and pay any further defense expenses as well as judgments/settlements exceeding the amount offered by the insurer to settle the claim. This provision is called the "hammer clause" because it compels the insured to agree to the insurer's proposed settlement.

7-4. Physicians can be held liable for medical errors (for example, injury to a patient) and administrative errors or omissions (for example, inappropriately withholding staff privileges from another doctor).

7-5. An agent or a broker can be held liable to the client for failure to properly advise the client regarding insurance needs or appropriate limits, failure to obtain insurance in a timely manner, or failure to renew a policy without prior notice. An agent or a broker who exceeds binding authority or who fails to cancel a policy when directed by the insurer can be held liable for any resulting claims that the insurer is required to pay.

7-6. A typical insurance agent's errors and omissions policy has the following provisions:

   a. A typical insurance agent's errors and omissions policy covers the insured against liability resulting from negligent acts or errors or omissions in the conduct of the insured's rendering of services as an insurance agent or broker.

   b. A typical insurance agent's errors and omissions policy might exclude bodily injury or damage to tangible property, overlaps with workers compensation and employer's liability policies, and overlaps with pollution liability policies.

Educational Objective 8

8-1. Directors are typically selected by an organization's owners, and officers are typically selected by the board of directors.

8-2. Even corporations with no public stockholders need D&O liability insurance because claimants can include not only stockholders but also employees, competitors, customers, and regulators.

8-3. A typical D&O policy contains the following coverages:
   a. Coverage A—Covers directors and officers for their personal liability as directors and officers resulting from a wrongful act.
   b. Coverage B—Covers the sums that the insured corporation is required or permitted by law to pay for suits alleging wrongful acts by directors or officers.

8-4. In a directors and officers (D&O) liability policy, one of the insuring agreements covers the directors and officers for their personal liability against liability for wrongful acts they commit in their capacities as directors or officers of the named corporation. The second insuring agreement covers the named corporation for all sums that it pays, as required or permitted by law, to indemnify its directors and officers who have been held liable for wrongful acts.

8-5. D&O policies are usually subject to both a flat deductible amount and a specified percentage of participation by the insured in all losses exceeding the retention.

8-6. Four examples of wrongful acts usually covered under employment practices liability policies are as follows:
   (1) Sexual harassment
   (2) Wrongful termination
   (3) Unlawful discrimination
   (4) Wrongful failure to promote

8-7. a. Employee benefits liability insurance basically covers an employer against liability claims alleging improper advice or other errors or omissions committed while administering the employer's employee benefit plans. Examples of administrative errors are providing negligent advice on the selection of employee benefit programs and failing to enroll an employee in the employer's group health insurance program.
   b. Fiduciary liability insurance covers employee benefit plan officials against liability resulting from breaching their fiduciary duties involving *discretionary* judgment. If, for example, the fiduciaries of an employee benefit plan make negligent investment decisions that result in financial harm to the plan's participants, the participants can sue the fiduciaries. (To summarize: employee benefits liability insurance covers *administrative* errors and omissions, whereas fiduciary liability insurance covers *discretionary* errors and omissions.)

8-8. The doctor's professional liability policy is likely to cover the following errors and omissions:
   - Improperly diagnosing a disease that results in a more serious illness, disability, or death
   - Leaving a surgical instrument or other foreign object in a patient following surgery

8-9. Ace Company would need an employment practices liability insurance policy to provide coverage for this age discrimination suit.

Educational Objective 9

9-1. The two most common aircraft hull coverages are as follows:
   (1) "All risks—ground and flight": Covers most causes of loss in flight or on the ground at the time of loss.
   (2) "All risks—not in motion": Covers the plane when it is on the ground and not moving under its own power, including being towed, but not while taxiing.

9-2. Aircraft liability coverage usually applies a combined single limit to all third-party claims except in cases where insurers impose a sublimit on claims by passengers. Aircraft liability is usually not subject to an aggregate limit.

9-3. In addition to liability and physical damage coverage, aircraft medical payments coverage and passenger voluntary settlement coverage (admitted liability coverage), and nonowned aircraft liability coverage are often included in aircraft policies.

9-4. Vicki and Associates' exposures from the aircraft and the coverages available to address those exposures are as follows:
   - Physical damage to the aircraft—Aircraft hull coverage "all risks—ground and flight" will protect the plane in flight or on the ground
   - Bodily injury and property damage resulting from the ownership, maintenance, or use of the aircraft—Aircraft liability coverage will address coverage for liability to others as well as bodily injury to passengers
   - Medical payments losses for Vicki—Aircraft medical payments coverage

Educational Objective 10

10-1. Standard commercial insurance policies contain a coverage territory that typically consists of the United States, its territories or possessions, and Canada. Although some standard policies, such as the CGL, provide worldwide coverage under narrowly defined circumstances, even these policies do not provide adequate coverage for insureds with regular operations in foreign countries.

10-2. For the needs of firms with foreign loss exposures, insurers offer these specialized coverages: foreign property and business income; foreign liability; foreign supplemental and excess auto; foreign voluntary workers compensation and employers liability; foreign crime, including kidnap and ransom and political risk.

10-3. Foreign voluntary workers compensation policies often include coverage for transportation expense to return disabled or deceased employees to the U.S. ("repatriation expense").

10-4. Julia's policies will respond to the loss in the following ways:
   - The business auto policy will cover losses only within the U.S. and its territories and possessions, Puerto Rico, and Canada. Therefore, no coverage applies.
   - Foreign supplemental and excess auto policies are nonstandard forms. Assuming that coverage is extended by this policy to Mexico and to nonowned vehicles, this policy would respond to the loss.

Educational Objective 11

11-1. Four characteristics of surety bonds that distinguish them from insurance policies are as follows:
   (1) Three parties to the contract are the surety, the obligee, and the principal. (Insurance policies are a two-party contract.)
   (2) The principal is liable to the surety for losses paid by the surety. (An insurer cannot subrogate against its own insured.)
   (3) The surety should not sustain any losses on any surety contracts.
   (4) The surety bond coverage period is indefinite. Surety bonds terminate after the principal has fulfilled its obligations. (Insurance policies usually have a definite policy period of one year or less.)

11-2. Surety bonds are often required by municipal ordinance or federal or state regulations or statutes; the provisions of such bonds, and thus the obligations of the three parties to the bond, are spelled out in the law.

11-3. The set limit of a surety bond is sometimes called the "penalty."

11-4. Charlie is the principal, BBI is the obligee, and the insurer (or bonding company) furnishing the bond is the surety.

Educational Objective 12

12-1. A bid bond guarantees that the bidder will enter into a contract at the price bid.

12-2. A payment bond guarantees payment when due for labor and material costs from work that the contractor is obligated to perform.

12-3. A maintenance bond guarantees the principal's work against defects in workmanship or materials for a specified period after completion.

12-4. A court bond guarantees (for example) that the judgment in a lawsuit will be paid after an unsuccessful appeal.

12-5. The following types of surety bonds would be appropriate for the specified situations:
   a. Performance bond
   b. License (or permit) bond
   c. Public official bond
   d. Fiduciary bond

Exam Information

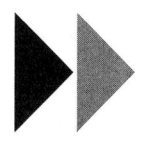

About Institute Exams
Exam questions are based on the Educational Objectives stated in the course guide and textbook. The exam is designed to measure whether you have met those Educational Objectives. The exam does not test every Educational Objective. Instead, it tests over a balanced sample of Educational Objectives.

How to Prepare for Institute Exams
What can you do to prepare for an Institute exam? Students who pass Institute exams do the following:

- Use the assigned study materials. Focus your study on the Educational Objectives presented at the beginning of each course guide assignment. Thoroughly read the textbook and any other assigned materials, and then complete the course guide exercises. Choose a study method that best suits your needs; for example, participate in a traditional class, online class, or informal study group; or study on your own. Use the Institutes' SMART Study Aids (if available) for practice and review. If this course has an associated SMART Online Practice Exams product, you will find an access code on the inside back cover of this course guide. This access code allows you to print (in PDF format) a full practice exam and to take additional online practice exams that will simulate an actual credentialing exam.

- Become familiar with the types of test questions asked on the exam. The practice exam in this course guide or in the SMART Online Practice Exams product will help you understand the different types of questions you will encounter on the exam.

- Maximize your test-taking time. Successful students use the sample exam in the course guide or in the SMART Online Practice Exams product to practice pacing themselves. Learning how to manage your time during the exam ensures that you will complete all of the test questions in the time allotted.

Types of Exam Questions

The exam for this course consists of objective questions of several types.

The Correct-Answer Type

In this type of question, the question stem is followed by four responses, one of which is absolutely correct. Select the *correct* answer.

> Which one of the following persons evaluates requests for insurance to determine which applicants are accepted and which are rejected?
>
> a. The premium auditor
>
> b. The loss control representative
>
> c. The underwriter
>
> d. The risk manager

The Best-Answer Type

In this type of question, the question stem is followed by four responses, only one of which is best, given the statement made or facts provided in the stem. Select the *best* answer.

> Several people within an insurer might be involved in determining whether an applicant for insurance is accepted. Which one of the following positions is primarily responsible for determining whether an applicant for insurance is accepted?
>
> a. The loss control representative
>
> b. The customer service representative
>
> c. The underwriter
>
> d. The premium auditor

The Incomplete-Statement or Sentence-Completion Type

In this type of question, the last part of the question stem consists of a portion of a statement rather than a direct question. Select the phrase that *correctly* or *best* completes the sentence.

> Residual market plans designed for individuals who are unable to obtain insurance on their personal property in the voluntary market are called
>
> a. VIN plans.
>
> b. Self-insured retention plans.
>
> c. Premium discount plans.
>
> d. FAIR plans.

"All of the Above" Type

In this type of question, only one of the first three answers could be correct, or all three might be correct, in which case the best answer would be "All of the above." Read all the answers and select the *best* answer.

> When a large commercial insured's policy is up for renewal, who is likely to provide input to the renewal decision process?
>
> a. The underwriter
>
> b. The loss control representative
>
> c. The producer
>
> d. All of the above

"All of the following, EXCEPT:" Type

In this type of question, responses include three correct answers and one answer that is incorrect or is clearly the least correct. Select the *incorrect* or *least correct* answer.

> All of the following adjust insurance claims, EXCEPT:
>
> a. Insurer claim representatives
>
> b. Premium auditors
>
> c. Producers
>
> d. Independent adjusters

Appendix

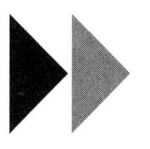

Sample Policies and Forms

Common Forms (Commercial Package Policy)
Common Policy Declarations 6
Common Policy Conditions 8

Commercial Property Forms
Commercial Property Coverage Part Declarations Page 9
Commercial Property Conditions 10
Building and Personal Property Coverage Form 12
Causes of Loss—Special Form 26

Commercial General Liability Forms
Commercial General Liability Declarations 35
Commercial General Liability Coverage Form 37

Commercial Auto Forms
Business Auto Declarations 52
Business Auto Coverage Form 60

POLICY NUMBER:

IL DS 00 09 07

COMMON POLICY DECLARATIONS

COMPANY NAME AREA	PRODUCER NAME AREA

NAMED INSURED: AMR Corporation
MAILING ADDRESS: 2000 Industrial Highway
Workingtown, PA 19000

POLICY PERIOD: FROM 10/1/07 TO 10/1/08 AT 12:01 A.M. STANDARD TIME AT YOUR MAILING ADDRESS SHOWN ABOVE.

BUSINESS DESCRIPTION: Storm Door Manufacturing

IN RETURN FOR THE PAYMENT OF THE PREMIUM, AND SUBJECT TO ALL THE TERMS OF THIS POLICY, WE AGREE WITH YOU TO PROVIDE THE INSURANCE AS STATED IN THIS POLICY.

THIS POLICY CONSISTS OF THE FOLLOWING COVERAGE PARTS FOR WHICH A PREMIUM IS INDICATED. THIS PREMIUM MAY BE SUBJECT TO ADJUSTMENT.

	PREMIUM
CAPITAL ASSETS PROGRAM (OUTPUT POLICY) COVERAGE PART	$ XXX
COMMERCIAL AUTOMOBILE COVERAGE PART	$ XXX
COMMERCIAL GENERAL LIABILITY COVERAGE PART	$ XXX
COMMERCIAL INLAND MARINE COVERAGE PART	$ XXX
COMMERCIAL LIABILITY UMBRELLA	$ XXX
COMMERCIAL PROPERTY COVERAGE PART	$ XXX
CRIME AND FIDELITY COVERAGE PART	$ XXX
EMPLOYMENT-RELATED PRACTICES LIABILITY COVERAGE PART	$ XXX
EQUIPMENT BREAKDOWN COVERAGE PART	$ XXX
FARM COVERAGE PART	$ XXX
LIQUOR LIABILITY COVERAGE PART	$ XXX
POLLUTION LIABILITY COVERAGE PART	$ XXX
PROFESSIONAL LIABILITY COVERAGE PART	$ XXX
	$ XXX
TOTAL:	$ XXX

Premium shown is payable: $ XXX at inception. $ XXX

Appendix 7

FORMS APPLICABLE TO ALL COVERAGE PARTS (SHOW NUMBERS):

Countersigned:	10/1/07	By:	A. M. Abel
	(Date)		(Authorized Representative)

NOTE

OFFICERS' FACSIMILE SIGNATURES MAY BE INSERTED HERE, ON THE POLICY COVER OR ELSEWHERE AT THE COMPANY'S OPTION.

COMMON POLICY CONDITIONS

All Coverage Parts included in this policy are subject to the following conditions.

A. Cancellation

1. The first Named Insured shown in the Declarations may cancel this policy by mailing or delivering to us advance written notice of cancellation.

2. We may cancel this policy by mailing or delivering to the first Named Insured written notice of cancellation at least:

   a. 10 days before the effective date of cancellation if we cancel for nonpayment of premium; or

   b. 30 days before the effective date of cancellation if we cancel for any other reason.

3. We will mail or deliver our notice to the first Named Insured's last mailing address known to us.

4. Notice of cancellation will state the effective date of cancellation. The policy period will end on that date.

5. If this policy is cancelled, we will send the first Named Insured any premium refund due. If we cancel, the refund will be pro rata. If the first Named Insured cancels, the refund may be less than pro rata. The cancellation will be effective even if we have not made or offered a refund.

6. If notice is mailed, proof of mailing will be sufficient proof of notice.

B. Changes

This policy contains all the agreements between you and us concerning the insurance afforded. The first Named Insured shown in the Declarations is authorized to make changes in the terms of this policy with our consent. This policy's terms can be amended or waived only by endorsement issued by us and made a part of this policy.

C. Examination Of Your Books And Records

We may examine and audit your books and records as they relate to this policy at any time during the policy period and up to three years afterward.

D. Inspections And Surveys

1. We have the right to:

   a. Make inspections and surveys at any time;

   b. Give you reports on the conditions we find; and

   c. Recommend changes.

2. We are not obligated to make any inspections, surveys, reports or recommendations and any such actions we do undertake relate only to insurability and the premiums to be charged. We do not make safety inspections. We do not undertake to perform the duty of any person or organization to provide for the health or safety of workers or the public. And we do not warrant that conditions:

   a. Are safe or healthful; or

   b. Comply with laws, regulations, codes or standards.

3. Paragraphs **1.** and **2.** of this condition apply not only to us, but also to any rating, advisory, rate service or similar organization which makes insurance inspections, surveys, reports or recommendations.

4. Paragraph **2.** of this condition does not apply to any inspections, surveys, reports or recommendations we may make relative to certification, under state or municipal statutes, ordinances or regulations, of boilers, pressure vessels or elevators.

E. Premiums

The first Named Insured shown in the Declarations:

1. Is responsible for the payment of all premiums; and

2. Will be the payee for any return premiums we pay.

F. Transfer Of Your Rights And Duties Under This Policy

Your rights and duties under this policy may not be transferred without our written consent except in the case of death of an individual named insured.

If you die, your rights and duties will be transferred to your legal representative but only while acting within the scope of duties as your legal representative. Until your legal representative is appointed, anyone having proper temporary custody of your property will have your rights and duties but only with respect to that property.

IL 00 17 11 98   Copyright, Insurance Services Office, Inc., 1998

Appendix 9

COMMERCIAL PROPERTY
CP DS 00 10 00

COMMERCIAL PROPERTY COVERAGE PART
DECLARATIONS PAGE

POLICY NO. SP 0001   EFFECTIVE DATE 10 / 1 / 07   "X" If Supplemental
                                                       Declarations Is Attached

NAMED INSURED

AMR Corporation

DESCRIPTION OF PREMISES

Prem. No.	Bldg. No.	Location, Construction And Occupancy
001	001	2000 Industrial Highway, Workingtown, PA 19000
		Joisted Masonry
		Storm Door Manufacturing

COVERAGES PROVIDED — Insurance At The Described Premises Applies Only For Coverages For Which A Limit Of Insurance Is Shown

Prem. No.	Bldg. No.	Coverage	Limit Of Insurance	Covered Causes Of Loss	Coinsurance*	Rates
001	001	Building	600,000	Special	80%	(See Schedule)
		Personal Prop. of Others	1,120,000	Special	80%	
		Your Business Personal Prop.	50,000	Special	80%	
		Business Income w/o	680,000	Special	80%	
		Extra Expense	*If Extra Expense Coverage, Limits On Loss Payment			

OPTIONAL COVERAGES — Applicable Only When Entries Are Made In The Schedule Below

Prem. No.	Bldg. No.	Agreed Value Expiration Date	Cov.	Amount	Replacement Cost (X) Building	Pers. Prop.	Including "Stock"
001	001				X		

	Inflation Guard (%) Bldg.	Pers. Prop.	*Monthly Limit Of Indemnity (Fraction)	Maximum Period Of Indemnity (X)	*Extended Period Of Indemnity (Days)
	3%	3%			

*Applies to Business Income Only

MORTGAGEHOLDERS

Prem. No.	Bldg. No.	Mortgageholder Name And Mailing Address
001	001	Workingtown Federal Savings and Loan Assn. P.O. Box 100 Workingtown, PA 19000

DEDUCTIBLE

$1,000

FORMS APPLICABLE

CP 00 10, CP 00 32, CP 00 90, CP 10 30

Prem. No.	Bldg. No.	Coverages	Form Number

CP DS 00 10 00   Copyright, Insurance Services Office, Inc., 1999   Page 1 of 1

COMMERCIAL PROPERTY

COMMERCIAL PROPERTY CONDITIONS

This Coverage Part is subject to the following conditions, the Common Policy Conditions and applicable Loss Conditions and Additional Conditions in Commercial Property Coverage Forms.

A. CONCEALMENT, MISREPRESENTATION OR FRAUD

This Coverage Part is void in any case of fraud by you as it relates to this Coverage Part at any time. It is also void if you or any other insured, at any time, intentionally conceal or misrepresent a material fact concerning:

1. This Coverage Part;
2. The Covered Property;
3. Your interest in the Covered Property; or
4. A claim under this Coverage Part.

B. CONTROL OF PROPERTY

Any act or neglect of any person other than you beyond your direction or control will not affect this insurance.

The breach of any condition of this Coverage Part at any one or more locations will not affect coverage at any location where, at the time of loss or damage, the breach of condition does not exist.

C. INSURANCE UNDER TWO OR MORE COVERAGES

If two or more of this policy's coverages apply to the same loss or damage, we will not pay more than the actual amount of the loss or damage.

D. LEGAL ACTION AGAINST US

No one may bring a legal action against us under this Coverage Part unless:

1. There has been full compliance with all of the terms of this Coverage Part; and
2. The action is brought within 2 years after the date on which the direct physical loss or damage occurred.

E. LIBERALIZATION

If we adopt any revision that would broaden the coverage under this Coverage Part without additional premium within 45 days prior to or during the policy period, the broadened coverage will immediately apply to this Coverage Part.

F. NO BENEFIT TO BAILEE

No person or organization, other than you, having custody of Covered Property will benefit from this insurance.

G. OTHER INSURANCE

1. You may have other insurance subject to the same plan, terms, conditions and provisions as the insurance under this Coverage Part. If you do, we will pay our share of the covered loss or damage. Our share is the proportion that the applicable Limit of Insurance under this Coverage Part bears to the Limits of Insurance of all insurance covering on the same basis.
2. If there is other insurance covering the same loss or damage, other than that described in 1. above, we will pay only for the amount of covered loss or damage in excess of the amount due from that other insurance, whether you can collect on it or not. But we will not pay more than the applicable Limit of Insurance.

H. POLICY PERIOD, COVERAGE TERRITORY

Under this Coverage Part:

1. We cover loss or damage commencing:
   a. During the policy period shown in the Declarations; and
   b. Within the coverage territory.
2. The coverage territory is:
   a. The United States of America (including its territories and possessions);
   b. Puerto Rico; and
   c. Canada.

CP 00 90 07 88   Copyright, ISO Commercial Risk Services, Inc., 1983, 1987

Appendix 11

I. TRANSFER OF RIGHTS OF RECOVERY AGAINST OTHERS TO US

If any person or organization to or for whom we make payment under this Coverage Part has rights to recover damages from another, those rights are transferred to us to the extent of our payment. That person or organization must do everything necessary to secure our rights and must do nothing after loss to impair them. But you may waive your rights against another party in writing:

1. Prior to a loss to your Covered Property or Covered Income.
2. After a loss to your Covered Property or Covered Income only if, at time of loss, that party is one of the following:
   a. Someone insured by this insurance;
   b. A business firm:
      (1) Owned or controlled by you; or
      (2) That owns or controls you; or
   c. Your tenant.

This will not restrict your insurance.

COMMERCIAL PROPERTY
CP 00 10 04 02

BUILDING AND PERSONAL PROPERTY COVERAGE FORM

Various provisions in this policy restrict coverage. Read the entire policy carefully to determine rights, duties and what is and is not covered.

Throughout this policy the words "you" and "your" refer to the Named Insured shown in the Declarations. The words "we", "us" and "our" refer to the Company providing this insurance.

Other words and phrases that appear in quotation marks have special meaning. Refer to Section **H. – Definitions.**

A. Coverage

We will pay for direct physical loss of or damage to Covered Property at the premises described in the Declarations caused by or resulting from any Covered Cause of Loss.

1. Covered Property

Covered Property, as used in this Coverage Part, means the type of property described in this Section, **A.1.**, and limited in **A.2.**, Property Not Covered, if a Limit of Insurance is shown in the Declarations for that type of property.

  a. Building, meaning the building or structure described in the Declarations, including:

  (1) Completed additions;

  (2) Fixtures, including outdoor fixtures;

  (3) Permanently installed:

   (a) Machinery and

   (b) Equipment;

  (4) Personal property owned by you that is used to maintain or service the building or structure or its premises, including:

   (a) Fire extinguishing equipment;

   (b) Outdoor furniture;

   (c) Floor coverings; and

   (d) Appliances used for refrigerating, ventilating, cooking, dishwashing or laundering;

  (5) If not covered by other insurance:

   (a) Additions under construction, alterations and repairs to the building or structure;

   (b) Materials, equipment, supplies and temporary structures, on or within 100 feet of the described premises, used for making additions, alterations or repairs to the building or structure.

  b. Your Business Personal Property located in or on the building described in the Declarations or in the open (or in a vehicle) within 100 feet of the described premises, consisting of the following unless otherwise specified in the Declarations or on the Your Business Personal Property – Separation of Coverage form:

  (1) Furniture and fixtures;

  (2) Machinery and equipment;

  (3) "Stock";

  (4) All other personal property owned by you and used in your business;

  (5) Labor, materials or services furnished or arranged by you on personal property of others;

  (6) Your use interest as tenant in improvements and betterments. Improvements and betterments are fixtures, alterations, installations or additions:

   (a) Made a part of the building or structure you occupy but do not own; and

   (b) You acquired or made at your expense but cannot legally remove;

  (7) Leased personal property for which you have a contractual responsibility to insure, unless otherwise provided for under Personal Property of Others.

c. **Personal Property Of Others** that is:
      (1) In your care, custody or control; and
      (2) Located in or on the building described in the Declarations or in the open (or in a vehicle) within 100 feet of the described premises.

      However, our payment for loss of or damage to personal property of others will only be for the account of the owner of the property.

2. **Property Not Covered**

   Covered Property does not include:
   a. Accounts, bills, currency, food stamps or other evidences of debt, money, notes or securities. Lottery tickets held for sale are not securities;
   b. Animals, unless owned by others and boarded by you, or if owned by you, only as "stock" while inside of buildings;
   c. Automobiles held for sale;
   d. Bridges, roadways, walks, patios or other paved surfaces;
   e. Contraband, or property in the course of illegal transportation or trade;
   f. The cost of excavations, grading, backfilling or filling;
   g. Foundations of buildings, structures, machinery or boilers if their foundations are below:
      (1) The lowest basement floor; or
      (2) The surface of the ground, if there is no basement;
   h. Land (including land on which the property is located), water, growing crops or lawns;
   i. Personal property while airborne or waterborne;
   j. Bulkheads, pilings, piers, wharves or docks;
   k. Property that is covered under another coverage form of this or any other policy in which it is more specifically described, except for the excess of the amount due (whether you can collect on it or not) from that other insurance;
   l. Retaining walls that are not part of a building;
   m. Underground pipes, flues or drains;
   n. Electronic data, except as provided under Additional Coverages – Electronic Data. Electronic data means information, facts or computer programs stored as or on, created or used on, or transmitted to or from computer software (including systems and applications software), on hard or floppy disks, CD-ROMs, tapes, drives, cells, data processing devices or any other repositories of computer software which are used with electronically controlled equipment. The term computer programs, referred to in the foregoing description of electronic data, means a set of related electronic instructions which direct the operations and functions of a computer or device connected to it, which enable the computer or device to receive, process, store, retrieve or send data. This Paragraph **n.**, does not apply to your "stock" of prepackaged software.
   o. The cost to replace or restore the information on valuable papers and records, including those which exist as electronic data. Valuable papers and records include but are not limited to proprietary information, books of account, deeds, manuscripts, abstracts, drawings and card index systems. Refer to the Coverage Extension for Valuable Papers And Records (Other Than Electronic Data) for limited coverage for valuable papers and records other than those which exist as electronic data.
   p. Vehicles or self-propelled machines (including aircraft or watercraft) that:
      (1) Are licensed for use on public roads; or
      (2) Are operated principally away from the described premises.

      This paragraph does not apply to:
      (a) Vehicles or self-propelled machines or autos you manufacture, process or warehouse;
      (b) Vehicles or self-propelled machines, other than autos, you hold for sale;
      (c) Rowboats or canoes out of water at the described premises; or
      (d) Trailers, but only to the extent provided for in the Coverage Extension for Non-Owned Detached Trailers.

q. The following property while outside of buildings:

(1) Grain, hay, straw or other crops;

(2) Fences, radio or television antennas (including satellite dishes) and their lead-in wiring, masts or towers, signs (other than signs attached to buildings), trees, shrubs or plants (other than "stock" of trees, shrubs or plants), all except as provided in the Coverage Extensions.

3. **Covered Causes Of Loss**

   See applicable Causes of Loss Form as shown in the Declarations.

4. **Additional Coverages**

   a. **Debris Removal**

   (1) Subject to Paragraphs (3) and (4), we will pay your expense to remove debris of Covered Property caused by or resulting from a Covered Cause of Loss that occurs during the policy period. The expenses will be paid only if they are reported to us in writing within 180 days of the date of direct physical loss or damage.

   (2) Debris Removal does not apply to costs to:

   (a) Extract "pollutants" from land or water; or

   (b) Remove, restore or replace polluted land or water.

   (3) Subject to the exceptions in Paragraph (4), the following provisions apply:

   (a) The most we will pay for the total of direct physical loss or damage plus debris removal expense is the Limit of Insurance applicable to the Covered Property that has sustained loss or damage.

   (b) Subject to (a) above, the amount we will pay for debris removal expense is limited to 25% of the sum of the deductible plus the amount that we pay for direct physical loss or damage to the Covered Property that has sustained loss or damage.

   (4) We will pay up to an additional $10,000 for debris removal expense, for each location, in any one occurrence of physical loss or damage to Covered Property, if one or both of the following circumstances apply:

   (a) The total of the actual debris removal expense plus the amount we pay for direct physical loss or damage exceeds the Limit of Insurance on the Covered Property that has sustained loss or damage.

   (b) The actual debris removal expense exceeds 25% of the sum of the deductible plus the amount that we pay for direct physical loss or damage to the Covered Property that has sustained loss or damage.

   Therefore, if (4)(a) and/or (4)(b) apply, our total payment for direct physical loss or damage and debris removal expense may reach but will never exceed the Limit of Insurance on the Covered Property that has sustained loss or damage, plus $10,000.

   (5) Examples

   The following examples assume that there is no coinsurance penalty.

   Example #1

Limit of Insurance	$ 90,000
Amount of Deductible	$ 500
Amount of Loss	$ 50,000
Amount of Loss Payable	$ 49,500
	($50,000 - $500)
Debris Removal Expense	$ 10,000
Debris Removal Expense Payable	$ 10,000
($10,000 is 20% of $50,000)	

   The debris removal expense is less than 25% of the sum of the loss payable plus the deductible. The sum of the loss payable and the debris removal expense ($49,500 + $10,000 = $59,500) is less than the Limit of Insurance. Therefore the full amount of debris removal expense is payable in accordance with the terms of Paragraph (3).

Example #2

Limit of Insurance	$ 90,000
Amount of Deductible	$ 500
Amount of Loss	$ 80,000
Amount of Loss Payable	$ 79,500
	($80,000 - $500)
Debris Removal Expense	$ 30,000
Debris Removal Expense Payable	
Basic Amount	$ 10,500
Additional Amount	$ 10,000

The basic amount payable for debris removal expense under the terms of Paragraph **(3)** is calculated as follows: $80,000 ($79,500 + $500) x .25 = $20,000; capped at $10,500. The cap applies because the sum of the loss payable ($79,500) and the basic amount payable for debris removal expense ($10,500) cannot exceed the Limit of Insurance ($90,000).

The additional amount payable for debris removal expense is provided in accordance with the terms of Paragraph **(4)**, because the debris removal expense ($30,000) exceeds 25% of the loss payable plus the deductible ($30,000 is 37.5% of $80,000), and because the sum of the loss payable and debris removal expense ($79,500 + $30,000 = $109,500) would exceed the Limit of Insurance ($90,000). The additional amount of covered debris removal expense is $10,000, the maximum payable under Paragraph **(4)**. Thus the total payable for debris removal expense in this example is $20,500; $9,500 of the debris removal expense is not covered.

b. Preservation Of Property

If it is necessary to move Covered Property from the described premises to preserve it from loss or damage by a Covered Cause of Loss, we will pay for any direct physical loss or damage to that property:

(1) While it is being moved or while temporarily stored at another location; and

(2) Only if the loss or damage occurs within 30 days after the property is first moved.

c. Fire Department Service Charge

When the fire department is called to save or protect Covered Property from a Covered Cause of Loss, we will pay up to $1,000 for your liability for fire department service charges:

(1) Assumed by contract or agreement prior to loss; or

(2) Required by local ordinance.

No Deductible applies to this Additional Coverage.

d. Pollutant Clean Up And Removal

We will pay your expense to extract "pollutants" from land or water at the described premises if the discharge, dispersal, seepage, migration, release or escape of the "pollutants" is caused by or results from a Covered Cause of Loss that occurs during the policy period. The expenses will be paid only if they are reported to us in writing within 180 days of the date on which the Covered Cause of Loss occurs.

This Additional Coverage does not apply to costs to test for, monitor or assess the existence, concentration or effects of "pollutants". But we will pay for testing which is performed in the course of extracting the "pollutants" from the land or water.

The most we will pay under this Additional Coverage for each described premises is $10,000 for the sum of all covered expenses arising out of Covered Causes of Loss occurring during each separate 12 month period of this policy.

e. Increased Cost Of Construction

(1) This Additional Coverage applies only to buildings to which the Replacement Cost Optional Coverage applies.

(2) In the event of damage by a Covered Cause of Loss to a building that is Covered Property, we will pay the increased costs incurred to comply with enforcement of an ordinance or law in the course of repair, rebuilding or replacement of damaged parts of that property, subject to the limitations stated in **e.(3)** through **e.(9)** of this Additional Coverage.

(3) The ordinance or law referred to in **e.(2)** of this Additional Coverage is an ordinance or law that regulates the construction or repair of buildings or establishes zoning or land use requirements at the described premises, and is in force at the time of loss.

(4) Under this Additional Coverage, we will not pay any costs due to an ordinance or law that:

   (a) You were required to comply with before the loss, even when the building was undamaged; and

   (b) You failed to comply with.

(5) Under this Additional Coverage, we will not pay for:

   (a) The enforcement of any ordinance or law which requires demolition, repair, replacement, reconstruction, remodeling or remediation of property due to contamination by "pollutants" or due to the presence, growth, proliferation, spread or any activity of "fungus", wet or dry rot or bacteria; or

   (b) Any costs associated with the enforcement of an ordinance or law which requires any insured or others to test for, monitor, clean up, remove, contain, treat, detoxify or neutralize, or in any way respond to, or assess the effects of "pollutants", "fungus", wet or dry rot or bacteria.

(6) The most we will pay under this Additional Coverage, for each described building insured under this Coverage Form, is $10,000 or 5% of the Limit of Insurance applicable to that building, whichever is less. If a damaged building is covered under a blanket Limit of Insurance which applies to more than one building or item of property, then the most we will pay under this Additional Coverage, for that damaged building, is the lesser of: $10,000 or 5% times the value of the damaged building as of the time of loss times the applicable coinsurance percentage.

The amount payable under this Additional Coverage is additional insurance.

(7) With respect to this Additional Coverage:

   (a) We will not pay for the Increased Cost of Construction:

      (i) Until the property is actually repaired or replaced, at the same or another premises; and

      (ii) Unless the repairs or replacement are made as soon as reasonably possible after the loss or damage, not to exceed two years. We may extend this period in writing during the two years.

   (b) If the building is repaired or replaced at the same premises, or if you elect to rebuild at another premises, the most we will pay for the Increased Cost of Construction, subject to the provisions of **e.(6)** of this Additional Coverage, is the increased cost of construction at the same premises.

   (c) If the ordinance or law requires relocation to another premises, the most we will pay for the Increased Cost of Construction, subject to the provisions of **e.(6)** of this Additional Coverage, is the increased cost of construction at the new premises.

(8) This Additional Coverage is not subject to the terms of the Ordinance or Law Exclusion, to the extent that such Exclusion would conflict with the provisions of this Additional Coverage.

(9) The costs addressed in the Loss Payment and Valuation Conditions, and the Replacement Cost Optional Coverage, in this Coverage Form, do not include the increased cost attributable to enforcement of an ordinance or law. The amount payable under this Additional Coverage, as stated in **e.(6)** of this Additional Coverage, is not subject to such limitation.

f. Electronic Data

(1) Under this Additional Coverage, electronic data has the meaning described under Property Not Covered – Electronic Data.

(2) Subject to the provisions of this Additional Coverage, we will pay for the cost to replace or restore electronic data which has been destroyed or corrupted by a Covered Cause of Loss. To the extent that electronic data is not replaced or restored, the loss will be valued at the cost of replacement of the media on which the electronic data was stored, with blank media of substantially identical type.

(3) The Covered Causes of Loss applicable to Your Business Personal Property apply to this Additional Coverage – Electronic Data, subject to the following:

(a) If the Causes Of Loss – Special Form applies, coverage under this Additional Coverage – Electronic Data is limited to the "specified causes of loss" as defined in that form, and Collapse as set forth in that form.

(b) If the Causes Of Loss – Broad Form applies, coverage under this Additional Coverage – Electronic Data includes Collapse as set forth in that form.

(c) If the Causes Of Loss Form is endorsed to add a Covered Cause of Loss, the additional Covered Cause of Loss does not apply to the coverage provided under this Additional Coverage – Electronic Data.

(d) The Covered Causes of Loss include a virus, harmful code or similar instruction introduced into or enacted on a computer system (including electronic data) or a network to which it is connected, designed to damage or destroy any part of the system or disrupt its normal operation. But there is no coverage for loss or damage caused by or resulting from manipulation of a computer system (including electronic data) by any employee, including a temporary or leased employee, or by an entity retained by you or for you to inspect, design, install, modify, maintain, repair or replace that system.

(4) The most we will pay under this Additional Coverage – Electronic Data is $2,500 for all loss or damage sustained in any one policy year, regardless of the number of occurrences of loss or damage or the number of premises, locations or computer systems involved. If loss payment on the first occurrence does not exhaust this amount, then the balance is available for subsequent loss or damage sustained in but not after that policy year. With respect to an occurrence which begins in one policy year and continues or results in additional loss or damage in a subsequent policy year(s), all loss or damage is deemed to be sustained in the policy year in which the occurrence began.

5. **Coverage Extensions**

    Except as otherwise provided, the following Extensions apply to property located in or on the building described in the Declarations or in the open (or in a vehicle) within 100 feet of the described premises.

    If a Coinsurance percentage of 80% or more or, a Value Reporting period symbol, is shown in the Declarations, you may extend the insurance provided by this Coverage Part as follows:

    a. **Newly Acquired Or Constructed Property**

        (1) **Buildings**

            If this policy covers Building, you may extend that insurance to apply to:

            (a) Your new buildings while being built on the described premises; and

            (b) Buildings you acquire at locations, other than the described premises, intended for:

                (i) Similar use as the building described in the Declarations; or

                (ii) Use as a warehouse.

            The most we will pay for loss or damage under this Extension is $250,000 at each building.

        (2) **Your Business Personal Property**

            (a) If this policy covers Your Business Personal Property, you may extend that insurance to apply to:

                (i) Business personal property, including such property that you newly acquire, at any location you acquire other than at fairs, trade shows or exhibitions;

                (ii) Business personal property, including such property that you newly acquire, located at your newly constructed or acquired buildings at the location described in the Declarations; or

                (iii) Business personal property that you newly acquire, located at the described premises.

            The most we will pay for loss or damage under this Extension is $100,000 at each building.

            (b) This Extension does not apply to:

                (i) Personal property of others that is temporarily in your possession in the course of installing or performing work on such property; or

(ii) Personal property of others that is temporarily in your possession in the course of your manufacturing or wholesaling activities.

(3) Period Of Coverage

With respect to insurance on or at each newly acquired or constructed property, coverage will end when any of the following first occurs:

(a) This policy expires;

(b) 30 days expire after you acquire the property or begin construction of that part of the building that would qualify as covered property; or

(c) You report values to us.

We will charge you additional premium for values reported from the date you acquire the property or begin construction of that part of the building that would qualify as covered property.

b. Personal Effects And Property Of Others

You may extend the insurance that applies to Your Business Personal Property to apply to:

(1) Personal effects owned by you, your officers, your partners or members, your managers or your employees. This extension does not apply to loss or damage by theft.

(2) Personal property of others in your care, custody or control.

The most we will pay for loss or damage under this Extension is $2,500 at each described premises. Our payment for loss of or damage to personal property of others will only be for the account of the owner of the property.

c. Valuable Papers And Records (Other Than Electronic Data)

(1) You may extend the insurance that applies to Your Business Personal Property to apply to the cost to replace or restore the lost information on valuable papers and records for which duplicates do not exist. But this Extension does not apply to valuable papers and records which exist as electronic data. Electronic data has the meaning described under Property Not Covered – Electronic Data.

(2) If the Causes Of Loss – Special Form applies, coverage under this Extension is limited to the "specified causes of loss" as defined in that form, and Collapse as set forth in that form.

(3) If the Causes Of Loss – Broad Form applies, coverage under this Extension includes Collapse as set forth in that form.

(4) Under this Extension, the most we will pay to replace or restore the lost information is $2,500 at each described premises, unless a higher limit is shown in the Declarations. Such amount is additional insurance. We will also pay for the cost of blank material for reproducing the records (whether or not duplicates exist), and (when there is a duplicate) for the cost of labor to transcribe or copy the records. The costs of blank material and labor are subject to the applicable Limit of Insurance on Your Business Personal Property and therefore coverage of such costs is not additional insurance.

d. Property Off-Premises

(1) You may extend the insurance provided by this Coverage Form to apply to your Covered Property while it is away from the described premises, if it is:

(a) Temporarily at a location you do not own, lease or operate;

(b) In storage at a location you lease, provided the lease was executed after the beginning of the current policy term; or

(c) At any fair, trade show or exhibition.

(2) This Extension does not apply to property:

(a) In or on a vehicle; or

(b) In the care, custody or control of your salespersons, unless the property is in such care, custody or control at a fair, trade show or exhibition.

(3) The most we will pay for loss or damage under this Extension is $10,000.

e. Outdoor Property

You may extend the insurance provided by this Coverage Form to apply to your outdoor fences, radio and television antennas (including satellite dishes), signs (other than signs attached to buildings), trees, shrubs and plants (other than "stock" of trees, shrubs or plants), including debris removal expense, caused by or resulting from any of the following causes of loss if they are Covered Causes of Loss:

(1) Fire;

(2) Lightning;

(3) Explosion;

(4) Riot or Civil Commotion; or

(5) Aircraft.

The most we will pay for loss or damage under this Extension is $1,000, but not more than $250 for any one tree, shrub or plant. These limits apply to any one occurrence, regardless of the types or number of items lost or damaged in that occurrence.

f. Non-Owned Detached Trailers

(1) You may extend the insurance that applies to Your Business Personal Property to apply to loss or damage to trailers that you do not own, provided that:

(a) The trailer is used in your business;

(b) The trailer is in your care, custody or control at the premises described in the Declarations; and

(c) You have a contractual responsibility to pay for loss or damage to the trailer.

(2) We will not pay for any loss or damage that occurs:

(a) While the trailer is attached to any motor vehicle or motorized conveyance, whether or not the motor vehicle or motorized conveyance is in motion;

(b) During hitching or unhitching operations, or when a trailer becomes accidentally unhitched from a motor vehicle or motorized conveyance.

(3) The most we will pay for loss or damage under this Extension is $5,000, unless a higher limit is shown in the Declarations.

(4) This insurance is excess over the amount due (whether you can collect on it or not) from any other insurance covering such property.

Each of these Extensions is additional insurance unless otherwise indicated. The Additional Condition, Coinsurance, does not apply to these Extensions.

B. Exclusions And Limitations

See applicable Causes of Loss Form as shown in the Declarations.

C. Limits Of Insurance

The most we will pay for loss or damage in any one occurrence is the applicable Limit of Insurance shown in the Declarations.

The most we will pay for loss or damage to outdoor signs attached to buildings is $1,000 per sign in any one occurrence.

The limits applicable to the Fire Department Service Charge and Pollutant Clean Up and Removal Additional Coverages are in addition to the Limits of Insurance.

Payments under the Preservation of Property Additional Coverage will not increase the applicable Limit of Insurance.

D. Deductible

In any one occurrence of loss or damage (hereinafter referred to as loss), we will first reduce the amount of loss if required by the Coinsurance Condition or the Agreed Value Optional Coverage. If the adjusted amount of loss is less than or equal to the Deductible, we will not pay for that loss. If the adjusted amount of loss exceeds the Deductible, we will then subtract the Deductible from the adjusted amount of loss, and will pay the resulting amount or the Limit of Insurance, whichever is less.

When the occurrence involves loss to more than one item of Covered Property and separate Limits of Insurance apply, the losses will not be combined in determining application of the Deductible. But the Deductible will be applied only once per occurrence.

Example No. 1:

(This example assumes there is no coinsurance penalty.)

Deductible:	$ 250
Limit of Insurance – Bldg. 1:	$ 60,000
Limit of Insurance – Bldg. 2:	$ 80,000
Loss to Bldg. 1:	$ 60,100
Loss to Bldg. 2:	$ 90,000

The amount of loss to Bldg. 1 ($60,100) is less than the sum ($60,250) of the Limit of Insurance applicable to Bldg. 1 plus the Deductible.

The Deductible will be subtracted from the amount of loss in calculating the loss payable for Bldg. 1:

$ 60,100
− 250
$ 59,850 Loss Payable – Bldg. 1

The Deductible applies once per occurrence and therefore is not subtracted in determining the amount of loss payable for Bldg. 2. Loss payable for Bldg. 2 is the Limit of Insurance of $80,000.

Total amount of loss payable: $59,850 + 80,000 = $139,850

Example No. 2:

(This example, too, assumes there is no coinsurance penalty.)

The Deductible and Limits of Insurance are the same as those in Example No. 1.

Loss to Bldg. 1: $ 70,000
  (exceeds Limit of Insurance plus Deductible)
Loss to Bldg. 2: $ 90,000
  (exceeds Limit of Insurance plus Deductible)
Loss Payable – Bldg. 1: $60,000
  (Limit of Insurance)
Loss Payable – Bldg. 2: $80,000
  (Limit of Insurance)
Total amount of loss payable:
        $140,000

E. Loss Conditions

The following conditions apply in addition to the Common Policy Conditions and the Commercial Property Conditions.

1. Abandonment

There can be no abandonment of any property to us.

2. Appraisal

If we and you disagree on the value of the property or the amount of loss, either may make written demand for an appraisal of the loss. In this event, each party will select a competent and impartial appraiser. The two appraisers will select an umpire. If they cannot agree, either may request that selection be made by a judge of a court having jurisdiction. The appraisers will state separately the value of the property and amount of loss. If they fail to agree, they will submit their differences to the umpire. A decision agreed to by any two will be binding. Each party will:

a. Pay its chosen appraiser; and

b. Bear the other expenses of the appraisal and umpire equally.

If there is an appraisal, we will still retain our right to deny the claim.

3. Duties In The Event Of Loss Or Damage

a. You must see that the following are done in the event of loss or damage to Covered Property:

(1) Notify the police if a law may have been broken.

(2) Give us prompt notice of the loss or damage. Include a description of the property involved.

(3) As soon as possible, give us a description of how, when and where the loss or damage occurred.

(4) Take all reasonable steps to protect the Covered Property from further damage, and keep a record of your expenses necessary to protect the Covered Property, for consideration in the settlement of the claim. This will not increase the Limit of Insurance. However, we will not pay for any subsequent loss or damage resulting from a cause of loss that is not a Covered Cause of Loss. Also, if feasible, set the damaged property aside and in the best possible order for examination.

(5) At our request, give us complete inventories of the damaged and undamaged property. Include quantities, costs, values and amount of loss claimed.

(6) As often as may be reasonably required, permit us to inspect the property proving the loss or damage and examine your books and records.

Also permit us to take samples of damaged and undamaged property for inspection, testing and analysis, and permit us to make copies from your books and records.

(7) Send us a signed, sworn proof of loss containing the information we request to investigate the claim. You must do this within 60 days after our request. We will supply you with the necessary forms.

(8) Cooperate with us in the investigation or settlement of the claim.

b. We may examine any insured under oath, while not in the presence of any other insured and at such times as may be reasonably required, about any matter relating to this insurance or the claim, including an insured's books and records. In the event of an examination, an insured's answers must be signed.

4. Loss Payment

a. In the event of loss or damage covered by this Coverage Form, at our option, we will either:

(1) Pay the value of lost or damaged property;

(2) Pay the cost of repairing or replacing the lost or damaged property, subject to **b.** below;

(3) Take all or any part of the property at an agreed or appraised value; or

(4) Repair, rebuild or replace the property with other property of like kind and quality, subject to **b.** below.

We will determine the value of lost or damaged property, or the cost of its repair or replacement, in accordance with the applicable terms of the Valuation Condition in this Coverage Form or any applicable provision which amends or supersedes the Valuation Condition.

b. The cost to repair, rebuild or replace does not include the increased cost attributable to enforcement of any ordinance or law regulating the construction, use or repair of any property.

c. We will give notice of our intentions within 30 days after we receive the sworn proof of loss.

d. We will not pay you more than your financial interest in the Covered Property.

e. We may adjust losses with the owners of lost or damaged property if other than you. If we pay the owners, such payments will satisfy your claims against us for the owners' property. We will not pay the owners more than their financial interest in the Covered Property.

f. We may elect to defend you against suits arising from claims of owners of property. We will do this at our expense.

g. We will pay for covered loss or damage within 30 days after we receive the sworn proof of loss, if you have complied with all of the terms of this Coverage Part and:

(1) We have reached agreement with you on the amount of loss; or

(2) An appraisal award has been made.

5. Recovered Property

If either you or we recover any property after loss settlement, that party must give the other prompt notice. At your option, the property will be returned to you. You must then return to us the amount we paid to you for the property. We will pay recovery expenses and the expenses to repair the recovered property, subject to the Limit of Insurance.

6. Vacancy

a. **Description Of Terms**

(1) As used in this Vacancy Condition, the term building and the term vacant have the meanings set forth in **(1)(a)** and **(1)(b)** below:

(a) When this policy is issued to a tenant, and with respect to that tenant's interest in Covered Property, building means the unit or suite rented or leased to the tenant. Such building is vacant when it does not contain enough business personal property to conduct customary operations.

(b) When this policy is issued to the owner or general lessee of a building, building means the entire building. Such building is vacant unless at least 31% of its total square footage is:

(i) Rented to a lessee or sub-lessee and used by the lessee or sub-lessee to conduct its customary operations; and/or

(ii) Used by the building owner to conduct customary operations.

(2) Buildings under construction or renovation are not considered vacant.

b. **Vacancy Provisions**

If the building where loss or damage occurs has been vacant for more than 60 consecutive days before that loss or damage occurs:

(1) We will not pay for any loss or damage caused by any of the following even if they are Covered Causes of Loss:

(a) Vandalism;

(b) Sprinkler leakage, unless you have protected the system against freezing;

(c) Building glass breakage;

(d) Water damage;

(e) Theft; or

(f) Attempted theft.

(2) With respect to Covered Causes of Loss other than those listed in **b.(1)(a)** through **b.(1)(f)** above, we will reduce the amount we would otherwise pay for the loss or damage by 15%.

7. **Valuation**

We will determine the value of Covered Property in the event of loss or damage as follows:

a. At actual cash value as of the time of loss or damage, except as provided in **b., c., d.** and **e.** below.

b. If the Limit of Insurance for Building satisfies the Additional Condition, Coinsurance, and the cost to repair or replace the damaged building property is $2,500 or less, we will pay the cost of building repairs or replacement.

The cost of building repairs or replacement does not include the increased cost attributable to enforcement of any ordinance or law regulating the construction, use or repair of any property. However, the following property will be valued at the actual cash value even when attached to the building:

(1) Awnings or floor coverings;

(2) Appliances for refrigerating, ventilating, cooking, dishwashing or laundering; or

(3) Outdoor equipment or furniture.

c. "Stock" you have sold but not delivered at the selling price less discounts and expenses you otherwise would have had.

d. Glass at the cost of replacement with safety glazing material if required by law.

e. Tenant's Improvements and Betterments at:

(1) Actual cash value of the lost or damaged property if you make repairs promptly.

(2) A proportion of your original cost if you do not make repairs promptly. We will determine the proportionate value as follows:

(a) Multiply the original cost by the number of days from the loss or damage to the expiration of the lease; and

(b) Divide the amount determined in **(a)** above by the number of days from the installation of improvements to the expiration of the lease.

If your lease contains a renewal option, the expiration of the renewal option period will replace the expiration of the lease in this procedure.

(3) Nothing if others pay for repairs or replacement.

F. **Additional Conditions**

The following conditions apply in addition to the Common Policy Conditions and the Commercial Property Conditions.

1. **Coinsurance**

If a Coinsurance percentage is shown in the Declarations, the following condition applies.

a. We will not pay the full amount of any loss if the value of Covered Property at the time of loss times the Coinsurance percentage shown for it in the Declarations is greater than the Limit of Insurance for the property.

Instead, we will determine the most we will pay using the following steps:

(1) Multiply the value of Covered Property at the time of loss by the Coinsurance percentage;

(2) Divide the Limit of Insurance of the property by the figure determined in Step (1);

(3) Multiply the total amount of loss, before the application of any deductible, by the figure determined in Step **(2)**; and

(4) Subtract the deductible from the figure determined in Step **(3)**.

We will pay the amount determined in Step **(4)** or the limit of insurance, whichever is less. For the remainder, you will either have to rely on other insurance or absorb the loss yourself.

Example No. 1 (Underinsurance):

When:
The value of the property is	$	250,000
The Coinsurance percentage for it is		80%
The Limit of Insurance for it is	$	100,000
The Deductible is	$	250
The amount of loss is	$	40,000

Step **(1):** $250,000 x 80% = $200,000 (the minimum amount of insurance to meet your Coinsurance requirements)

Step **(2):** $100,000 ÷ $200,000 = .50

Step **(3):** $40,000 x .50 = $20,000

Step **(4):** $20,000 – $250 = $19,750

We will pay no more than $19,750. The remaining $20,250 is not covered.

Example No. 2 (Adequate Insurance):

When:
The value of the property is	$	250,000
The Coinsurance percentage for it is		80%
The Limit of Insurance for it is	$	200,000
The Deductible is	$	250
The amount of loss is	$	40,000

The minimum amount of insurance to meet your Coinsurance requirement is $200,000 ($250,000 x 80%). Therefore, the Limit of Insurance in this Example is adequate and no penalty applies. We will pay no more than $39,750 ($40,000 amount of loss minus the deductible of $250).

b. If one Limit of Insurance applies to two or more separate items, this condition will apply to the total of all property to which the limit applies.

Example No. 3:

When:
The value of property is:		
Bldg. at Location No. 1	$	75,000
Bldg. at Location No. 2	$	100,000
Personal Property at Location No. 2	$	75,000
	$	250,000
The Coinsurance percentage for it is		90%
The Limit of Insurance for Buildings and Personal Property at Location Nos. 1 and 2 is	$	180,000
The Deductible is	$	1,000
The amount of loss is:		
Bldg. at Location No. 2	$	30,000
Personal Property at Location No. 2.	$	20,000
	$	50,000

Step **(1):** $250,000 x 90% = $225,000 (the minimum amount of insurance to meet your Coinsurance requirements and to avoid the penalty shown below)

Step **(2):** $180,000 ÷ $225,000 = .80

Step **(3):** $50,000 x .80 = $40,000

Step **(4):** $40,000 – $1,000 = $39,000

We will pay no more than $39,000. The remaining $11,000 is not covered.

2. Mortgageholders

a. The term mortgageholder includes trustee.

b. We will pay for covered loss of or damage to buildings or structures to each mortgageholder shown in the Declarations in their order of precedence, as interests may appear.

c. The mortgageholder has the right to receive loss payment even if the mortgageholder has started foreclosure or similar action on the building or structure.

d. If we deny your claim because of your acts or because you have failed to comply with the terms of this Coverage Part, the mortgageholder will still have the right to receive loss payment if the mortgageholder:

(1) Pays any premium due under this Coverage Part at our request if you have failed to do so;

(2) Submits a signed, sworn proof of loss within 60 days after receiving notice from us of your failure to do so; and

(3) Has notified us of any change in ownership, occupancy or substantial change in risk known to the mortgageholder.

All of the terms of this Coverage Part will then apply directly to the mortgageholder.

e. If we pay the mortgageholder for any loss or damage and deny payment to you because of your acts or because you have failed to comply with the terms of this Coverage Part:

(1) The mortgageholder's rights under the mortgage will be transferred to us to the extent of the amount we pay; and

(2) The mortgageholder's right to recover the full amount of the mortgageholder's claim will not be impaired.

At our option, we may pay to the mortgageholder the whole principal on the mortgage plus any accrued interest. In this event, your mortgage and note will be transferred to us and you will pay your remaining mortgage debt to us.

f. If we cancel this policy, we will give written notice to the mortgageholder at least:

(1) 10 days before the effective date of cancellation if we cancel for your non-payment of premium; or

(2) 30 days before the effective date of cancellation if we cancel for any other reason.

g. If we elect not to renew this policy, we will give written notice to the mortgageholder at least 10 days before the expiration date of this policy.

G. Optional Coverages

If shown as applicable in the Declarations, the following Optional Coverages apply separately to each item.

1. Agreed Value

a. The Additional Condition, Coinsurance, does not apply to Covered Property to which this Optional Coverage applies. We will pay no more for loss of or damage to that property than the proportion that the Limit of Insurance under this Coverage Part for the property bears to the Agreed Value shown for it in the Declarations.

b. If the expiration date for this Optional Coverage shown in the Declarations is not extended, the Additional Condition, Coinsurance, is reinstated and this Optional Coverage expires.

c. The terms of this Optional Coverage apply only to loss or damage that occurs:

(1) On or after the effective date of this Optional Coverage; and

(2) Before the Agreed Value expiration date shown in the Declarations or the policy expiration date, whichever occurs first.

2. Inflation Guard

a. The Limit of Insurance for property to which this Optional Coverage applied will automatically increase by the annual percentage shown in the Declarations.

b. The amount of increase will be:

(1) The Limit of Insurance that applied on the most recent of the policy inception date, the policy anniversary date, or any other policy change amending the Limit of Insurance, times

(2) The percentage of annual increase shown in the Declarations, expressed as a decimal (example: 8% is .08), times

(3) The number of days since the beginning of the current policy year or the effective date of the most recent policy change amending the Limit of Insurance, divided by 365.

Example:

If:
The applicable Limit of Insurance is	$	100,000
The annual percentage increase is		8%
The number of days since the beginning of the policy year (or last policy change) is		146
The amount of increase is $100,000 x .08 x 146 ÷ 365 =	$	3,200

3. Replacement Cost

a. Replacement Cost (without deduction for depreciation) replaces Actual Cash Value in the Loss Condition, Valuation, of this Coverage Form.

b. This Optional Coverage does not apply to:

(1) Personal property of others;

(2) Contents of a residence;

- **(3)** Works of art, antiques or rare articles, including etchings, pictures, statuary, marbles, bronzes, porcelains and bric-a-brac; or
- **(4)** "Stock", unless the Including "Stock" option is shown in the Declarations.

Under the terms of this Replacement Cost Optional Coverage, tenants' improvements and betterments are not considered to be the personal property of others.

- **c.** You may make a claim for loss or damage covered by this insurance on an actual cash value basis instead of on a replacement cost basis. In the event you elect to have loss or damage settled on an actual cash value basis, you may still make a claim for the additional coverage this Optional Coverage provides if you notify us of your intent to do so within 180 days after the loss or damage.
- **d.** We will not pay on a replacement cost basis for any loss or damage:
  - **(1)** Until the lost or damaged property is actually repaired or replaced; and
  - **(2)** Unless the repairs or replacement are made as soon as reasonably possible after the loss or damage.

  With respect to tenants' improvements and betterments, the following also apply:
  - **(3)** If the conditions in **d.(1)** and **d.(2)** above are not met, the value of tenants' improvements and betterments will be determined as a proportion of your original cost, as set forth in the Valuation Condition of this Coverage Form; and
  - **(4)** We will not pay for loss or damage to tenants' improvements and betterments if others pay for repairs or replacement.
- **e.** We will not pay more for loss or damage on a replacement cost basis than the least of **(1)**, **(2)** or **(3)**, subject to **f.** below:
  - **(1)** The Limit of Insurance applicable to the lost or damaged property;
  - **(2)** The cost to replace the lost or damaged property with other property:
    - **(a)** Of comparable material and quality; and
    - **(b)** Used for the same purpose; or
  - **(3)** The amount actually spent that is necessary to repair or replace the lost or damaged property.

  If a building is rebuilt at a new premises, the cost described in **e.(2)** above is limited to the cost which would have been incurred if the building had been rebuilt at the original premises.
- **f.** The cost of repair or replacement does not include the increased cost attributable to enforcement of any ordinance or law regulating the construction, use or repair of any property.

4. Extension Of Replacement Cost To Personal Property Of Others

- **a.** If the Replacement Cost Optional Coverage is shown as applicable in the Declarations, then this Extension may also be shown as applicable. If the Declarations show this Extension as applicable, then Paragraph **3.b.(1)** of the Replacement Cost Optional Coverage is deleted and all other provisions of the Replacement Cost Optional Coverage apply to replacement cost on personal property of others.
- **b.** With respect to replacement cost on the personal property of others, the following limitation applies:

  If an item(s) of personal property of others is subject to a written contract which governs your liability for loss or damage to that item(s), then valuation of that item(s) will be based on the amount for which you are liable under such contract, but not to exceed the lesser of the replacement cost of the property or the applicable Limit of Insurance.

H. Definitions

1. "Fungus" means any type or form of fungus, including mold or mildew, and any mycotoxins, spores, scents or by-products produced or released by fungi.
2. "Pollutants" means any solid, liquid, gaseous or thermal irritant or contaminant, including smoke, vapor, soot, fumes, acids, alkalis, chemicals and waste. Waste includes materials to be recycled, reconditioned or reclaimed.
3. "Stock" means merchandise held in storage or for sale, raw materials and in-process or finished goods, including supplies used in their packing or shipping.

COMMERCIAL PROPERTY
CP 10 30 04 02

CAUSES OF LOSS – SPECIAL FORM

Words and phrases that appear in quotation marks have special meaning. Refer to Section **F.** – Definitions.

A. Covered Causes Of Loss

When Special is shown in the Declarations, Covered Causes of Loss means Risks Of Direct Physical Loss unless the loss is:

1. Excluded in Section **B.**, Exclusions; or
2. Limited in Section **C.**, Limitations;

that follow.

B. Exclusions

1. We will not pay for loss or damage caused directly or indirectly by any of the following. Such loss or damage is excluded regardless of any other cause or event that contributes concurrently or in any sequence to the loss.

    a. Ordinance Or Law

    The enforcement of any ordinance or law:

    (1) Regulating the construction, use or repair of any property; or

    (2) Requiring the tearing down of any property, including the cost of removing its debris.

    This exclusion, Ordinance Or Law, applies whether the loss results from:

    (1) An ordinance or law that is enforced even if the property has not been damaged; or

    (2) The increased costs incurred to comply with an ordinance or law in the course of construction, repair, renovation, remodeling or demolition of property, or removal of its debris, following a physical loss to that property.

    b. Earth Movement

    (1) Earthquake, including any earth sinking, rising or shifting related to such event;

    (2) Landslide, including any earth sinking, rising or shifting related to such event;

    (3) Mine subsidence, meaning subsidence of a man-made mine, whether or not mining activity has ceased;

    (4) Earth sinking (other than sinkhole collapse), rising or shifting including soil conditions which cause settling, cracking or other disarrangement of foundations or other parts of realty. Soil conditions include contraction, expansion, freezing, thawing, erosion, improperly compacted soil and the action of water under the ground surface.

    But if Earth Movement, as described in **b.**(1) through (4) above, results in fire or explosion, we will pay for the loss or damage caused by that fire or explosion.

    (5) Volcanic eruption, explosion or effusion. But if volcanic eruption, explosion or effusion results in fire, building glass breakage or Volcanic Action, we will pay for the loss or damage caused by that fire, building glass breakage or Volcanic Action.

    Volcanic action means direct loss or damage resulting from the eruption of a volcano when the loss or damage is caused by:

    (a) Airborne volcanic blast or airborne shock waves;

    (b) Ash, dust or particulate matter; or

    (c) Lava flow.

    All volcanic eruptions that occur within any 168 hour period will constitute a single occurrence.

    Volcanic action does not include the cost to remove ash, dust or particulate matter that does not cause direct physical loss or damage to the described property.

    c. Governmental Action

    Seizure or destruction of property by order of governmental authority.

    But we will pay for loss or damage caused by or resulting from acts of destruction ordered by governmental authority and taken at the time of a fire to prevent its spread, if the fire would be covered under this Coverage Part.

d. Nuclear Hazard

Nuclear reaction or radiation, or radioactive contamination, however caused.

But if nuclear reaction or radiation, or radioactive contamination, results in fire, we will pay for the loss or damage caused by that fire.

e. Utility Services

The failure of power or other utility service supplied to the described premises, however caused, if the failure occurs away from the described premises. Failure includes lack of sufficient capacity and reduction in supply.

But if the failure of power or other utility service results in a Covered Cause of Loss, we will pay for the loss or damage caused by that Covered Cause of Loss.

This exclusion does not apply to the Business Income coverage or to Extra Expense coverage. Instead, the Special Exclusion in Paragraph **B.4.a.(1)** applies to these coverages.

f. War And Military Action

(1) War, including undeclared or civil war;

(2) Warlike action by a military force, including action in hindering or defending against an actual or expected attack, by any government, sovereign or other authority using military personnel or other agents; or

(3) Insurrection, rebellion, revolution, usurped power, or action taken by governmental authority in hindering or defending against any of these.

g. Water

(1) Flood, surface water, waves, tides, tidal waves, overflow of any body of water, or their spray, all whether driven by wind or not;

(2) Mudslide or mudflow;

(3) Water that backs up or overflows from a sewer, drain or sump; or

(4) Water under the ground surface pressing on, or flowing or seeping through:

    (a) Foundations, walls, floors or paved surfaces;

    (b) Basements, whether paved or not; or

    (c) Doors, windows or other openings.

But if Water, as described in **g.(1)** through **g.(4)** above, results in fire, explosion or sprinkler leakage, we will pay for the loss or damage caused by that fire, explosion or sprinkler leakage.

h. "Fungus", Wet Rot, Dry Rot And Bacteria

Presence, growth, proliferation, spread or any activity of "fungus", wet or dry rot or bacteria.

But if "fungus", wet or dry rot or bacteria results in a "specified cause of loss", we will pay for the loss or damage caused by that "specified cause of loss".

This exclusion does not apply:

1. When "fungus", wet or dry rot or bacteria results from fire or lightning; or

2. To the extent that coverage is provided in the Additional Coverage – Limited Coverage For "Fungus", Wet Rot, Dry Rot And Bacteria with respect to loss or damage by a cause of loss other than fire or lightning.

Exclusions **B.1.a.** through **B.1.h.** apply whether or not the loss event results in widespread damage or affects a substantial area.

2. We will not pay for loss or damage caused by or resulting from any of the following:

a. Artificially generated electrical current, including electric arcing, that disturbs electrical devices, appliances or wires.

But if artificially generated electrical current results in fire, we will pay for the loss or damage caused by that fire.

b. Delay, loss of use or loss of market.

c. Smoke, vapor or gas from agricultural smudging or industrial operations.

d.(1) Wear and tear;

    (2) Rust or other corrosion, decay, deterioration, hidden or latent defect or any quality in property that causes it to damage or destroy itself;

    (3) Smog;

    (4) Settling, cracking, shrinking or expansion;

    (5) Nesting or infestation, or discharge or release of waste products or secretions, by insects, birds, rodents or other animals.

(6) Mechanical breakdown, including rupture or bursting caused by centrifugal force. But if mechanical breakdown results in elevator collision, we will pay for the loss or damage caused by that elevator collision.

(7) The following causes of loss to personal property:

    (a) Dampness or dryness of atmosphere;

    (b) Changes in or extremes of temperature; or

    (c) Marring or scratching.

But if an excluded cause of loss that is listed in **2.d.(1)** through **(7)** results in a "specified cause of loss" or building glass breakage, we will pay for the loss or damage caused by that "specified cause of loss" or building glass breakage.

e. Explosion of steam boilers, steam pipes, steam engines or steam turbines owned or leased by you, or operated under your control. But if explosion of steam boilers, steam pipes, steam engines or steam turbines results in fire or combustion explosion, we will pay for the loss or damage caused by that fire or combustion explosion. We will also pay for loss or damage caused by or resulting from the explosion of gases or fuel within the furnace of any fired vessel or within the flues or passages through which the gases of combustion pass.

f. Continuous or repeated seepage or leakage of water, or the presence or condensation of humidity, moisture or vapor, that occurs over a period of 14 days or more.

g. Water, other liquids, powder or molten material that leaks or flows from plumbing, heating, air conditioning or other equipment (except fire protective systems) caused by or resulting from freezing, unless:

    (1) You do your best to maintain heat in the building or structure; or

    (2) You drain the equipment and shut off the supply if the heat is not maintained.

h. Dishonest or criminal act by you, any of your partners, members, officers, managers, employees (including leased employees), directors, trustees, authorized representatives or anyone to whom you entrust the property for any purpose:

    (1) Acting alone or in collusion with others; or

    (2) Whether or not occurring during the hours of employment.

This exclusion does not apply to acts of destruction by your employees (including leased employees); but theft by employees (including leased employees) is not covered.

i. Voluntary parting with any property by you or anyone else to whom you have entrusted the property if induced to do so by any fraudulent scheme, trick, device or false pretense.

j. Rain, snow, ice or sleet to personal property in the open.

k. Collapse, except as provided below in the Additional Coverage for Collapse. But if collapse results in a Covered Cause of Loss at the described premises, we will pay for the loss or damage caused by that Covered Cause of Loss.

l. Discharge, dispersal, seepage, migration, release or escape of "pollutants" unless the discharge, dispersal, seepage, migration, release or escape is itself caused by any of the "specified causes of loss". But if the discharge, dispersal, seepage, migration, release or escape of "pollutants" results in a "specified cause of loss", we will pay for the loss or damage caused by that "specified cause of loss".

This exclusion, **l.**, does not apply to damage to glass caused by chemicals applied to the glass.

m. Neglect of an insured to use all reasonable means to save and preserve property from further damage at and after the time of loss.

3. We will not pay for loss or damage caused by or resulting from any of the following, **3.a.** through **3.c.** But if an excluded cause of loss that is listed in **3.a.** through **3.c.** results in a Covered Cause of Loss, we will pay for the loss or damage caused by that Covered Cause of Loss.

    a. Weather conditions. But this exclusion only applies if weather conditions contribute in any way with a cause or event excluded in Paragraph **1.** above to produce the loss or damage.

    b. Acts or decisions, including the failure to act or decide, of any person, group, organization or governmental body.

c. Faulty, inadequate or defective:

(1) Planning, zoning, development, surveying, siting;

(2) Design, specifications, workmanship, repair, construction, renovation, remodeling, grading, compaction;

(3) Materials used in repair, construction, renovation or remodeling; or

(4) Maintenance;

of part or all of any property on or off the described premises.

4. **Special Exclusions**

The following provisions apply only to the specified Coverage Forms.

a. **Business Income (And Extra Expense) Coverage Form, Business Income (Without Extra Expense) Coverage Form, Or Extra Expense Coverage Form**

We will not pay for:

(1) Any loss caused directly or indirectly by the failure of power or other utility service supplied to the described premises, however caused, if the failure occurs outside of a covered building. Failure includes lack of sufficient capacity and reduction in supply.

But if the failure of power or other utility service results in a Covered Cause of Loss, we will pay for the loss resulting from that Covered Cause of Loss.

(2) Any loss caused by or resulting from:

(a) Damage or destruction of "finished stock"; or

(b) The time required to reproduce "finished stock".

This exclusion does not apply to Extra Expense.

(3) Any loss caused by or resulting from direct physical loss or damage to radio or television antennas (including satellite dishes) and their lead-in wiring, masts or towers.

(4) Any increase of loss caused by or resulting from:

(a) Delay in rebuilding, repairing or replacing the property or resuming "operations", due to interference at the location of the rebuilding, repair or replacement by strikers or other persons; or

(b) Suspension, lapse or cancellation of any license, lease or contract. But if the suspension, lapse or cancellation is directly caused by the "suspension" of "operations", we will cover such loss that affects your Business Income during the "period of restoration" and any extension of the "period of restoration" in accordance with the terms of the Extended Business Income Additional Coverage and the Extended Period Of Indemnity Optional Coverage or any variation of these.

(5) Any Extra Expense caused by or resulting from suspension, lapse or cancellation of any license, lease or contract beyond the "period of restoration".

(6) Any other consequential loss.

b. **Leasehold Interest Coverage Form**

(1) Paragraph **B.1.a.** Ordinance Or Law, does not apply to insurance under this Coverage Form.

(2) We will not pay for any loss caused by:

(a) Your cancelling the lease;

(b) The suspension, lapse or cancellation of any license; or

(c) Any other consequential loss.

c. **Legal Liability Coverage Form**

(1) The following exclusions do not apply to insurance under this Coverage Form:

(a) Paragraph **B.1.a.**, Ordinance Or Law;

(b) Paragraph **B.1.c.**, Governmental Action;

(c) Paragraph **B.1.d.**, Nuclear Hazard;

(d) Paragraph **B.1.e.**, Utility Services; and

(e) Paragraph **B.1.f.**, War And Military Action.

(2) The following additional exclusions apply to insurance under this Coverage Form:

(a) **Contractual Liability**

We will not defend any claim or "suit", or pay damages that you are legally liable to pay, solely by reason of your assumption of liability in a contract or agreement. But this exclusion does not apply to a written lease agreement in which you have assumed liability for building damage resulting from an actual or attempted burglary or robbery, provided that:

(i) Your assumption of liability was executed prior to the accident; and

(ii) The building is Covered Property under this Coverage Form.

(b) **Nuclear Hazard**

We will not defend any claim or "suit", or pay any damages, loss, expense or obligation, resulting from nuclear reaction or radiation, or radioactive contamination, however caused.

C. Limitations

The following limitations apply to all policy forms and endorsements, unless otherwise stated.

1. We will not pay for loss of or damage to property, as described and limited in this section. In addition, we will not pay for any loss that is a consequence of loss or damage as described and limited in this section.

   a. Steam boilers, steam pipes, steam engines or steam turbines caused by or resulting from any condition or event inside such equipment. But we will pay for loss of or damage to such equipment caused by or resulting from an explosion of gases or fuel within the furnace of any fired vessel or within the flues or passages through which the gases of combustion pass.

   b. Hot water boilers or other water heating equipment caused by or resulting from any condition or event inside such boilers or equipment, other than an explosion.

   c. The interior of any building or structure, or to personal property in the building or structure, caused by or resulting from rain, snow, sleet, ice, sand or dust, whether driven by wind or not, unless:

   (1) The building or structure first sustains damage by a Covered Cause of Loss to its roof or walls through which the rain, snow, sleet, ice, sand or dust enters; or

   (2) The loss or damage is caused by or results from thawing of snow, sleet or ice on the building or structure.

   d. Building materials and supplies not attached as part of the building or structure, caused by or resulting from theft.

   However, this limitation does not apply to:

   (1) Building materials and supplies held for sale by you, unless they are insured under the Builders Risk Coverage Form; or

   (2) Business Income coverage or Extra Expense coverage.

   e. Property that is missing, where the only evidence of the loss or damage is a shortage disclosed on taking inventory, or other instances where there is no physical evidence to show what happened to the property.

   f. Property that has been transferred to a person or to a place outside the described premises on the basis of unauthorized instructions.

2. We will not pay for loss of or damage to the following types of property unless caused by the "specified causes of loss" or building glass breakage:

   a. Animals, and then only if they are killed or their destruction is made necessary.

   b. Fragile articles such as statuary, marbles, chinaware and porcelains, if broken. This restriction does not apply to:

   (1) Glass; or

   (2) Containers of property held for sale.

   c. Builders' machinery, tools and equipment owned by you or entrusted to you, provided such property is Covered Property.

However, this limitation does not apply:

(1) If the property is located on or within 100 feet of the described premises, unless the premises is insured under the Builders Risk Coverage Form; or

(2) To Business Income coverage or to Extra Expense coverage.

3. The special limit shown for each category, **a.** through **d.**, is the total limit for loss of or damage to all property in that category. The special limit applies to any one occurrence of theft, regardless of the types or number of articles that are lost or damaged in that occurrence. The special limits are:

   a. $2,500 for furs, fur garments and garments trimmed with fur.

   b. $2,500 for jewelry, watches, watch movements, jewels, pearls, precious and semi-precious stones, bullion, gold, silver, platinum and other precious alloys or metals. This limit does not apply to jewelry and watches worth $100 or less per item.

   c. $2,500 for patterns, dies, molds and forms.

   d. $250 for stamps, tickets, including lottery tickets held for sale, and letters of credit.

   These special limits are part of, not in addition to, the Limit of Insurance applicable to the Covered Property.

   This limitation, **C.3.**, does not apply to Business Income coverage or to Extra Expense coverage.

4. We will not pay the cost to repair any defect to a system or appliance from which water, other liquid, powder or molten material escapes. But we will pay the cost to repair or replace damaged parts of fire extinguishing equipment if the damage:

   a. Results in discharge of any substance from an automatic fire protection system; or

   b. Is directly caused by freezing.

   However, this limitation does not apply to Business Income coverage or to Extra Expense coverage.

D. Additional Coverage – Collapse

The term Covered Cause of Loss includes the Additional Coverage – Collapse as described and limited in **D.1.** through **D.5.** below.

1. With respect to buildings:

   a. Collapse means an abrupt falling down or caving in of a building or any part of a building with the result that the building or part of the building cannot be occupied for its intended purpose;

   b. A building or any part of a building that is in danger of falling down or caving in is not considered to be in a state of collapse;

   c. A part of a building that is standing is not considered to be in a state of collapse even if it has separated from another part of the building;

   d. A building that is standing or any part of a building that is standing is not considered to be in a state of collapse even if it shows evidence of cracking, bulging, sagging, bending, leaning, settling, shrinkage or expansion.

2. We will pay for direct physical loss or damage to Covered Property, caused by collapse of a building or any part of a building that is insured under this Coverage Form or that contains Covered Property insured under this Coverage Form, if the collapse is caused by one or more of the following:

   a. The "specified causes of loss" or breakage of building glass, all only as insured against in this Coverage Part;

   b. Decay that is hidden from view, unless the presence of such decay is known to an insured prior to collapse;

   c. Insect or vermin damage that is hidden from view, unless the presence of such damage is known to an insured prior to collapse;

   d. Weight of people or personal property;

   e. Weight of rain that collects on a roof;

f. Use of defective material or methods in construction, remodeling or renovation if the collapse occurs during the course of the construction, remodeling or renovation. However, if the collapse occurs after construction, remodeling or renovation is complete and is caused in part by a cause of loss listed in **2.a.** through **2.e.,** we will pay for the loss or damage even if use of defective material or methods, in construction, remodeling or renovation, contributes to the collapse.

The criteria set forth in **1.a.** through **1.d.** do not limit the coverage otherwise provided under this Causes of Loss Form for the causes of loss listed in **2.a., 2.d.** and **2.e.**

3. With respect to the following property:
   a. Outdoor radio or television antennas (including satellite dishes) and their lead-in wiring, masts or towers;
   b. Awnings, gutters and downspouts;
   c. Yard fixtures;
   d. Outdoor swimming pools;
   e. Fences;
   f. Piers, wharves and docks;
   g. Beach or diving platforms or appurtenances;
   h. Retaining walls; and
   i. Walks, roadways and other paved surfaces;

   if the collapse is caused by a cause of loss listed in **2.b.** through **2.f.,** we will pay for loss or damage to that property only if:
   a. Such loss or damage is a direct result of the collapse of a building insured under this Coverage Form; and
   b. The property is Covered Property under this Coverage Form.

4. If personal property abruptly falls down or caves in and such collapse is not the result of collapse of a building, we will pay for loss or damage to Covered Property caused by such collapse of personal property only if:
   a. The collapse was caused by a Cause of Loss listed in **2.a.** through **2.f.** above;
   b. The personal property which collapses is inside a building; and
   c. The property which collapses is not of a kind listed in **3.** above, regardless of whether that kind of property is considered to be personal property or real property.

The coverage stated in this Paragraph **4.** does not apply to personal property if marring and/or scratching is the only damage to that personal property caused by the collapse.

Collapse of personal property does not mean cracking, bulging, sagging, bending, leaning, settling, shrinkage or expansion.

5. This Additional Coverage, Collapse, will not increase the Limits of Insurance provided in this Coverage Part.

E. **Additional Coverage – Limited Coverage For "Fungus", Wet Rot, Dry Rot And Bacteria**

1. The coverage described in **E.2.** and **E.6.** only applies when the "fungus", wet or dry rot or bacteria is the result of one or more of the following causes that occurs during the policy period and only if all reasonable means were used to save and preserve the property from further damage at the time of and after that occurrence.
   a. A "specified cause of loss" other than fire or lightning; or
   b. Flood, if the Flood Coverage Endorsement applies to the affected premises.

2. We will pay for loss or damage by "fungus", wet or dry rot or bacteria. As used in this Limited Coverage, the term loss or damage means:
   a. Direct physical loss or damage to Covered Property caused by "fungus", wet or dry rot or bacteria, including the cost of removal of the "fungus", wet or dry rot or bacteria;
   b. The cost to tear out and replace any part of the building or other property as needed to gain access to the "fungus", wet or dry rot or bacteria; and
   c. The cost of testing performed after removal, repair, replacement or restoration of the damaged property is completed, provided there is a reason to believe that "fungus", wet or dry rot or bacteria are present.

3. The coverage described under **E.2.** of this Limited Coverage is limited to $15,000. Regardless of the number of claims, this limit is the most we will pay for the total of all loss or damage arising out of all occurrences of "specified causes of loss" (other than fire or lightning) and Flood which take place in a 12-month period (starting with the beginning of the present annual policy period). With respect to a particular occurrence of loss which results in "fungus", wet or dry rot or bacteria, we will not pay more than a total of $15,000 even if the "fungus", wet or dry rot or bacteria continues to be present or active, or recurs, in a later policy period.

CP 10 30 04 02 © ISO Properties, Inc., 2001

4. The coverage provided under this Limited Coverage does not increase the applicable Limit of Insurance on any Covered Property. If a particular occurrence results in loss or damage by "fungus", wet or dry rot or bacteria, and other loss or damage, we will not pay more, for the total of all loss or damage, than the applicable Limit of Insurance on the affected Covered Property.

   If there is covered loss or damage to Covered Property, not caused by "fungus", wet or dry rot or bacteria, loss payment will not be limited by the terms of this Limited Coverage, except to the extent that "fungus", wet or dry rot or bacteria causes an increase in the loss. Any such increase in the loss will be subject to the terms of this Limited Coverage.

5. The terms of this Limited Coverage do not increase or reduce the coverage provided under Paragraph **F.2.** (Water Damage, Other Liquids, Powder Or Molten Material Damage) of this Causes Of Loss Form or under the Additional Coverage – Collapse.

6. The following, **6.a.** or **6.b.**, applies only if Business Income and/or Extra Expense coverage applies to the described premises and only if the "suspension" of "operations" satisfies all terms and conditions of the applicable Business Income and/or Extra Expense coverage form.

   a. If the loss which resulted in "fungus", wet or dry rot or bacteria does not in itself necessitate a "suspension" of "operations", but such "suspension" is necessary due to loss or damage to property caused by "fungus", wet or dry rot or bacteria, then our payment under Business Income and/or Extra Expense is limited to the amount of loss and/or expense sustained in a period of not more than 30 days. The days need not be consecutive.

   b. If a covered "suspension" of "operations" was caused by loss or damage other than "fungus", wet or dry rot or bacteria but remediation of "fungus", wet or dry rot or bacteria prolongs the "period of restoration", we will pay for loss and/or expense sustained during the delay (regardless of when such a delay occurs during the "period of restoration"), but such coverage is limited to 30 days. The days need not be consecutive.

F. **Additional Coverage Extensions**
   1. **Property In Transit**

      This Extension applies only to your personal property to which this form applies.

      a. You may extend the insurance provided by this Coverage Part to apply to your personal property (other than property in the care, custody or control of your salespersons) in transit more than 100 feet from the described premises. Property must be in or on a motor vehicle you own, lease or operate while between points in the coverage territory.

      b. Loss or damage must be caused by or result from one of the following causes of loss:

         (1) Fire, lightning, explosion, windstorm or hail, riot or civil commotion, or vandalism.

         (2) Vehicle collision, upset or overturn. Collision means accidental contact of your vehicle with another vehicle or object. It does not mean your vehicle's contact with the road bed.

         (3) Theft of an entire bale, case or package by forced entry into a securely locked body or compartment of the vehicle. There must be visible marks of the forced entry.

      c. The most we will pay for loss or damage under this Extension is $5,000.

      This Coverage Extension is additional insurance. The Additional Condition, Coinsurance, does not apply to this Extension.

   2. **Water Damage, Other Liquids, Powder Or Molten Material Damage**

      If loss or damage caused by or resulting from covered water or other liquid, powder or molten material damage loss occurs, we will also pay the cost to tear out and replace any part of the building or structure to repair damage to the system or appliance from which the water or other substance escapes. This Coverage Extension does not increase the Limit of Insurance.

   3. **Glass**

      a. We will pay for expenses incurred to put up temporary plates or board up openings if repair or replacement of damaged glass is delayed.

b. We will pay for expenses incurred to remove or replace obstructions when repairing or replacing glass that is part of a building. This does not include removing or replacing window displays.

This Coverage Extension, **F.3.**, does not increase the Limit of Insurance.

G. Definitions

1. "Fungus" means any type or form of fungus, including mold or mildew, and any mycotoxins, spores, scents or by-products produced or released by fungi.

2. "Specified Causes of Loss" means the following: Fire; lightning; explosion; windstorm or hail; smoke; aircraft or vehicles; riot or civil commotion; vandalism; leakage from fire extinguishing equipment; sinkhole collapse; volcanic action; falling objects; weight of snow, ice or sleet; water damage.

    a. Sinkhole collapse means the sudden sinking or collapse of land into underground empty spaces created by the action of water on limestone or dolomite. This cause of loss does not include:

    (1) The cost of filling sinkholes; or

    (2) Sinking or collapse of land into man-made underground cavities.

    b. Falling objects does not include loss or damage to:

    (1) Personal property in the open; or

    (2) The interior of a building or structure, or property inside a building or structure, unless the roof or an outside wall of the building or structure is first damaged by a falling object.

    c. Water damage means accidental discharge or leakage of water or steam as the direct result of the breaking apart or cracking of a plumbing, heating, air conditioning or other system or appliance (other than a sump system including its related equipment and parts), that is located on the described premises and contains water or steam.

Appendix 35

POLICY NUMBER: COMMERCIAL GENERAL LIABILITY
                                                                                                       CG DS 01 10 01

COMMERCIAL GENERAL LIABILITY DECLARATIONS

XYZ Insurance Co.	A. M. Abel

NAMED INSURED: AMR Corporation
MAILING ADDRESS: 2000 Industrial Highway
                                Workingtown, PA 19000
POLICY PERIOD: FROM 10/1/07 TO 10/1/08 AT 12:01 A.M. TIME AT YOUR MAILING ADDRESS SHOWN ABOVE

IN RETURN FOR THE PAYMENT OF THE PREMIUM, AND SUBJECT TO ALL THE TERMS OF THIS POLICY, WE AGREE WITH YOU TO PROVIDE THE INSURANCE AS STATED IN THIS POLICY.

LIMITS OF INSURANCE

EACH OCCURRENCE LIMIT	$ 1,000,000	
DAMAGE TO PREMISES RENTED TO YOU LIMIT	$ 100,000	Any one premises
MEDICAL EXPENSE LIMIT	$ 5,000	Any one person
PERSONAL & ADVERTISING INJURY LIMIT	$ 1,000,000	Any one person or organization
GENERAL AGGREGATE LIMIT	$ 2,000,000	
PRODUCTS/COMPLETED OPERATIONS AGGREGATE LIMIT	$ 2,000,000	

RETROACTIVE DATE (CG 00 02 ONLY)

THIS INSURANCE DOES NOT APPLY TO "BODILY INJURY", "PROPERTY DAMAGE" OR "PERSONAL AND ADVERTISING INJURY" WHICH OCCURS BEFORE THE RETROACTIVE DATE, IF ANY, SHOWN BELOW.
RETROACTIVE DATE: _____
(ENTER DATE OR "NONE" IF NO RETROACTIVE DATE APPLIES)

DESCRIPTION OF BUSINESS

FORM OF BUSINESS:

☐ INDIVIDUAL   ☐ PARTNERSHIP   ☐ JOINT VENTURE   ☐ TRUST

☐ LIMITED LIABILITY COMPANY   ☒ ORGANIZATION, INCLUDING A CORPORATION (BUT NOT INCLUDING A PARTNERSHIP, JOINT VENTURE OR LIMITED LIABILITY COMPANY)

BUSINESS DESCRIPTION: Storm Door Manufacturing

CG DS 01 10 01   © ISO Properties, Inc., 2000   Page 1 of 2

ALL PREMISES YOU OWN, RENT OR OCCUPY	
LOCATION NUMBER	ADDRESS OF ALL PREMISES YOU OWN, RENT OR OCCUPY
1	2000 Industrial Highway Workingtown, PA 19000

CLASSIFICATION AND PREMIUM						
LOCATION NUMBER	CLASSIFICATION	CODE NO.	PREMIUM BASE	RATE		ADVANCE PREMIUM	
				Prem/Ops	Prod/Comp Ops	Prem/Ops	Prod/Comp Ops
1	Glass or Glassware Mfg.	54077	$2,000,000	$1.018	$2.589	$2,036	$5,178

PREMIUM SHOWN IS PAYABLE:	STATE TAX OR OTHER (if applicable)	$
	TOTAL PREMIUM (SUBJECT TO AUDIT)	$
	AT INCEPTION	$ XXX
	AT EACH ANNIVERSARY	$
	(IF POLICY PERIOD IS MORE THAN ONE YEAR AND PREMIUM IS PAID IN ANNUAL INSTALLMENTS)	

AUDIT PERIOD (IF APPLICABLE)	☒ ANNUALLY	☐ SEMI-ANNUALLY	☐ QUARTERLY	☐ MONTHLY

ENDORSEMENTS
ENDORSEMENTS ATTACHED TO THIS POLICY: IL 00 21 04 98 — Broad Form Nuclear Exclusion
Plus those listed on schedule

THESE DECLARATIONS, TOGETHER WITH THE COMMON POLICY CONDITIONS AND COVERAGE FORM(S) AND ANY ENDORSEMENT(S), COMPLETE THE ABOVE NUMBERED POLICY.

Countersigned:	AMR Corporation	By:	A. M. Abel
	10/1/07		(Authorized Representative)

NOTE

OFFICERS' FACSIMILE SIGNATURES MAY BE INSERTED HERE, ON THE POLICY COVER OR ELSEWHERE AT THE COMPANY'S OPTION.

COMMERCIAL GENERAL LIABILITY
CG 00 01 12 04

COMMERCIAL GENERAL LIABILITY COVERAGE FORM

Various provisions in this policy restrict coverage. Read the entire policy carefully to determine rights, duties and what is and is not covered.

Throughout this policy the words "you" and "your" refer to the Named Insured shown in the Declarations, and any other person or organization qualifying as a Named Insured under this policy. The words "we", "us" and "our" refer to the company providing this insurance.

The word "insured" means any person or organization qualifying as such under Section II – Who Is An Insured.

Other words and phrases that appear in quotation marks have special meaning. Refer to Section V – Definitions.

SECTION I – COVERAGES

COVERAGE A BODILY INJURY AND PROPERTY DAMAGE LIABILITY

1. **Insuring Agreement**

   a. We will pay those sums that the insured becomes legally obligated to pay as damages because of "bodily injury" or "property damage" to which this insurance applies. We will have the right and duty to defend the insured against any "suit" seeking those damages. However, we will have no duty to defend the insured against any "suit" seeking damages for "bodily injury" or "property damage" to which this insurance does not apply. We may, at our discretion, investigate any "occurrence" and settle any claim or "suit" that may result. But:

   (1) The amount we will pay for damages is limited as described in Section III – Limits Of Insurance; and

   (2) Our right and duty to defend ends when we have used up the applicable limit of insurance in the payment of judgments or settlements under Coverages **A** or **B** or medical expenses under Coverage **C**.

   No other obligation or liability to pay sums or perform acts or services is covered unless explicitly provided for under Supplementary Payments – Coverages **A** and **B**.

   b. This insurance applies to "bodily injury" and "property damage" only if:

   (1) The "bodily injury" or "property damage" is caused by an "occurrence" that takes place in the "coverage territory";

   (2) The "bodily injury" or "property damage" occurs during the policy period; and

   (3) Prior to the policy period, no insured listed under Paragraph **1.** of Section II – Who Is An Insured and no "employee" authorized by you to give or receive notice of an "occurrence" or claim, knew that the "bodily injury" or "property damage" had occurred, in whole or in part. If such a listed insured or authorized "employee" knew, prior to the policy period, that the "bodily injury" or "property damage" occurred, then any continuation, change or resumption of such "bodily injury" or "property damage" during or after the policy period will be deemed to have been known prior to the policy period.

   c. "Bodily injury" or "property damage" which occurs during the policy period and was not, prior to the policy period, known to have occurred by any insured listed under Paragraph **1.** of Section II – Who Is An Insured or any "employee" authorized by you to give or receive notice of an "occurrence" or claim, includes any continuation, change or resumption of that "bodily injury" or "property damage" after the end of the policy period.

   d. "Bodily injury" or "property damage" will be deemed to have been known to have occurred at the earliest time when any insured listed under Paragraph **1.** of Section II – Who Is An Insured or any "employee" authorized by you to give or receive notice of an "occurrence" or claim:

   (1) Reports all, or any part, of the "bodily injury" or "property damage" to us or any other insurer;

   (2) Receives a written or verbal demand or claim for damages because of the "bodily injury" or "property damage"; or

   (3) Becomes aware by any other means that "bodily injury" or "property damage" has occurred or has begun to occur.

CG 00 01 12 04 © ISO Properties, Inc., 2003 Page 1 of 15

e. Damages because of "bodily injury" include damages claimed by any person or organization for care, loss of services or death resulting at any time from the "bodily injury".

2. **Exclusions**

   This insurance does not apply to:

   a. **Expected Or Intended Injury**

   "Bodily injury" or "property damage" expected or intended from the standpoint of the insured. This exclusion does not apply to "bodily injury" resulting from the use of reasonable force to protect persons or property.

   b. **Contractual Liability**

   "Bodily injury" or "property damage" for which the insured is obligated to pay damages by reason of the assumption of liability in a contract or agreement. This exclusion does not apply to liability for damages:

   (1) That the insured would have in the absence of the contract or agreement; or

   (2) Assumed in a contract or agreement that is an "insured contract", provided the "bodily injury" or "property damage" occurs subsequent to the execution of the contract or agreement. Solely for the purposes of liability assumed in an "insured contract", reasonable attorney fees and necessary litigation expenses incurred by or for a party other than an insured are deemed to be damages because of "bodily injury" or "property damage", provided:

   (a) Liability to such party for, or for the cost of, that party's defense has also been assumed in the same "insured contract"; and

   (b) Such attorney fees and litigation expenses are for defense of that party against a civil or alternative dispute resolution proceeding in which damages to which this insurance applies are alleged.

   c. **Liquor Liability**

   "Bodily injury" or "property damage" for which any insured may be held liable by reason of:

   (1) Causing or contributing to the intoxication of any person;

   (2) The furnishing of alcoholic beverages to a person under the legal drinking age or under the influence of alcohol; or

   (3) Any statute, ordinance or regulation relating to the sale, gift, distribution or use of alcoholic beverages.

   This exclusion applies only if you are in the business of manufacturing, distributing, selling, serving or furnishing alcoholic beverages.

   d. **Workers' Compensation And Similar Laws**

   Any obligation of the insured under a workers' compensation, disability benefits or unemployment compensation law or any similar law.

   e. **Employer's Liability**

   "Bodily injury" to:

   (1) An "employee" of the insured arising out of and in the course of:

   (a) Employment by the insured; or

   (b) Performing duties related to the conduct of the insured's business; or

   (2) The spouse, child, parent, brother or sister of that "employee" as a consequence of Paragraph **(1)** above.

   This exclusion applies:

   (1) Whether the insured may be liable as an employer or in any other capacity; and

   (2) To any obligation to share damages with or repay someone else who must pay damages because of the injury.

   This exclusion does not apply to liability assumed by the insured under an "insured contract".

f. Pollution

(1) "Bodily injury" or "property damage" arising out of the actual, alleged or threatened discharge, dispersal, seepage, migration, release or escape of "pollutants":

(a) At or from any premises, site or location which is or was at any time owned or occupied by, or rented or loaned to, any insured. However, this subparagraph does not apply to:

  (i) "Bodily injury" if sustained within a building and caused by smoke, fumes, vapor or soot produced by or originating from equipment that is used to heat, cool or dehumidify the building, or equipment that is used to heat water for personal use, by the building's occupants or their guests;

  (ii) "Bodily injury" or "property damage" for which you may be held liable, if you are a contractor and the owner or lessee of such premises, site or location has been added to your policy as an additional insured with respect to your ongoing operations performed for that additional insured at that premises, site or location and such premises, site or location is not and never was owned or occupied by, or rented or loaned to, any insured, other than that additional insured; or

  (iii) "Bodily injury" or "property damage" arising out of heat, smoke or fumes from a "hostile fire";

(b) At or from any premises, site or location which is or was at any time used by or for any insured or others for the handling, storage, disposal, processing or treatment of waste;

(c) Which are or were at any time transported, handled, stored, treated, disposed of, or processed as waste by or for:

  (i) Any insured; or

  (ii) Any person or organization for whom you may be legally responsible; or

(d) At or from any premises, site or location on which any insured or any contractors or subcontractors working directly or indirectly on any insured's behalf are performing operations if the "pollutants" are brought on or to the premises, site or location in connection with such operations by such insured, contractor or subcontractor. However, this subparagraph does not apply to:

  (i) "Bodily injury" or "property damage" arising out of the escape of fuels, lubricants or other operating fluids which are needed to perform the normal electrical, hydraulic or mechanical functions necessary for the operation of "mobile equipment" or its parts, if such fuels, lubricants or other operating fluids escape from a vehicle part designed to hold, store or receive them. This exception does not apply if the "bodily injury" or "property damage" arises out of the intentional discharge, dispersal or release of the fuels, lubricants or other operating fluids, or if such fuels, lubricants or other operating fluids are brought on or to the premises, site or location with the intent that they be discharged, dispersed or released as part of the operations being performed by such insured, contractor or subcontractor;

  (ii) "Bodily injury" or "property damage" sustained within a building and caused by the release of gases, fumes or vapors from materials brought into that building in connection with operations being performed by you or on your behalf by a contractor or subcontractor; or

  (iii) "Bodily injury" or "property damage" arising out of heat, smoke or fumes from a "hostile fire".

(e) At or from any premises, site or location on which any insured or any contractors or subcontractors working directly or indirectly on any insured's behalf are performing operations if the operations are to test for, monitor, clean up, remove, contain, treat, detoxify or neutralize, or in any way respond to, or assess the effects of, "pollutants".

(2) Any loss, cost or expense arising out of any:

(a) Request, demand, order or statutory or regulatory requirement that any insured or others test for, monitor, clean up, remove, contain, treat, detoxify or neutralize, or in any way respond to, or assess the effects of, "pollutants"; or

(b) Claim or "suit" by or on behalf of a governmental authority for damages because of testing for, monitoring, cleaning up, removing, containing, treating, detoxifying or neutralizing, or in any way responding to, or assessing the effects of, "pollutants".

However, this paragraph does not apply to liability for damages because of "property damage" that the insured would have in the absence of such request, demand, order or statutory or regulatory requirement, or such claim or "suit" by or on behalf of a governmental authority.

g. Aircraft, Auto Or Watercraft

"Bodily injury" or "property damage" arising out of the ownership, maintenance, use or entrustment to others of any aircraft, "auto" or watercraft owned or operated by or rented or loaned to any insured. Use includes operation and "loading or unloading".

This exclusion applies even if the claims against any insured allege negligence or other wrongdoing in the supervision, hiring, employment, training or monitoring of others by that insured, if the "occurrence" which caused the "bodily injury" or "property damage" involved the ownership, maintenance, use or entrustment to others of any aircraft, "auto" or watercraft that is owned or operated by or rented or loaned to any insured.

This exclusion does not apply to:

(1) A watercraft while ashore on premises you own or rent;

(2) A watercraft you do not own that is:

(a) Less than 26 feet long; and

(b) Not being used to carry persons or property for a charge;

(3) Parking an "auto" on, or on the ways next to, premises you own or rent, provided the "auto" is not owned by or rented or loaned to you or the insured;

(4) Liability assumed under any "insured contract" for the ownership, maintenance or use of aircraft or watercraft; or

(5) "Bodily injury" or "property damage" arising out of:

(a) The operation of machinery or equipment that is attached to, or part of, a land vehicle that would qualify under the definition of "mobile equipment" if it were not subject to a compulsory or financial responsibility law or other motor vehicle insurance law in the state where it is licensed or principally garaged; or

(b) the operation of any of the machinery or equipment listed in Paragraph **f.(2)** or **f.(3)** of the definition of "mobile equipment".

h. Mobile Equipment

"Bodily injury" or "property damage" arising out of:

(1) The transportation of "mobile equipment" by an "auto" owned or operated by or rented or loaned to any insured; or

(2) The use of "mobile equipment" in, or while in practice for, or while being prepared for, any prearranged racing, speed, demolition, or stunting activity.

i. War

"Bodily injury" or "property damage", however caused, arising, directly or indirectly, out of:

(1) War, including undeclared or civil war;

(2) Warlike action by a military force, including action in hindering or defending against an actual or expected attack, by any government, sovereign or other authority using military personnel or other agents; or

(3) Insurrection, rebellion, revolution, usurped power, or action taken by governmental authority in hindering or defending against any of these.

j. Damage To Property

"Property damage" to:

(1) Property you own, rent, or occupy, including any costs or expenses incurred by you, or any other person, organization or entity, for repair, replacement, enhancement, restoration or maintenance of such property for any reason, including prevention of injury to a person or damage to another's property;

(2) Premises you sell, give away or abandon, if the "property damage" arises out of any part of those premises;

(3) Property loaned to you;

(4) Personal property in the care, custody or control of the insured;

(5) That particular part of real property on which you or any contractors or subcontractors working directly or indirectly on your behalf are performing operations, if the "property damage" arises out of those operations; or

(6) That particular part of any property that must be restored, repaired or replaced because "your work" was incorrectly performed on it.

Paragraphs **(1)**, **(3)** and **(4)** of this exclusion do not apply to "property damage" (other than damage by fire) to premises, including the contents of such premises, rented to you for a period of 7 or fewer consecutive days. A separate limit of insurance applies to Damage To Premises Rented To You as described in Section **III** – Limits Of Insurance.

Paragraph **(2)** of this exclusion does not apply if the premises are "your work" and were never occupied, rented or held for rental by you.

Paragraphs **(3)**, **(4)**, **(5)** and **(6)** of this exclusion do not apply to liability assumed under a sidetrack agreement.

Paragraph **(6)** of this exclusion does not apply to "property damage" included in the "products-completed operations hazard".

k. **Damage To Your Product**

"Property damage" to "your product" arising out of it or any part of it.

l. **Damage To Your Work**

"Property damage" to "your work" arising out of it or any part of it and included in the "products-completed operations hazard".

This exclusion does not apply if the damaged work or the work out of which the damage arises was performed on your behalf by a subcontractor.

m. **Damage To Impaired Property Or Property Not Physically Injured**

"Property damage" to "impaired property" or property that has not been physically injured, arising out of:

(1) A defect, deficiency, inadequacy or dangerous condition in "your product" or "your work"; or

(2) A delay or failure by you or anyone acting on your behalf to perform a contract or agreement in accordance with its terms.

This exclusion does not apply to the loss of use of other property arising out of sudden and accidental physical injury to "your product" or "your work" after it has been put to its intended use.

n. **Recall Of Products, Work Or Impaired Property**

Damages claimed for any loss, cost or expense incurred by you or others for the loss of use, withdrawal, recall, inspection, repair, replacement, adjustment, removal or disposal of:

(1) "Your product";

(2) "Your work"; or

(3) "Impaired property";

if such product, work, or property is withdrawn or recalled from the market or from use by any person or organization because of a known or suspected defect, deficiency, inadequacy or dangerous condition in it.

o. **Personal And Advertising Injury**

"Bodily injury" arising out of "personal and advertising injury".

p. **Electronic Data**

Damages arising out of the loss of, loss of use of, damage to, corruption of, inability to access, or inability to manipulate electronic data.

As used in this exclusion, electronic data means information, facts or programs stored as or on, created or used on, or transmitted to or from computer software, including systems and applications software, hard or floppy disks, CD-ROMS, tapes, drives, cells, data processing devices or any other media which are used with electronically controlled equipment.

Exclusions **c.** through **n.** do not apply to damage by fire to premises while rented to you or temporarily occupied by you with permission of the owner. A separate limit of insurance applies to this coverage as described in Section **III** – Limits Of Insurance.

COVERAGE B PERSONAL AND ADVERTISING INJURY LIABILITY

1. **Insuring Agreement**

   a. We will pay those sums that the insured becomes legally obligated to pay as damages because of "personal and advertising injury" to which this insurance applies. We will have the right and duty to defend the insured against any "suit" seeking those damages. However, we will have no duty to defend the insured against any "suit" seeking damages for "personal and advertising injury" to which this insurance does not apply. We may, at our discretion, investigate any offense and settle any claim or "suit" that may result. But:

   (1) The amount we will pay for damages is limited as described in Section **III** – Limits Of Insurance; and

(2) Our right and duty to defend end when we have used up the applicable limit of insurance in the payment of judgments or settlements under Coverages **A** or **B** or medical expenses under Coverage **C**.

No other obligation or liability to pay sums or perform acts or services is covered unless explicitly provided for under Supplementary Payments – Coverages **A** and **B**.

b. This insurance applies to "personal and advertising injury" caused by an offense arising out of your business but only if the offense was committed in the "coverage territory" during the policy period.

2. **Exclusions**

This insurance does not apply to:

a. **Knowing Violation Of Rights Of Another**

"Personal and advertising injury" caused by or at the direction of the insured with the knowledge that the act would violate the rights of another and would inflict "personal and advertising injury".

b. **Material Published With Knowledge Of Falsity**

"Personal and advertising injury" arising out of oral or written publication of material, if done by or at the direction of the insured with knowledge of its falsity.

c. **Material Published Prior To Policy Period**

"Personal and advertising injury" arising out of oral or written publication of material whose first publication took place before the beginning of the policy period.

d. **Criminal Acts**

"Personal and advertising injury" arising out of a criminal act committed by or at the direction of the insured.

e. **Contractual Liability**

"Personal and advertising injury" for which the insured has assumed liability in a contract or agreement. This exclusion does not apply to liability for damages that the insured would have in the absence of the contract or agreement.

f. **Breach Of Contract**

"Personal and advertising injury" arising out of a breach of contract, except an implied contract to use another's advertising idea in your "advertisement".

g. **Quality Or Performance Of Goods – Failure To Conform To Statements**

"Personal and advertising injury" arising out of the failure of goods, products or services to conform with any statement of quality or performance made in your "advertisement".

h. **Wrong Description Of Prices**

"Personal and advertising injury" arising out of the wrong description of the price of goods, products or services stated in your "advertisement".

i. **Infringement Of Copyright, Patent, Trademark Or Trade Secret**

"Personal and advertising injury" arising out of the infringement of copyright, patent, trademark, trade secret or other intellectual property rights.

However, this exclusion does not apply to infringement, in your "advertisement", of copyright, trade dress or slogan.

j. **Insureds In Media And Internet Type Businesses**

"Personal and advertising injury" committed by an insured whose business is:

(1) Advertising, broadcasting, publishing or telecasting;

(2) Designing or determining content of websites for others; or

(3) An Internet search, access, content or service provider.

However, this exclusion does not apply to Paragraphs **14.a.**, **b.** and **c.** of "personal and advertising injury" under the Definitions Section.

For the purposes of this exclusion, the placing of frames, borders or links, or advertising, for you or others anywhere on the Internet, is not by itself, considered the business of advertising, broadcasting, publishing or telecasting.

k. **Electronic Chatrooms Or Bulletin Boards**

"Personal and advertising injury" arising out of an electronic chatroom or bulletin board the insured hosts, owns, or over which the insured exercises control.

l. **Unauthorized Use Of Another's Name Or Product**

"Personal and advertising injury" arising out of the unauthorized use of another's name or product in your e-mail address, domain name or metatag, or any other similar tactics to mislead another's potential customers.

m. Pollution

"Personal and advertising injury" arising out of the actual, alleged or threatened discharge, dispersal, seepage, migration, release or escape of "pollutants" at any time.

n. Pollution-Related

Any loss, cost or expense arising out of any:

(1) Request, demand, order or statutory or regulatory requirement that any insured or others test for, monitor, clean up, remove, contain, treat, detoxify or neutralize, or in any way respond to, or assess the effects of, "pollutants"; or

(2) Claim or suit by or on behalf of a governmental authority for damages because of testing for, monitoring, cleaning up, removing, containing, treating, detoxifying or neutralizing, or in any way responding to, or assessing the effects of, "pollutants".

o. War

"Personal and advertising injury", however caused, arising, directly or indirectly, out of:

(1) War, including undeclared or civil war;

(2) Warlike action by a military force, including action in hindering or defending against an actual or expected attack, by any government, sovereign or other authority using military personnel or other agents; or

(3) Insurrection, rebellion, revolution, usurped power, or action taken by governmental authority in hindering or defending against any of these.

COVERAGE C MEDICAL PAYMENTS

1. Insuring Agreement

a. We will pay medical expenses as described below for "bodily injury" caused by an accident:

(1) On premises you own or rent;

(2) On ways next to premises you own or rent; or

(3) Because of your operations;

provided that:

(1) The accident takes place in the "coverage territory" and during the policy period;

(2) The expenses are incurred and reported to us within one year of the date of the accident; and

(3) The injured person submits to examination, at our expense, by physicians of our choice as often as we reasonably require.

b. We will make these payments regardless of fault. These payments will not exceed the applicable limit of insurance. We will pay reasonable expenses for:

(1) First aid administered at the time of an accident;

(2) Necessary medical, surgical, x-ray and dental services, including prosthetic devices; and

(3) Necessary ambulance, hospital, professional nursing and funeral services.

2. Exclusions

We will not pay expenses for "bodily injury":

a. **Any Insured**

To any insured, except "volunteer workers".

b. **Hired Person**

To a person hired to do work for or on behalf of any insured or a tenant of any insured.

c. **Injury On Normally Occupied Premises**

To a person injured on that part of premises you own or rent that the person normally occupies.

d. **Workers Compensation And Similar Laws**

To a person, whether or not an "employee" of any insured, if benefits for the "bodily injury" are payable or must be provided under a workers' compensation or disability benefits law or a similar law.

e. **Athletics Activities**

To a person injured while practicing, instructing or participating in any physical exercises or games, sports, or athletic contests.

f. **Products-Completed Operations Hazard**

Included within the "products-completed operations hazard".

g. **Coverage A Exclusions**

Excluded under Coverage A.

SUPPLEMENTARY PAYMENTS – COVERAGES A AND B

1. We will pay, with respect to any claim we investigate or settle, or any "suit" against an insured we defend:

a. All expenses we incur.

b. Up to $250 for cost of bail bonds required because of accidents or traffic law violations arising out of the use of any vehicle to which the Bodily Injury Liability Coverage applies. We do not have to furnish these bonds.

c. The cost of bonds to release attachments, but only for bond amounts within the applicable limit of insurance. We do not have to furnish these bonds.

d. All reasonable expenses incurred by the insured at our request to assist us in the investigation or defense of the claim or "suit", including actual loss of earnings up to $250 a day because of time off from work.

e. All costs taxed against the insured in the "suit".

f. Prejudgment interest awarded against the insured on that part of the judgment we pay. If we make an offer to pay the applicable limit of insurance, we will not pay any prejudgment interest based on that period of time after the offer.

g. All interest on the full amount of any judgment that accrues after entry of the judgment and before we have paid, offered to pay, or deposited in court the part of the judgment that is within the applicable limit of insurance.

These payments will not reduce the limits of insurance.

2. If we defend an insured against a "suit" and an indemnitee of the insured is also named as a party to the "suit", we will defend that indemnitee if all of the following conditions are met:

   a. The "suit" against the indemnitee seeks damages for which the insured has assumed the liability of the indemnitee in a contract or agreement that is an "insured contract";

   b. This insurance applies to such liability assumed by the insured;

   c. The obligation to defend, or the cost of the defense of, that indemnitee, has also been assumed by the insured in the same "insured contract";

   d. The allegations in the "suit" and the information we know about the "occurrence" are such that no conflict appears to exist between the interests of the insured and the interests of the indemnitee;

   e. The indemnitee and the insured ask us to conduct and control the defense of that indemnitee against such "suit" and agree that we can assign the same counsel to defend the insured and the indemnitee; and

   f. The indemnitee:

      (1) Agrees in writing to:

         (a) Cooperate with us in the investigation, settlement or defense of the "suit";

         (b) Immediately send us copies of any demands, notices, summonses or legal papers received in connection with the "suit";

         (c) Notify any other insurer whose coverage is available to the indemnitee; and

         (d) Cooperate with us with respect to coordinating other applicable insurance available to the indemnitee; and

      (2) Provides us with written authorization to:

         (a) Obtain records and other information related to the "suit"; and

         (b) Conduct and control the defense of the indemnitee in such "suit".

So long as the above conditions are met, attorneys' fees incurred by us in the defense of that indemnitee, necessary litigation expenses incurred by us and necessary litigation expenses incurred by the indemnitee at our request will be paid as Supplementary Payments. Notwithstanding the provisions of Paragraph **2.b.(2)** of Section **I** – Coverage **A** – Bodily Injury And Property Damage Liability, such payments will not be deemed to be damages for "bodily injury" and "property damage" and will not reduce the limits of insurance.

Our obligation to defend an insured's indemnitee and to pay for attorneys' fees and necessary litigation expenses as Supplementary Payments ends when:

a. We have used up the applicable limit of insurance in the payment of judgments or settlements; or

b. The conditions set forth above, or the terms of the agreement described in Paragraph **f.** above, are no longer met.

SECTION II – WHO IS AN INSURED

1. If you are designated in the Declarations as:

   a. An individual, you and your spouse are insureds, but only with respect to the conduct of a business of which you are the sole owner.

   b. A partnership or joint venture, you are an insured. Your members, your partners, and their spouses are also insureds, but only with respect to the conduct of your business.

   c. A limited liability company, you are an insured. Your members are also insureds, but only with respect to the conduct of your business. Your managers are insureds, but only with respect to their duties as your managers.

d. An organization other than a partnership, joint venture or limited liability company, you are an insured. Your "executive officers" and directors are insureds, but only with respect to their duties as your officers or directors. Your stockholders are also insureds, but only with respect to their liability as stockholders.

e. A trust, you are an insured. Your trustees are also insureds, but only with respect to their duties as trustees.

2. Each of the following is also an insured:

a. Your "volunteer workers" only while performing duties related to the conduct of your business, or your "employees", other than either your "executive officers" (if you are an organization other than a partnership, joint venture or limited liability company) or your managers (if you are a limited liability company), but only for acts within the scope of their employment by you or while performing duties related to the conduct of your business. However, none of these "employees" or "volunteer workers" are insureds for:

(1) "Bodily injury" or "personal and advertising injury":

(a) To you, to your partners or members (if you are a partnership or joint venture), to your members (if you are a limited liability company), to a co-"employee" while in the course of his or her employment or performing duties related to the conduct of your business, or to your other "volunteer workers" while performing duties related to the conduct of your business;

(b) To the spouse, child, parent, brother or sister of that co-"employee" or "volunteer worker" as a consequence of Paragraph **(1)(a)** above;

(c) For which there is any obligation to share damages with or repay someone else who must pay damages because of the injury described in Paragraphs **(1)(a)** or **(b)** above; or

(d) Arising out of his or her providing or failing to provide professional health care services.

(2) "Property damage" to property:

(a) Owned, occupied or used by,

(b) Rented to, in the care, custody or control of, or over which physical control is being exercised for any purpose by

you, any of your "employees", "volunteer workers", any partner or member (if you are a partnership or joint venture), or any member (if you are a limited liability company).

b. Any person (other than your "employee" or "volunteer worker"), or any organization while acting as your real estate manager.

c. Any person or organization having proper temporary custody of your property if you die, but only:

(1) With respect to liability arising out of the maintenance or use of that property; and

(2) Until your legal representative has been appointed.

d. Your legal representative if you die, but only with respect to duties as such. That representative will have all your rights and duties under this Coverage Part.

3. Any organization you newly acquire or form, other than a partnership, joint venture or limited liability company, and over which you maintain ownership or majority interest, will qualify as a Named Insured if there is no other similar insurance available to that organization. However:

a. Coverage under this provision is afforded only until the 90th day after you acquire or form the organization or the end of the policy period, whichever is earlier;

b. Coverage **A** does not apply to "bodily injury" or "property damage" that occurred before you acquired or formed the organization; and

c. Coverage **B** does not apply to "personal and advertising injury" arising out of an offense committed before you acquired or formed the organization.

No person or organization is an insured with respect to the conduct of any current or past partnership, joint venture or limited liability company that is not shown as a Named Insured in the Declarations.

SECTION III – LIMITS OF INSURANCE

1. The Limits of Insurance shown in the Declarations and the rules below fix the most we will pay regardless of the number of:

a. Insureds;

b. Claims made or "suits" brought; or

c. Persons or organizations making claims or bringing "suits".

2. The General Aggregate Limit is the most we will pay for the sum of:
   a. Medical expenses under Coverage **C**;
   b. Damages under Coverage **A**, except damages because of "bodily injury" or "property damage" included in the "products-completed operations hazard"; and
   c. Damages under Coverage **B**.
3. The Products-Completed Operations Aggregate Limit is the most we will pay under Coverage **A** for damages because of "bodily injury" and "property damage" included in the "products-completed operations hazard".
4. Subject to **2.** above, the Personal and Advertising Injury Limit is the most we will pay under Coverage **B** for the sum of all damages because of all "personal and advertising injury" sustained by any one person or organization.
5. Subject to **2.** or **3.** above, whichever applies, the Each Occurrence Limit is the most we will pay for the sum of:
   a. Damages under Coverage **A**; and
   b. Medical expenses under Coverage **C**

   because of all "bodily injury" and "property damage" arising out of any one "occurrence".
6. Subject to **5.** above, the Damage To Premises Rented To You Limit is the most we will pay under Coverage **A** for damages because of "property damage" to any one premises, while rented to you, or in the case of damage by fire, while rented to you or temporarily occupied by you with permission of the owner.
7. Subject to **5.** above, the Medical Expense Limit is the most we will pay under Coverage **C** for all medical expenses because of "bodily injury" sustained by any one person.

The Limits of Insurance of this Coverage Part apply separately to each consecutive annual period and to any remaining period of less than 12 months, starting with the beginning of the policy period shown in the Declarations, unless the policy period is extended after issuance for an additional period of less than 12 months. In that case, the additional period will be deemed part of the last preceding period for purposes of determining the Limits of Insurance.

SECTION IV – COMMERCIAL GENERAL LIABILITY CONDITIONS

1. **Bankruptcy**

   Bankruptcy or insolvency of the insured or of the insured's estate will not relieve us of our obligations under this Coverage Part.

2. **Duties In The Event Of Occurrence, Offense, Claim Or Suit**
   a. You must see to it that we are notified as soon as practicable of an "occurrence" or an offense which may result in a claim. To the extent possible, notice should include:
      (1) How, when and where the "occurrence" or offense took place;
      (2) The names and addresses of any injured persons and witnesses; and
      (3) The nature and location of any injury or damage arising out of the "occurrence" or offense.
   b. If a claim is made or "suit" is brought against any insured, you must:
      (1) Immediately record the specifics of the claim or "suit" and the date received; and
      (2) Notify us as soon as practicable.

      You must see to it that we receive written notice of the claim or "suit" as soon as practicable.
   c. You and any other involved insured must:
      (1) Immediately send us copies of any demands, notices, summonses or legal papers received in connection with the claim or "suit";
      (2) Authorize us to obtain records and other information;
      (3) Cooperate with us in the investigation or settlement of the claim or defense against the "suit"; and
      (4) Assist us, upon our request, in the enforcement of any right against any person or organization which may be liable to the insured because of injury or damage to which this insurance may also apply.
   d. No insured will, except at that insured's own cost, voluntarily make a payment, assume any obligation, or incur any expense, other than for first aid, without our consent.

3. **Legal Action Against Us**

   No person or organization has a right under this Coverage Part:
   a. To join us as a party or otherwise bring us into a "suit" asking for damages from an insured; or

b. To sue us on this Coverage Part unless all of its terms have been fully complied with.

A person or organization may sue us to recover on an agreed settlement or on a final judgment against an insured; but we will not be liable for damages that are not payable under the terms of this Coverage Part or that are in excess of the applicable limit of insurance. An agreed settlement means a settlement and release of liability signed by us, the insured and the claimant or the claimant's legal representative.

4. Other Insurance

If other valid and collectible insurance is available to the insured for a loss we cover under Coverages **A** or **B** of this Coverage Part, our obligations are limited as follows:

a. Primary Insurance

This insurance is primary except when **b.** below applies. If this insurance is primary, our obligations are not affected unless any of the other insurance is also primary. Then, we will share with all that other insurance by the method described in **c.** below.

b. Excess Insurance

This insurance is excess over:

(1) Any of the other insurance, whether primary, excess, contingent or on any other basis:

(a) That is Fire, Extended Coverage, Builder's Risk, Installation Risk or similar coverage for "your work";

(b) That is Fire insurance for premises rented to you or temporarily occupied by you with permission of the owner;

(c) That is insurance purchased by you to cover your liability as a tenant for "property damage" to premises rented to you or temporarily occupied by you with permission of the owner; or

(d) If the loss arises out of the maintenance or use of aircraft, "autos" or watercraft to the extent not subject to Exclusion **g.** of Section I – Coverage **A** – Bodily Injury And Property Damage Liability.

(2) Any other primary insurance available to you covering liability for damages arising out of the premises or operations, or the products and completed operations, for which you have been added as an additional insured by attachment of an endorsement.

When this insurance is excess, we will have no duty under Coverages **A** or **B** to defend the insured against any "suit" if any other insurer has a duty to defend the insured against that "suit". If no other insurer defends, we will undertake to do so, but we will be entitled to the insured's rights against all those other insurers.

When this insurance is excess over other insurance, we will pay only our share of the amount of the loss, if any, that exceeds the sum of:

(1) The total amount that all such other insurance would pay for the loss in the absence of this insurance; and

(2) The total of all deductible and self-insured amounts under all that other insurance.

We will share the remaining loss, if any, with any other insurance that is not described in this Excess Insurance provision and was not bought specifically to apply in excess of the Limits of Insurance shown in the Declarations of this Coverage Part.

c. Method Of Sharing

If all of the other insurance permits contribution by equal shares, we will follow this method also. Under this approach each insurer contributes equal amounts until it has paid its applicable limit of insurance or none of the loss remains, whichever comes first.

If any of the other insurance does not permit contribution by equal shares, we will contribute by limits. Under this method, each insurer's share is based on the ratio of its applicable limit of insurance to the total applicable limits of insurance of all insurers.

5. Premium Audit

a. We will compute all premiums for this Coverage Part in accordance with our rules and rates.

b. Premium shown in this Coverage Part as advance premium is a deposit premium only. At the close of each audit period we will compute the earned premium for that period and send notice to the first Named Insured. The due date for audit and retrospective premiums is the date shown as the due date on the bill. If the sum of the advance and audit premiums paid for the policy period is greater than the earned premium, we will return the excess to the first Named Insured.

c. The first Named Insured must keep records of the information we need for premium computation, and send us copies at such times as we may request.

6. **Representations**

    By accepting this policy, you agree:

    a. The statements in the Declarations are accurate and complete;

    b. Those statements are based upon representations you made to us; and

    c. We have issued this policy in reliance upon your representations.

7. **Separation Of Insureds**

    Except with respect to the Limits of Insurance, and any rights or duties specifically assigned in this Coverage Part to the first Named Insured, this insurance applies:

    a. As if each Named Insured were the only Named Insured; and

    b. Separately to each insured against whom claim is made or "suit" is brought.

8. **Transfer Of Rights Of Recovery Against Others To Us**

    If the insured has rights to recover all or part of any payment we have made under this Coverage Part, those rights are transferred to us. The insured must do nothing after loss to impair them. At our request, the insured will bring "suit" or transfer those rights to us and help us enforce them.

9. **When We Do Not Renew**

    If we decide not to renew this Coverage Part, we will mail or deliver to the first Named Insured shown in the Declarations written notice of the nonrenewal not less than 30 days before the expiration date.

    If notice is mailed, proof of mailing will be sufficient proof of notice.

SECTION V – DEFINITIONS

1. "Advertisement" means a notice that is broadcast or published to the general public or specific market segments about your goods, products or services for the purpose of attracting customers or supporters. For the purposes of this definition:

    a. Notices that are published include material placed on the Internet or on similar electronic means of communication; and

    b. Regarding web-sites, only that part of a web-site that is about your goods, products or services for the purposes of attracting customers or supporters is considered an advertisement.

2. "Auto" means:

    a. A land motor vehicle, trailer or semitrailer designed for travel on public roads, including any attached machinery or equipment; or

    b. Any other land vehicle that is subject to a compulsory or financial responsibility law or other motor vehicle insurance law in the state where it is licensed or principally garaged.

    However, "auto" does not include "mobile equipment".

3. "Bodily injury" means bodily injury, sickness or disease sustained by a person, including death resulting from any of these at any time.

4. "Coverage territory" means:

    a. The United States of America (including its territories and possessions), Puerto Rico and Canada;

    b. International waters or airspace, but only if the injury or damage occurs in the course of travel or transportation between any places included in a. above; or

    c. All other parts of the world if the injury or damage arises out of:

        (1) Goods or products made or sold by you in the territory described in a. above;

        (2) The activities of a person whose home is in the territory described in a. above, but is away for a short time on your business; or

        (3) "Personal and advertising injury" offenses that take place through the Internet or similar electronic means of communication

    provided the insured's responsibility to pay damages is determined in a "suit" on the merits, in the territory described in a. above or in a settlement we agree to.

5. "Employee" includes a "leased worker". "Employee" does not include a "temporary worker".

6. "Executive officer" means a person holding any of the officer positions created by your charter, constitution, by-laws or any other similar governing document.

7. "Hostile fire" means one which becomes uncontrollable or breaks out from where it was intended to be.

8. "Impaired property" means tangible property, other than "your product" or "your work", that cannot be used or is less useful because:

    a. It incorporates "your product" or "your work" that is known or thought to be defective, deficient, inadequate or dangerous; or

    b. You have failed to fulfill the terms of a contract or agreement;

    if such property can be restored to use by:

    a. The repair, replacement, adjustment or removal of "your product" or "your work"; or

b. Your fulfilling the terms of the contract or agreement.
9. "Insured contract" means:
   a. A contract for a lease of premises. However, that portion of the contract for a lease of premises that indemnifies any person or organization for damage by fire to premises while rented to you or temporarily occupied by you with permission of the owner is not an "insured contract";
   b. A sidetrack agreement;
   c. Any easement or license agreement, except in connection with construction or demolition operations on or within 50 feet of a railroad;
   d. An obligation, as required by ordinance, to indemnify a municipality, except in connection with work for a municipality;
   e. An elevator maintenance agreement;
   f. That part of any other contract or agreement pertaining to your business (including an indemnification of a municipality in connection with work performed for a municipality) under which you assume the tort liability of another party to pay for "bodily injury" or "property damage" to a third person or organization. Tort liability means a liability that would be imposed by law in the absence of any contract or agreement.

   Paragraph **f.** does not include that part of any contract or agreement:

   (1) That indemnifies a railroad for "bodily injury" or "property damage" arising out of construction or demolition operations, within 50 feet of any railroad property and affecting any railroad bridge or trestle, tracks, road-beds, tunnel, underpass or crossing;

   (2) That indemnifies an architect, engineer or surveyor for injury or damage arising out of:

   (a) Preparing, approving, or failing to prepare or approve, maps, shop drawings, opinions, reports, surveys, field orders, change orders or drawings and specifications; or

   (b) Giving directions or instructions, or failing to give them, if that is the primary cause of the injury or damage; or

   (3) Under which the insured, if an architect, engineer or surveyor, assumes liability for an injury or damage arising out of the insured's rendering or failure to render professional services, including those listed in **(2)** above and supervisory, inspection, architectural or engineering activities.

10. "Leased worker" means a person leased to you by a labor leasing firm under an agreement between you and the labor leasing firm, to perform duties related to the conduct of your business. "Leased worker" does not include a "temporary worker".

11. "Loading or unloading" means the handling of property:
    a. After it is moved from the place where it is accepted for movement into or onto an aircraft, watercraft or "auto";
    b. While it is in or on an aircraft, watercraft or "auto"; or
    c. While it is being moved from an aircraft, watercraft or "auto" to the place where it is finally delivered;

    but "loading or unloading" does not include the movement of property by means of a mechanical device, other than a hand truck, that is not attached to the aircraft, watercraft or "auto".

12. "Mobile equipment" means any of the following types of land vehicles, including any attached machinery or equipment:
    a. Bulldozers, farm machinery, forklifts and other vehicles designed for use principally off public roads;
    b. Vehicles maintained for use solely on or next to premises you own or rent;
    c. Vehicles that travel on crawler treads;
    d. Vehicles, whether self-propelled or not, maintained primarily to provide mobility to permanently mounted:

    (1) Power cranes, shovels, loaders, diggers or drills; or

    (2) Road construction or resurfacing equipment such as graders, scrapers or rollers;

    e. Vehicles not described in **a., b., c.** or **d.** above that are not self-propelled and are maintained primarily to provide mobility to permanently attached equipment of the following types:

    (1) Air compressors, pumps and generators, including spraying, welding, building cleaning, geophysical exploration, lighting and well servicing equipment; or

    (2) Cherry pickers and similar devices used to raise or lower workers;

    f. Vehicles not described in **a., b., c.** or **d.** above maintained primarily for purposes other than the transportation of persons or cargo.

    However, self-propelled vehicles with the following types of permanently attached equipment are not "mobile equipment" but will be considered "autos":

(1) Equipment designed primarily for:
  (a) Snow removal;
  (b) Road maintenance, but not construction or resurfacing; or
  (c) Street cleaning;
(2) Cherry pickers and similar devices mounted on automobile or truck chassis and used to raise or lower workers; and
(3) Air compressors, pumps and generators, including spraying, welding, building cleaning, geophysical exploration, lighting and well servicing equipment.

However, "mobile equipment" does not include any land vehicles that are subject to a compulsory or financial responsibility law or other motor vehicle insurance law in the state where it is licensed or principally garaged. Land vehicles subject to a compulsory or financial responsibility law or other motor vehicle insurance law are considered "autos".

13. "Occurrence" means an accident, including continuous or repeated exposure to substantially the same general harmful conditions.

14. "Personal and advertising injury" means injury, including consequential "bodily injury", arising out of one or more of the following offenses:
  a. False arrest, detention or imprisonment;
  b. Malicious prosecution;
  c. The wrongful eviction from, wrongful entry into, or invasion of the right of private occupancy of a room, dwelling or premises that a person occupies, committed by or on behalf of its owner, landlord or lessor;
  d. Oral or written publication, in any manner, of material that slanders or libels a person or organization or disparages a person's or organization's goods, products or services;
  e. Oral or written publication, in any manner, of material that violates a person's right of privacy;
  f. The use of another's advertising idea in your "advertisement"; or
  g. Infringing upon another's copyright, trade dress or slogan in your "advertisement".

15. "Pollutants" mean any solid, liquid, gaseous or thermal irritant or contaminant, including smoke, vapor, soot, fumes, acids, alkalis, chemicals and waste. Waste includes materials to be recycled, reconditioned or reclaimed.

16. "Products-completed operations hazard":
  a. Includes all "bodily injury" and "property damage" occurring away from premises you own or rent and arising out of "your product" or "your work" except:
    (1) Products that are still in your physical possession; or
    (2) Work that has not yet been completed or abandoned. However, "your work" will be deemed completed at the earliest of the following times:
      (a) When all of the work called for in your contract has been completed.
      (b) When all of the work to be done at the job site has been completed if your contract calls for work at more than one job site.
      (c) When that part of the work done at a job site has been put to its intended use by any person or organization other than another contractor or subcontractor working on the same project.
    Work that may need service, maintenance, correction, repair or replacement, but which is otherwise complete, will be treated as completed.
  b. Does not include "bodily injury" or "property damage" arising out of:
    (1) The transportation of property, unless the injury or damage arises out of a condition in or on a vehicle not owned or operated by you, and that condition was created by the "loading or unloading" of that vehicle by any insured;
    (2) The existence of tools, uninstalled equipment or abandoned or unused materials; or
    (3) Products or operations for which the classification, listed in the Declarations or in a policy schedule, states that products-completed operations are subject to the General Aggregate Limit.

17. "Property damage" means:
  a. Physical injury to tangible property, including all resulting loss of use of that property. All such loss of use shall be deemed to occur at the time of the physical injury that caused it; or

Appendix

b. Loss of use of tangible property that is not physically injured. All such loss of use shall be deemed to occur at the time of the "occurrence" that caused it.

For the purposes of this insurance, electronic data is not tangible property.

As used in this definition, electronic data means information, facts or programs stored as or on, created or used on, or transmitted to or from computer software, including systems and applications software, hard or floppy disks, CD-ROMS, tapes, drives, cells, data processing devices or any other media which are used with electronically controlled equipment.

18. "Suit" means a civil proceeding in which damages because of "bodily injury", "property damage" or "personal and advertising injury" to which this insurance applies are alleged. "Suit" includes:

   a. An arbitration proceeding in which such damages are claimed and to which the insured must submit or does submit with our consent; or

   b. Any other alternative dispute resolution proceeding in which such damages are claimed and to which the insured submits with our consent.

19. "Temporary worker" means a person who is furnished to you to substitute for a permanent "employee" on leave or to meet seasonal or short-term workload conditions.

20. "Volunteer worker" means a person who is not your "employee", and who donates his or her work and acts at the direction of and within the scope of duties determined by you, and is not paid a fee, salary or other compensation by you or anyone else for their work performed for you.

21. "Your product":

   a. Means:

      (1) Any goods or products, other than real property, manufactured, sold, handled, distributed or disposed of by:

         (a) You;

         (b) Others trading under your name; or

         (c) A person or organization whose business or assets you have acquired; and

      (2) Containers (other than vehicles), materials, parts or equipment furnished in connection with such goods or products.

   b. Includes

      (1) Warranties or representations made at any time with respect to the fitness, quality, durability, performance or use of "your product"; and

      (2) The providing of or failure to provide warnings or instructions.

   c. Does not include vending machines or other property rented to or located for the use of others but not sold.

22. "Your work":

   a. Means:

      (1) Work or operations performed by you or on your behalf; and

      (2) Materials, parts or equipment furnished in connection with such work or operations.

   b. Includes

      (1) Warranties or representations made at any time with respect to the fitness, quality, durability, performance or use of "your work", and

      (2) The providing of or failure to provide warnings or instructions.

POLICY NUMBER: SP 0001

COMMERCIAL AUTO
CA DS 03 03 06

BUSINESS AUTO DECLARATIONS

COMPANY NAME AREA	PRODUCER NAME AREA

ITEM ONE

Named Insured: AMR Corporation

Mailing Address: 2000 Industrial Highway
Workingtown, PA 19000

Policy Period

From: 10/1/07

To: 10/1/08
At 12:01 A.M. Standard Time at your mailing address.

Previous Policy Number:

Form Of Business:
☒ Corporation ☐ Limited Liability Company ☐ Individual
☐ Partnership ☐ Other:

In return for the payment of the premium, and subject to all the terms of this policy, we agree with you to provide the insurance as stated in this policy.

Premium shown is payable at inception: $ XXX
Audit Period (If Applicable): ☒ Annually ☐ Semi-Annually ☐ Quarterly ☐ Monthly

Endorsements Attached To This Policy:
IL 00 17 . Common Policy Conditions (**IL 01 46** in Washington)
IL 00 21 . Broad Form Nuclear Exclusion (Not applicable in New York)

CA DS 03 03 06 © ISO Properties, Inc., 2005 Page 1 of 11

Countersignature Of Authorized Representative
Name: A.M. Abel
Title:
Signature:
Date: 10/1/07

Note
Officers' facsimile signatures may be inserted here, on the policy cover or elsewhere at the company's option.

ITEM TWO

Schedule Of Coverages And Covered Autos

This policy provides only those coverages where a charge is shown in the premium column below. Each of these
coverages will apply only to those "autos" shown as covered "autos". **"Autos" are shown as covered "autos" for a particular coverage by the entry of one or more of the symbols from the Covered Autos Section of the Business Auto Coverage Form next to the name of the coverage.**

Coverages	Covered Autos	Limit	Premium
Liability	1	$ 1,000,000	$ XXX
Personal Injury Protection (Or Equivalent No-Fault Coverage)	5	Separately Stated In Each Personal Injury Protection Endorsement Minus $ Deductible.	$ XXX
Added Personal Injury Protection (Or Equivalent Added No-Fault Coverage)		Separately Stated In Each Added Personal Injury Protection Endorsement.	$
Property Protection Insurance (Michigan Only)		Separately Stated In The Property Protection Insurance Endorsement Minus $ Deductible For Each Accident.	$
Auto Medical Payments		$	$
Medical Expense And Income Loss Benefits (Virginia Only)		Separately Stated In Each Medical Expense And Income Loss Benefits Endorsement.	$
Uninsured Motorists	6	$ 1,000,000	$ XXX
Underinsured Motorists (When Not Included In Uninsured Motorists Coverage)	6	$ 1,000,000	$ XXX

ITEM TWO
Schedule Of Coverages And Covered Autos (Cont'd)

Coverages	Covered Autos	Limit	Premium
Physical Damage Comprehensive Coverage	7,8	Actual Cash Value Or Cost Of Repair, Whichever Is Less, Minus $ 1,000 Deductible For Each Covered Auto, But No Deductible Applies To Loss Caused By Fire Or Lightning. See Item Four For Hired Or Borrowed Autos.	$ XXX
Physical Damage Specified Causes Of Loss Coverage		Actual Cash Value Or Cost Of Repair, Whichever Is Less, Minus $ Deductible For Each Covered Auto For Loss Caused By Mischief Or Vandalism. See Item Four For Hired Or Borrowed Autos.	$
Physical Damage Collision Coverage	7,8	Actual Cash Value Or Cost Of Repair, Whichever Is Less, Minus $ 1,000 Deductible For Each Covered Auto, See Item Four For Hired Or Borrowed Autos.	$ XXX
Physical Damage Towing And Labor		For Each Disablement Of A Private Passenger Auto.	$
			$ XXX
		Premium For Endorsements	$
		Estimated Total Premium*	$ XXX

*This Policy May Be Subject To Final Audit.

CA DS 03 03 06

ITEM THREE
Schedule Of Covered Autos You Own

Covered Auto Number: 1	
Town And State Where The Covered Auto Will Be Principally Garaged	PA 041
Description (Year, Model, Trade Name, Body Type, Serial Number (S), Vehicle Identification Number (VIN))	20xx Lincoln Navigator VIN xxx
Purchased: Original Cost New Actual Cost New (N) Or Used (U)	$ XXX

CLASSIFICATION

Radius Of Operation	Business Use s=service r=retail c=commercial	Size GVW, GCW Or Vehicle Seating Capacity	Age Group	Primary Rating Factor Liab.	Primary Rating Factor Phy. Dam.	Secondary Rating Factor	Code

Except For Towing, All Physical Damage Loss Is Payable To You And The Loss Payee Named To The Right As Interests May Appear At the Time Of The Loss.	

Coverages – Premiums, Limits And Deductibles
(Absence of a deductible or limit entry in any column below means that the limit or deductible entry in the corresponding Item Two column applies instead.)

Coverages	Limit	Premium
Liability	$	$
Personal Injury Protection	Stated In Each Personal Injury Protection Endorsement Minus $ Deductible Shown	$
Added Personal Injury Protection	Stated In Each Added Personal Injury Protection Endorsement	$
Property Protection Insurance (Michigan Only)	Stated In The Property Protection Insurance Endorsement Minus $ Deductible Shown	$
Auto Medical Payments	$	$
Medical Expense And Income Loss Benefits (Virginia Only)	Stated In Each Medical Expense And Income Loss Benefits Endorsement For Each Person	$
Comprehensive	Stated In Item Two Minus $ Deductible Shown	$
Specified Causes Of Loss	Stated In Item Two Minus $ Deductible Shown	$
Collision	Stated In Item Two Minus $ Deductible Shown	$
Towing And Labor	$ Per Disablement	$

© ISO Properties, Inc., 2005   CA DS 03 03 06

ITEM THREE
Schedule Of Covered Autos You Own

Covered Auto Number:	
2	

Town And State Where The Covered Auto Will Be Principally Garaged	PA 041
Description (Year, Model, Trade Name, Body Type, Serial Number (S), Vehicle Identification Number (VIN))	20xx Acura Legend VIN xxx
Purchased: Original Cost New Actual Cost New (N) Or Used (U)	$ XXX

CLASSIFICATION

Radius Of Operation	Business Use s=service r=retail c=commercial	Size GVW, GCW Or Vehicle Seating Capacity	Age Group	Primary Rating Factor Liab.	Primary Rating Factor Phy. Dam.	Secondary Rating Factor	Code

Except For Towing, All Physical Damage Loss Is Payable To You And The Loss Payee Named To The Right As Interests May Appear At the Time Of The Loss.

Coverages – Premiums, Limits And Deductibles
(Absence of a deductible or limit entry in any column below means that the limit or deductible entry in the corresponding Item Two column applies instead.)

Coverages	Limit	Premium
Liability	$	$
Personal Injury Protection	Stated In Each Personal Injury Protection Endorsement Minus $ Deductible Shown	$
Added Personal Injury Protection	Stated In Each Added Personal Injury Protection Endorsement	$
Property Protection Insurance (Michigan Only)	Stated In The Property Protection Insurance Endorsement Minus $ Deductible Shown	$
Auto Medical Payments	$	$
Medical Expense And Income Loss Benefits (Virginia Only)	Stated In Each Medical Expense And Income Loss Benefits Endorsement For Each Person	$
Comprehensive	Stated In Item Two Minus $ Deductible Shown	$
Specified Causes Of Loss	Stated In Item Two Minus $ Deductible Shown	$
Collision	Stated In Item Two Minus $ Deductible Shown	$
Towing And Labor	$ Per Disablement	$

CA DS 03 03 06   © ISO Properties, Inc., 2005

Appendix 57

ITEM THREE
Schedule Of Covered Autos You Own

Covered Auto Number: 3	
Town And State Where The Covered Auto Will Be Principally Garaged	PA 041
Description (Year, Model, Trade Name, Body Type, Serial Number (S), Vehicle Identification Number (VIN))	20xx Nissan Altima VIN xxx
Purchased: Original Cost New Actual Cost New (N) Or Used (U)	$ XXX

CLASSIFICATION

Radius Of Operation	Business Use s=service r=retail c=commercial	Size GVW, GCW Or Vehicle Seating Capacity	Age Group	Primary Rating Factor Liab.	Primary Rating Factor Phy. Dam.	Secondary Rating Factor	Code

Except For Towing, All Physical Damage Loss Is Payable To You And The Loss Payee Named To The Right As Interests May Appear At the Time Of The Loss.	

Coverages – Premiums, Limits And Deductibles
(Absence of a deductible or limit entry in any column below means that the limit or deductible entry in the corresponding Item Two column applies instead.)

Coverages	Limit	Premium
Liability	$	$
Personal Injury Protection	Stated In Each Personal Injury Protection Endorsement Minus $ Deductible Shown	$
Added Personal Injury Protection	Stated In Each Added Personal Injury Protection Endorsement	$
Property Protection Insurance (Michigan Only)	Stated In The Property Protection Insurance Endorsement Minus $ Deductible Shown	$
Auto Medical Payments	$	$
Medical Expense And Income Loss Benefits (Virginia Only)	Stated In Each Medical Expense And Income Loss Benefits Endorsement For Each Person	$
Comprehensive	Stated In Item Two Minus $ Deductible Shown	$
Specified Causes Of Loss	Stated In Item Two Minus $ Deductible Shown	$
Collision	Stated In Item Two Minus $ Deductible Shown	$
Towing And Labor	$ Per Disablement	$

ITEM THREE
Schedule Of Covered Autos You Own (Cont'd)

Total Premiums	
Liability	$ XXX
Personal Injury Protection	$ XXX
Added Personal Injury Protection	$
Property Protection Insurance (Michigan Only)	$
Auto Medical Payments	$
Medical Expense And Income Loss Benefits (Virginia Only)	$
Comprehensive	$ XXX
Specified Causes Of Loss	$
Collision	$ XXX
Towing And Labor	$

ITEM FOUR
Schedule Of Hired Or Borrowed Covered Auto Coverage And Premiums

Liability Coverage – Rating Basis, Cost Of Hire				
State	Estimated Cost Of Hire For Each State	Rate Per Each $100 Cost Of Hire	Factor (If Liability Coverage Is Primary)	Premium
PA	$ If any	$ XXX	$ NA	$ XXX
Liability Coverage . Rating Basis, Number Of Days . (For Mobile Or Farm Equipment . Rental Period Basis)				
State	Estimated Number Of Days Equipment Will Be Rented	Base Premium	Factor	Premium
		$		$
			Total Premium	$ XXX

Cost of hire means the total amount you incur for the hire of "autos" you don't own (not including "autos" you borrow
or rent from your partners or "employees" or their family members). Cost of hire does not include charges for services performed by motor carriers of property or passengers.

ITEM FOUR
Schedule Of Hired Or Borrowed Covered Auto Coverage And Premiums (Cont'd)
Physical Damage Coverage

Coverages	Limit Of Insurance		
Comprehensive	Actual Cash Value Or Cost Of Repair, Whichever Is Less, Minus $ Deductible For Each Covered Auto, But No Deductible Applies To Loss Caused By Fire Or Lightning.		
	Estimated Annual Cost Of Hire	Rate Per Each $100 Annual Cost Of Hire	Premium
	$ If any	$	$ XXX
Specified Causes Of Loss	Actual Cash Value Or Cost Of Repair, Whichever Is Less, Minus $ Deductible For Each Covered Auto For Loss Caused By Mischief Or Vandalism.		
	Estimated Annual Cost Of Hire	Rate Per Each $100 Annual Cost Of Hire	Premium
	$	$	$
Collision	Actual Cash Value Or Cost Of Repair, Whichever Is Less, Minus $ Deductible For Each Covered Auto.		
	Estimated Annual Cost Of Hire	Rate Per Each $100 Annual Cost Of Hire	Premium
	$ If any	$	$ Incl.

Total Premium:	$ XXX

ITEM FIVE
Schedule For Non-Ownership Liability

Named Insured's Business	Rating Basis	Number	Premium
Other Than Garage Service Operations And Other Than Social Service Agencies	Number Of Employees	32	$ XXX
	Number Of Partners		$
Garage Service Operations	Number Of Employees Whose Principal Duty Involves The Operation Of Autos		$
Social Service Agencies	Number Of Employees		$
	Number Of Volunteers		$
		Total Premiums	$ XXX

Note: Item 6, Schedule for Public Auto or Leasing Rental Concerns, Has Been Omitted.

COMMERCIAL AUTO
CA 00 01 03 06

BUSINESS AUTO COVERAGE FORM

Various provisions in this policy restrict coverage. Read the entire policy carefully to determine rights, duties and what is and is not covered.

Throughout this policy the words "you" and "your" refer to the Named Insured shown in the Declarations. The words "we", "us" and "our" refer to the Company providing this insurance.

Other words and phrases that appear in quotation marks have special meaning. Refer to Section **V** – Definitions.

SECTION I – COVERED AUTOS

Item Two of the Declarations shows the "autos" that are covered "autos" for each of your coverages. The following numerical symbols describe the "autos" that may be covered "autos". The symbols entered next to a coverage on the Declarations designate the only "autos" that are covered "autos".

A. Description Of Covered Auto Designation Symbols

Symbol	Description Of Covered Auto Designation Symbols	
1	Any "Auto"	
2	Owned "Autos" Only	Only those "autos" you own (and for Liability Coverage any "trailers" you don't own while attached to power units you own). This includes those "autos" you acquire ownership of after the policy begins.
3	Owned Private Passenger "Autos" Only	Only the private passenger "autos" you own. This includes those private passenger "autos" you acquire ownership of after the policy begins.
4	Owned "Autos" Other Than Private Passenger "Autos" Only	Only those "autos" you own that are not of the private passenger type (and for Liability Coverage any "trailers" you don't own while attached to power units you own). This includes those "autos" not of the private passenger type you acquire ownership of after the policy begins.
5	Owned "Autos" Subject To No-Fault	Only those "autos" you own that are required to have No-Fault benefits in the state where they are licensed or principally garaged. This includes those "autos" you acquire ownership of after the policy begins provided they are required to have No-Fault benefits in the state where they are licensed or principally garaged.
6	Owned "Autos" Subject To A Compulsory Uninsured Motorists Law	Only those "autos" you own that because of the law in the state where they are licensed or principally garaged are required to have and cannot reject Uninsured Motorists Coverage. This includes those "autos" you acquire ownership of after the policy begins provided they are subject to the same state uninsured motorists requirement.
7	Specifically Described "Autos"	Only those "autos" described in Item Three of the Declarations for which a premium charge is shown (and for Liability Coverage any "trailers" you don't own while attached to any power unit described in Item Three).
8	Hired "Autos" Only	Only those "autos" you lease, hire, rent or borrow. This does not include any "auto" you lease, hire, rent, or borrow from any of your "employees", partners (if you are a partnership), members (if you are a limited liability company) or members of their households.
9	Nonowned "Autos" Only	Only those "autos" you do not own, lease, hire, rent or borrow that are used in connection with your business. This includes "autos" owned by your "employees", partners (if you are a partnership), members (if you are a limited liability company), or members of their households but only while used in your business or your personal affairs.

CA 00 01 03 06 © ISO Properties, Inc., 2005 Page 1 of 12

| 19 | Mobile Equipment Subject To Compulsory Or Financial Responsibility Or Other Motor Vehicle Insurance Law Only | Only those "autos" that are land vehicles and that would qualify under the definition of "mobile equipment" under this policy if they were not subject to a compulsory or financial responsibility law or other motor vehicle insurance law where they are licensed or principally garaged. |

B. Owned Autos You Acquire After The Policy Begins

1. If Symbols **1, 2, 3, 4, 5, 6** or **19** are entered next to a coverage in Item Two of the Declarations, then you have coverage for "autos" that you acquire of the type described for the remainder of the policy period.

2. But, if Symbol **7** is entered next to a coverage in Item Two of the Declarations, an "auto" you acquire will be a covered "auto" for that coverage only if:

    a. We already cover all "autos" that you own for that coverage or it replaces an "auto" you previously owned that had that coverage; and

    b. You tell us within 30 days after you acquire it that you want us to cover it for that coverage.

C. Certain Trailers, Mobile Equipment And Temporary Substitute Autos

If Liability Coverage is provided by this Coverage Form, the following types of vehicles are also covered "autos" for Liability Coverage:

1. "Trailers" with a load capacity of 2,000 pounds or less designed primarily for travel on public roads.

2. "Mobile equipment" while being carried or towed by a covered "auto".

3. Any "auto" you do not own while used with the permission of its owner as a temporary substitute for a covered "auto" you own that is out of service because of its:

    a. Breakdown;
    b. Repair;
    c. Servicing;
    d. "Loss"; or
    e. Destruction.

SECTION II – LIABILITY COVERAGE

A. Coverage

We will pay all sums an "insured" legally must pay as damages because of "bodily injury" or "property damage" to which this insurance applies, caused by an "accident" and resulting from the ownership, maintenance or use of a covered "auto".

We will also pay all sums an "insured" legally must pay as a "covered pollution cost or expense" to which this insurance applies, caused by an "accident" and resulting from the ownership, maintenance or use of covered "autos". However, we will only pay for the "covered pollution cost or expense" if there is either "bodily injury" or "property damage" to which this insurance applies that is caused by the same "accident".

We have the right and duty to defend any "insured" against a "suit" asking for such damages or a "covered pollution cost or expense". However, we have no duty to defend any "insured" against a "suit" seeking damages for "bodily injury" or "property damage" or a "covered pollution cost or expense" to which this insurance does not apply. We may investigate and settle any claim or "suit" as we consider appropriate. Our duty to defend or settle ends when the Liability Coverage Limit of Insurance has been exhausted by payment of judgments or settlements.

1. **Who Is An Insured**

    The following are "insureds":

    a. You for any covered "auto".

    b. Anyone else while using with your permission a covered "auto" you own, hire or borrow except:

        (1) The owner or anyone else from whom you hire or borrow a covered "auto". This exception does not apply if the covered "auto" is a "trailer" connected to a covered "auto" you own.

(2) Your "employee" if the covered "auto" is owned by that "employee" or a member of his or her household.

(3) Someone using a covered "auto" while he or she is working in a business of selling, servicing, repairing, parking or storing "autos" unless that business is yours.

(4) Anyone other than your "employees", partners (if you are a partnership), members (if you are a limited liability company), or a lessee or borrower or any of their "employees", while moving property to or from a covered "auto".

(5) A partner (if you are a partnership), or a member (if you are a limited liability company) for a covered "auto" owned by him or her or a member of his or her household.

c. Anyone liable for the conduct of an "insured" described above but only to the extent of that liability.

2. **Coverage Extensions**

a. **Supplementary Payments**

We will pay for the "insured":

(1) All expenses we incur.

(2) Up to $2,000 for cost of bail bonds (including bonds for related traffic law violations) required because of an "accident" we cover. We do not have to furnish these bonds.

(3) The cost of bonds to release attachments in any "suit" against the "insured" we defend, but only for bond amounts within our Limit of Insurance.

(4) All reasonable expenses incurred by the "insured" at our request, including actual loss of earnings up to $250 a day because of time off from work.

(5) All costs taxed against the "insured" in any "suit" against the "insured" we defend.

(6) All interest on the full amount of any judgment that accrues after entry of the judgment in any "suit" against the "insured" we defend, but our duty to pay interest ends when we have paid, offered to pay or deposited in court the part of the judgment that is within our Limit of Insurance.

These payments will not reduce the Limit of Insurance.

b. **Out-Of-State Coverage Extensions**

While a covered "auto" is away from the state where it is licensed we will:

(1) Increase the Limit of Insurance for Liability Coverage to meet the limits specified by a compulsory or financial responsibility law of the jurisdiction where the covered "auto" is being used. This extension does not apply to the limit or limits specified by any law governing motor carriers of passengers or property.

(2) Provide the minimum amounts and types of other coverages, such as no-fault, required of out-of-state vehicles by the jurisdiction where the covered "auto" is being used.

We will not pay anyone more than once for the same elements of loss because of these extensions.

B. **Exclusions**

This insurance does not apply to any of the following:

1. **Expected Or Intended Injury**

"Bodily injury" or "property damage" expected or intended from the standpoint of the "insured".

2. **Contractual**

Liability assumed under any contract or agreement.

But this exclusion does not apply to liability for damages:

a. Assumed in a contract or agreement that is an "insured contract" provided the "bodily injury" or "property damage" occurs subsequent to the execution of the contract or agreement; or

b. That the "insured" would have in the absence of the contract or agreement.

3. **Workers' Compensation**

Any obligation for which the "insured" or the "insured's" insurer may be held liable under any workers' compensation, disability benefits or unemployment compensation law or any similar law.

4. **Employee Indemnification And Employer's Liability**

"Bodily injury" to:

a. An "employee" of the "insured" arising out of and in the course of:

(1) Employment by the "insured"; or

(2) Performing the duties related to the conduct of the "insured's" business; or

b. The spouse, child, parent, brother or sister of that "employee" as a consequence of Paragraph **a.** above.

This exclusion applies:

(1) Whether the "insured" may be liable as an employer or in any other capacity; and

(2) To any obligation to share damages with or repay someone else who must pay damages because of the injury.

But this exclusion does not apply to "bodily injury" to domestic "employees" not entitled to workers' compensation benefits or to liability assumed by the "insured" under an "insured contract". For the purposes of the Coverage Form, a domestic "employee" is a person engaged in household or domestic work performed principally in connection with a residence premises.

5. Fellow Employee

"Bodily injury" to any fellow "employee" of the "insured" arising out of and in the course of the fellow "employee's" employment or while performing duties related to the conduct of your business.

6. Care, Custody Or Control

"Property damage" to or "covered pollution cost or expense" involving property owned or transported by the "insured" or in the "insured's" care, custody or control. But this exclusion does not apply to liability assumed under a sidetrack agreement.

7. Handling Of Property

"Bodily injury" or "property damage" resulting from the handling of property:

a. Before it is moved from the place where it is accepted by the "insured" for movement into or onto the covered "auto"; or

b. After it is moved from the covered "auto" to the place where it is finally delivered by the "insured".

8. Movement Of Property By Mechanical Device

"Bodily injury" or "property damage" resulting from the movement of property by a mechanical device (other than a hand truck) unless the device is attached to the covered "auto".

9. Operations

"Bodily injury" or "property damage" arising out of the operation of:

a. Any equipment listed in Paragraphs **6.b.** and **6.c.** of the definition of "mobile equipment"; or

b. Machinery or equipment that is on, attached to, or part of, a land vehicle that would qualify under the definition of "mobile equipment" if it were not subject to a compulsory or financial responsibility law or other motor vehicle insurance law where it is licensed or principally garaged.

10. Completed Operations

"Bodily injury" or "property damage" arising out of your work after that work has been completed or abandoned.

In this exclusion, your work means:

a. Work or operations performed by you or on your behalf; and

b. Materials, parts or equipment furnished in connection with such work or operations.

Your work includes warranties or representations made at any time with respect to the fitness, quality, durability or performance of any of the items included in Paragraph **a.** or **b.** above.

Your work will be deemed completed at the earliest of the following times:

(1) When all of the work called for in your contract has been completed.

(2) When all of the work to be done at the site has been completed if your contract calls for work at more than one site.

(3) When that part of the work done at a job site has been put to its intended use by any person or organization other than another contractor or subcontractor working on the same project.

Work that may need service, maintenance, correction, repair or replacement, but which is otherwise complete, will be treated as completed.

11. Pollution

"Bodily injury" or "property damage" arising out of the actual, alleged or threatened discharge, dispersal, seepage, migration, release or escape of "pollutants":

a. That are, or that are contained in any property that is:

(1) Being transported or towed by, handled, or handled for movement into, onto or from, the covered "auto";

(2) Otherwise in the course of transit by or on behalf of the "insured"; or

(3) Being stored, disposed of, treated or processed in or upon the covered "auto";

b. Before the "pollutants" or any property in which the "pollutants" are contained are moved from the place where they are accepted by the "insured" for movement into or onto the covered "auto"; or

c. After the "pollutants" or any property in which the "pollutants" are contained are moved from the covered "auto" to the place where they are finally delivered, disposed of or abandoned by the "insured".

Paragraph **a.** above does not apply to fuels, lubricants, fluids, exhaust gases or other similar "pollutants" that are needed for or result from the normal electrical, hydraulic or mechanical functioning of the covered "auto" or its parts, if:

(1) The "pollutants" escape, seep, migrate, or are discharged, dispersed or released directly from an "auto" part designed by its manufacturer to hold, store, receive or dispose of such "pollutants"; and

(2) The "bodily injury", "property damage" or "covered pollution cost or expense" does not arise out of the operation of any equipment listed in Paragraphs **6.b.** and **6.c.** of the definition of "mobile equipment".

Paragraphs **b.** and **c.** above of this exclusion do not apply to "accidents" that occur away from premises owned by or rented to an "insured" with respect to "pollutants" not in or upon a covered "auto" if:

(1) The "pollutants" or any property in which the "pollutants" are contained are upset, overturned or damaged as a result of the maintenance or use of a covered "auto"; and

(2) The discharge, dispersal, seepage, migration, release or escape of the "pollutants" is caused directly by such upset, overturn or damage.

12. War

"Bodily injury" or "property damage" arising directly or indirectly out of:

a. War, including undeclared or civil war;

b. Warlike action by a military force, including action in hindering or defending against an actual or expected attack, by any government, sovereign or other authority using military personnel or other agents; or

c. Insurrection, rebellion, revolution, usurped power, or action taken by governmental authority in hindering or defending against any of these.

13. Racing

Covered "autos" while used in any professional or organized racing or demolition contest or stunting activity, or while practicing for such contest or activity. This insurance also does not apply while that covered "auto" is being prepared for such a contest or activity.

C. Limit Of Insurance

Regardless of the number of covered "autos", "insureds", premiums paid, claims made or vehicles involved in the "accident", the most we will pay for the total of all damages and "covered pollution cost or expense" combined, resulting from any one "accident" is the Limit of Insurance for Liability Coverage shown in the Declarations.

All "bodily injury", "property damage" and "covered pollution cost or expense" resulting from continuous or repeated exposure to substantially the same conditions will be considered as resulting from one "accident".

No one will be entitled to receive duplicate payments for the same elements of "loss" under this Coverage Form and any Medical Payments Coverage Endorsement, Uninsured Motorists Coverage Endorsement or Underinsured Motorists Coverage Endorsement attached to this Coverage Part.

SECTION III – PHYSICAL DAMAGE COVERAGE

A. Coverage

1. We will pay for "loss" to a covered "auto" or its equipment under:

    a. **Comprehensive Coverage**

    From any cause except:

    (1) The covered "auto's" collision with another object; or

    (2) The covered "auto's" overturn.

    b. **Specified Causes Of Loss Coverage**

    Caused by:

    (1) Fire, lightning or explosion;

    (2) Theft;

    (3) Windstorm, hail or earthquake;

    (4) Flood;

    (5) Mischief or vandalism; or

    (6) The sinking, burning, collision or derailment of any conveyance transporting the covered "auto".

c. **Collision Coverage**

Caused by:

(1) The covered "auto's" collision with another object; or

(2) The covered "auto's" overturn.

2. **Towing**

We will pay up to the limit shown in the Declarations for towing and labor costs incurred each time a covered "auto" of the private passenger type is disabled. However, the labor must be performed at the place of disablement.

3. **Glass Breakage – Hitting A Bird Or Animal – Falling Objects Or Missiles**

If you carry Comprehensive Coverage for the damaged covered "auto", we will pay for the following under Comprehensive Coverage:

a. Glass breakage;

b. "Loss" caused by hitting a bird or animal; and

c. "Loss" caused by falling objects or missiles.

However, you have the option of having glass breakage caused by a covered "auto's" collision or overturn considered a "loss" under Collision Coverage.

4. **Coverage Extensions**

a. **Transportation Expenses**

We will pay up to $20 per day to a maximum of $600 for temporary transportation expense incurred by you because of the total theft of a covered "auto" of the private passenger type. We will pay only for those covered "autos" for which you carry either Comprehensive or Specified Causes of Loss Coverage. We will pay for temporary transportation expenses incurred during the period beginning 48 hours after the theft and ending, regardless of the policy's expiration, when the covered "auto" is returned to use or we pay for its "loss".

b. **Loss Of Use Expenses**

For Hired Auto Physical Damage, we will pay expenses for which an "insured" becomes legally responsible to pay for loss of use of a vehicle rented or hired without a driver, under a written rental contract or agreement. We will pay for loss of use expenses if caused by:

(1) Other than collision only if the Declarations indicate that Comprehensive Coverage is provided for any covered "auto";

(2) Specified Causes Of Loss only if the Declarations indicate that Specified Causes Of Loss Coverage is provided for any covered "auto"; or

(3) Collision only if the Declarations indicate that Collision Coverage is provided for any covered "auto".

However, the most we will pay for any expenses for loss of use is $20 per day, to a maximum of $600.

B. **Exclusions**

1. We will not pay for "loss" caused by or resulting from any of the following. Such "loss" is excluded regardless of any other cause or event that contributes concurrently or in any sequence to the "loss".

a. **Nuclear Hazard**

(1) The explosion of any weapon employing atomic fission or fusion; or

(2) Nuclear reaction or radiation, or radioactive contamination, however caused.

b. **War Or Military Action**

(1) War, including undeclared or civil war;

(2) Warlike action by a military force, including action in hindering or defending against an actual or expected attack, by any government, sovereign or other authority using military personnel or other agents; or

(3) Insurrection, rebellion, revolution, usurped power or action taken by governmental authority in hindering or defending against any of these.

2. We will not pay for "loss" to any covered "auto" while used in any professional or organized racing or demolition contest or stunting activity, or while practicing for such contest or activity. We will also not pay for "loss" to any covered "auto" while that covered "auto" is being prepared for such a contest or activity.

3. We will not pay for "loss" caused by or resulting from any of the following unless caused by other "loss" that is covered by this insurance:

a. Wear and tear, freezing, mechanical or electrical breakdown.

b. Blowouts, punctures or other road damage to tires.

4. We will not pay for "loss" to any of the following:

a. Tapes, records, discs or other similar audio, visual or data electronic devices designed for use with audio, visual or data electronic equipment.

b. Any device designed or used to detect speed measuring equipment such as radar or laser detectors and any jamming apparatus intended to elude or disrupt speed measurement equipment.

c. Any electronic equipment, without regard to whether this equipment is permanently installed, that receives or transmits audio, visual or data signals and that is not designed solely for the reproduction of sound.

d. Any accessories used with the electronic equipment described in Paragraph **c.** above.

Exclusions **4.c.** and **4.d.** do not apply to:

a. Equipment designed solely for the reproduction of sound and accessories used with such equipment, provided such equipment is permanently installed in the covered "auto" at the time of the "loss" or such equipment is removable from a housing unit which is permanently installed in the covered "auto" at the time of the "loss", and such equipment is designed to be solely operated by use of the power from the "auto's" electrical system, in or upon the covered "auto"; or

b. Any other electronic equipment that is:

(1) Necessary for the normal operation of the covered "auto" or the monitoring of the covered "auto's" operating system; or

(2) An integral part of the same unit housing any sound reproducing equipment described in Paragraph **a.** above and permanently installed in the opening of the dash or console of the covered "auto" normally used by the manufacturer for installation of a radio.

5. We will not pay for "loss" to a covered "auto" due to "diminution in value".

C. Limit Of Insurance

1. The most we will pay for "loss" in any one "accident" is the lesser of:

    a. The actual cash value of the damaged or stolen property as of the time of the "loss"; or

    b. The cost of repairing or replacing the damaged or stolen property with other property of like kind and quality.

2. An adjustment for depreciation and physical condition will be made in determining actual cash value in the event of a total "loss".

3. If a repair or replacement results in better than like kind or quality, we will not pay for the amount of the betterment.

D. Deductible

For each covered "auto", our obligation to pay for, repair, return or replace damaged or stolen property will be reduced by the applicable deductible shown in the Declarations. Any Comprehensive Coverage deductible shown in the Declarations does not apply to "loss" caused by fire or lightning.

SECTION IV – BUSINESS AUTO CONDITIONS

The following conditions apply in addition to the Common Policy Conditions:

A. Loss Conditions

1. **Appraisal For Physical Damage Loss**

    If you and we disagree on the amount of "loss", either may demand an appraisal of the "loss". In this event, each party will select a competent appraiser. The two appraisers will select a competent and impartial umpire. The appraisers will state separately the actual cash value and amount of "loss". If they fail to agree, they will submit their differences to the umpire. A decision agreed to by any two will be binding. Each party will:

    a. Pay its chosen appraiser; and

    b. Bear the other expenses of the appraisal and umpire equally.

    If we submit to an appraisal, we will still retain our right to deny the claim.

2. **Duties In The Event Of Accident, Claim, Suit Or Loss**

    We have no duty to provide coverage under this policy unless there has been full compliance with the following duties:

    a. In the event of "accident", claim, "suit" or "loss", you must give us or our authorized representative prompt notice of the "accident" or "loss". Include:

    (1) How, when and where the "accident" or "loss" occurred;

    (2) The "insured's" name and address; and

    (3) To the extent possible, the names and addresses of any injured persons and witnesses.

    b. Additionally, you and any other involved "insured" must:

    (1) Assume no obligation, make no payment or incur no expense without our consent, except at the "insured's" own cost.

Appendix 67

(2) Immediately send us copies of any request, demand, order, notice, summons or legal paper received concerning the claim or "suit".

(3) Cooperate with us in the investigation or settlement of the claim or defense against the "suit".

(4) Authorize us to obtain medical records or other pertinent information.

(5) Submit to examination, at our expense, by physicians of our choice, as often as we reasonably require.

c. If there is "loss" to a covered "auto" or its equipment you must also do the following:

(1) Promptly notify the police if the covered "auto" or any of its equipment is stolen.

(2) Take all reasonable steps to protect the covered "auto" from further damage. Also keep a record of your expenses for consideration in the settlement of the claim.

(3) Permit us to inspect the covered "auto" and records proving the "loss" before its repair or disposition.

(4) Agree to examinations under oath at our request and give us a signed statement of your answers.

3. **Legal Action Against Us**

No one may bring a legal action against us under this Coverage Form until:

a. There has been full compliance with all the terms of this Coverage Form; and

b. Under Liability Coverage, we agree in writing that the "insured" has an obligation to pay or until the amount of that obligation has finally been determined by judgment after trial. No one has the right under this policy to bring us into an action to determine the "insured's" liability.

4. **Loss Payment – Physical Damage Coverages**

At our option we may:

a. Pay for, repair or replace damaged or stolen property;

b. Return the stolen property, at our expense. We will pay for any damage that results to the "auto" from the theft; or

c. Take all or any part of the damaged or stolen property at an agreed or appraised value.

If we pay for the "loss", our payment will include the applicable sales tax for the damaged or stolen property.

5. **Transfer Of Rights Of Recovery Against Others To Us**

If any person or organization to or for whom we make payment under this Coverage Form has rights to recover damages from another, those rights are transferred to us. That person or organization must do everything necessary to secure our rights and must do nothing after "accident" or "loss" to impair them.

B. **General Conditions**

1. **Bankruptcy**

Bankruptcy or insolvency of the "insured" or the "insured's" estate will not relieve us of any obligations under this Coverage Form.

2. **Concealment, Misrepresentation Or Fraud**

This Coverage Form is void in any case of fraud by you at any time as it relates to this Coverage Form. It is also void if you or any other "insured", at any time, intentionally conceal or misrepresent a material fact concerning:

a. This Coverage Form;

b. The covered "auto";

c. Your interest in the covered "auto"; or

d. A claim under this Coverage Form.

3. **Liberalization**

If we revise this Coverage Form to provide more coverage without additional premium charge, your policy will automatically provide the additional coverage as of the day the revision is effective in your state.

4. **No Benefit To Bailee – Physical Damage Coverages**

We will not recognize any assignment or grant any coverage for the benefit of any person or organization holding, storing or transporting property for a fee regardless of any other provision of this Coverage Form.

5. Other Insurance

a. For any covered "auto" you own, this Coverage Form provides primary insurance. For any covered "auto" you don't own, the insurance provided by this Coverage Form is excess over any other collectible insurance. However, while a covered "auto" which is a "trailer" is connected to another vehicle, the Liability Coverage this Coverage Form provides for the "trailer" is:

   (1) Excess while it is connected to a motor vehicle you do not own.

   (2) Primary while it is connected to a covered "auto" you own.

b. For Hired Auto Physical Damage Coverage, any covered "auto" you lease, hire, rent or borrow is deemed to be a covered "auto" you own. However, any "auto" that is leased, hired, rented or borrowed with a driver is not a covered "auto".

c. Regardless of the provisions of Paragraph a. above, this Coverage Form's Liability Coverage is primary for any liability assumed under an "insured contract".

d. When this Coverage Form and any other Coverage Form or policy covers on the same basis, either excess or primary, we will pay only our share. Our share is the proportion that the Limit of Insurance of our Coverage Form bears to the total of the limits of all the Coverage Forms and policies covering on the same basis.

6. Premium Audit

a. The estimated premium for this Coverage Form is based on the exposures you told us you would have when this policy began. We will compute the final premium due when we determine your actual exposures. The estimated total premium will be credited against the final premium due and the first Named Insured will be billed for the balance, if any. The due date for the final premium or retrospective premium is the date shown as the due date on the bill. If the estimated total premium exceeds the final premium due, the first Named Insured will get a refund.

b. If this policy is issued for more than one year, the premium for this Coverage Form will be computed annually based on our rates or premiums in effect at the beginning of each year of the policy.

7. Policy Period, Coverage Territory

Under this Coverage Form, we cover "accidents" and "losses" occurring:

a. During the policy period shown in the Declarations; and

b. Within the coverage territory.

The coverage territory is:

a. The United States of America;

b. The territories and possessions of the United States of America;

c. Puerto Rico;

d. Canada; and

e. Anywhere in the world if:

   (1) A covered "auto" of the private passenger type is leased, hired, rented or borrowed without a driver for a period of 30 days or less; and

   (2) The "insured's" responsibility to pay damages is determined in a "suit" on the merits, in the United States of America, the territories and possessions of the United States of America, Puerto Rico, or Canada or in a settlement we agree to.

We also cover "loss" to, or "accidents" involving, a covered "auto" while being transported between any of these places.

8. Two Or More Coverage Forms Or Policies Issued By Us

If this Coverage Form and any other Coverage Form or policy issued to you by us or any company affiliated with us apply to the same "accident", the aggregate maximum Limit of Insurance under all the Coverage Forms or policies shall not exceed the highest applicable Limit of Insurance under any one Coverage Form or policy. This condition does not apply to any Coverage Form or policy issued by us or an affiliated company specifically to apply as excess insurance over this Coverage Form.

SECTION V – DEFINITIONS

A. "Accident" includes continuous or repeated exposure to the same conditions resulting in "bodily injury" or "property damage".

B. "Auto" means:

1. A land motor vehicle, "trailer" or semitrailer designed for travel on public roads; or

2. Any other land vehicle that is subject to a compulsory or financial responsibility law or other motor vehicle insurance law where it is licensed or principally garaged.

However, "auto" does not include "mobile equipment".

C. "Bodily injury" means bodily injury, sickness or disease sustained by a person including death resulting from any of these.

D. "Covered pollution cost or expense" means any cost or expense arising out of:

1. Any request, demand, order or statutory or regulatory requirement that any "insured" or others test for, monitor, clean up, remove, contain, treat, detoxify or neutralize, or in any way respond to, or assess the effects of "pollutants"; or

2. Any claim or "suit" by or on behalf of a governmental authority for damages because of testing for, monitoring, cleaning up, removing, containing, treating, detoxifying or neutralizing, or in any way responding to or assessing the effects of "pollutants".

"Covered pollution cost or expense" does not include any cost or expense arising out of the actual, alleged or threatened discharge, dispersal, seepage, migration, release or escape of "pollutants":

a. That are, or that are contained in any property that is:

(1) Being transported or towed by, handled, or handled for movement into, onto or from the covered "auto";

(2) Otherwise in the course of transit by or on behalf of the "insured";

(3) Being stored, disposed of, treated or processed in or upon the covered "auto";

b. Before the "pollutants" or any property in which the "pollutants" are contained are moved from the place where they are accepted by the "insured" for movement into or onto the covered "auto"; or

c. After the "pollutants" or any property in which the "pollutants" are contained are moved from the covered "auto" to the place where they are finally delivered, disposed of or abandoned by the "insured".

Paragraph **a.** above does not apply to fuels, lubricants, fluids, exhaust gases or other similar "pollutants" that are needed for or result from the normal electrical, hydraulic or mechanical functioning of the covered "auto" or its parts, if:

(1) The "pollutants" escape, seep, migrate, or are discharged, dispersed or released directly from an "auto" part designed by its manufacturer to hold, store, receive or dispose of such "pollutants"; and

(2) The "bodily injury", "property damage" or "covered pollution cost or expense" does not arise out of the operation of any equipment listed in Paragraph **6.b.** or **6.c.** of the definition of "mobile equipment".

Paragraphs **b.** and **c.** above do not apply to "accidents" that occur away from premises owned by or rented to an "insured" with respect to "pollutants" not in or upon a covered "auto" if:

(1) The "pollutants" or any property in which the "pollutants" are contained are upset, overturned or damaged as a result of the maintenance or use of a covered "auto"; and

(2) The discharge, dispersal, seepage, migration, release or escape of the "pollutants" is caused directly by such upset, overturn or damage.

E. "Diminution in value" means the actual or perceived loss in market value or resale value which results from a direct and accidental "loss".

F. "Employee" includes a "leased worker". "Employee" does not include a "temporary worker".

G. "Insured" means any person or organization qualifying as an insured in the Who Is An Insured provision of the applicable coverage. Except with respect to the Limit of Insurance, the coverage afforded applies separately to each insured who is seeking coverage or against whom a claim or "suit" is brought.

H. "Insured contract" means:

1. A lease of premises;

2. A sidetrack agreement;

3. Any easement or license agreement, except in connection with construction or demolition operations on or within 50 feet of a railroad;

4. An obligation, as required by ordinance, to indemnify a municipality, except in connection with work for a municipality;

5. That part of any other contract or agreement pertaining to your business (including an indemnification of a municipality in connection with work performed for a municipality) under which you assume the tort liability of another to pay for "bodily injury" or "property damage" to a third party or organization. Tort liability means a liability that would be imposed by law in the absence of any contract or agreement;

6. That part of any contract or agreement entered into, as part of your business, pertaining to the rental or lease, by you or any of your "employees", of any "auto". However, such contract or agreement shall not be considered an "insured contract" to the extent that it obligates you or any of your "employees" to pay for "property damage" to any "auto" rented or leased by you or any of your "employees".

An "insured contract" does not include that part of any contract or agreement:

a. That indemnifies a railroad for "bodily injury" or "property damage" arising out of construction or demolition operations, within 50 feet of any railroad property and affecting any railroad bridge or trestle, tracks, roadbeds, tunnel, underpass or crossing; or

b. That pertains to the loan, lease or rental of an "auto" to you or any of your "employees", if the "auto" is loaned, leased or rented with a driver; or

c. That holds a person or organization engaged in the business of transporting property by "auto" for hire harmless for your use of a covered "auto" over a route or territory that person or organization is authorized to serve by public authority.

I. "Leased worker" means a person leased to you by a labor leasing firm under an agreement between you and the labor leasing firm, to perform duties related to the conduct of your business. "Leased worker" does not include a "temporary worker".

J. "Loss" means direct and accidental loss or damage.

K. "Mobile equipment" means any of the following types of land vehicles, including any attached machinery or equipment:

1. Bulldozers, farm machinery, forklifts and other vehicles designed for use principally off public roads;

2. Vehicles maintained for use solely on or next to premises you own or rent;

3. Vehicles that travel on crawler treads;

4. Vehicles, whether self-propelled or not, maintained primarily to provide mobility to permanently mounted:

   a. Power cranes, shovels, loaders, diggers or drills; or

   b. Road construction or resurfacing equipment such as graders, scrapers or rollers.

5. Vehicles not described in Paragraph **1.**, **2.**, **3.**, or **4.** above that are not self-propelled and are maintained primarily to provide mobility to permanently attached equipment of the following types:

   a. Air compressors, pumps and generators, including spraying, welding, building cleaning, geophysical exploration, lighting and well servicing equipment; or

   b. Cherry pickers and similar devices used to raise or lower workers.

6. Vehicles not described in Paragraph **1.**, **2.**, **3.** or **4.** above maintained primarily for purposes other than the transportation of persons or cargo. However, self-propelled vehicles with the following types of permanently attached equipment are not "mobile equipment" but will be considered "autos":

   a. Equipment designed primarily for:

      (1) Snow removal;

      (2) Road maintenance, but not construction or resurfacing; or

      (3) Street cleaning;

   b. Cherry pickers and similar devices mounted on automobile or truck chassis and used to raise or lower workers; and

   c. Air compressors, pumps and generators, including spraying, welding, building cleaning, geophysical exploration, lighting or well servicing equipment.

However, "mobile equipment" does not include land vehicles that are subject to a compulsory or financial responsibility law or other motor vehicle insurance law where it is licensed or principally garaged. Land vehicles subject to a compulsory or financial responsibility law or other motor vehicle insurance law are considered "autos".

L. "Pollutants" means any solid, liquid, gaseous or thermal irritant or contaminant, including smoke, vapor, soot, fumes, acids, alkalis, chemicals and waste. Waste includes materials to be recycled, reconditioned or reclaimed.

M. "Property damage" means damage to or loss of use of tangible property.

N. "Suit" means a civil proceeding in which:
1. Damages because of "bodily injury" or "property damage"; or
2. A "covered pollution cost or expense",

to which this insurance applies, are alleged.

"Suit" includes:
  a. An arbitration proceeding in which such damages or "covered pollution costs or expenses" are claimed and to which the "insured" must submit or does submit with our consent; or
  b. Any other alternative dispute resolution proceeding in which such damages or "covered pollution costs or expenses" are claimed and to which the insured submits with our consent.

O. "Temporary worker" means a person who is furnished to you to substitute for a permanent "employee" on leave or to meet seasonal or short-term workload conditions.

P. "Trailer" includes semitrailer.